COLLEGE ORIENTATION
Education for Relevance

"It was in making education not only common to all but in some sense compulsory on all that the destiny of the free republic of America was practically settled."

James Russell Lowell

COLLEGE ORIENTATION
Education for Relevance

CHARLES C. COLLINS

Associate Director
Junior College Leadership Program
University of California, Berkeley

HOLBROOK PRESS, INC., BOSTON

Second Printing ....September, 1969

Library of Congress Catalog Card Number 69–11624

Printed in United States of America

Frontispiece and photos on pages 16, 30, 48, 70, 108, 126, 144, 178, 198, 218, 238, and 240 by John M. Dixon and James R. Ney, Grossmont College Art Department.

Photo on page 92 by Wide World Photos.

Photo on page 160 by United Press International.

PREFACE

THIS BOOK WAS WRITTEN TO PROVOKE THE COLLEGE FRESHMAN into giving serious thought to the new phase of his life, for only by such thought can he shape the experience to his will. An attempt has been made to pose some of the big questions which have to be asked but which rarely, if ever, have answers which will fit in every case. The student must address himself to these overriding questions ("Who and what am I?" "What am I doing here?" "What is worth learning?") in order to force what he is experiencing into sharp focus. The answers at which he arrives are likely to be personal, relative, tentative —and frequently in contradiction to the biases of the author of this book.

Every book read should be a dialogue between the author and the reader. This book was designed to be somewhat more than that. It is actually a series of position papers in which a stand is taken to provide a beginning point for group discussions. Students should read each chapter, supplement it with suggested reading and/or listening, and then, using a professional counselor as a catalyst, meet in groups of fifteen to twenty for depth discussion of the personal implications of what they have read. Hopefully, that will make the dialogue into a colloquy: instead of the idea being shuttled back and forth between author and reader, it will be explored and enlarged by all participants.

Orientation involves discovering where you are and then finding the best way to get from where you are to where you want to be. In the final analysis, each person has to orient himself. The author simply hopes this book will help.

Charles C. Collins

Colombo, Ceylon

CONTENTS

PART I
PHILOSOPHIC CONSIDERATIONS 1

PART 1

Philosophic Considerations

SOMETIMES READING A BOOK IS LIKE LOOKING THROUGH A microscope: the reader has to know what he is looking for before he can see it. He needs a frame through which to view the subject, and he needs to have some notion of the subject matter so he can adjust his mental mechanisms to bring the picture into sharp focus. The subject matter of this book is the student experiencing a college education. The five chapters of Part 1 were designed to provide the frame and to adjust the focus to help the student take a long, close look at himself experiencing a college education. The hope is that this self-conscious viewing of a crucial experience will make it a more rewarding experience.

The first chapter deals with how perception determines behavior and the implications of this fact for the process of learning. Chapter 2 zeroes in on the impact of values on perceptions—and therefore on behavior—and proposes that values can to some degree be chosen. Next, the student is asked to consider the assumptions undergirding the whole idea of higher education, especially universal higher education. Chapters 4 and 5 then spell out in a critical way the functions of higher education so the student knows what he should get and can better evaluate the quality of what he is getting.

"There is nothing either good or bad but thinking makes it so."

William Shakespeare

1 Perception ⟶ Behavior

ANY NONCONFORMIST, WHETHER HE BE HENRY THOREAU IN the eighteen-fifty's or some beaded, bearded, belled hippie of the nineteen-sixty's, says in effect, "I reject the way you people in the establishment insist on seeing the world, and since I see it differently, I'll act differently." How any person perceives his world will determine how he will respond to it. How a student perceives the college experience will determine how he will react to it and how he will shape it to his will.

To say that action is determined by perception may be to say the obvious. However, the psychological explanation of this simple statement and the implications that ramify from the truth of this statement are not so simple. They deserve to be explored.

BEHAVIOR IS CAUSED

To begin then at the beginning: All behavior is caused. This premise holds whether the behavior is scratching an itch, dropping from college, getting married, or committing murder. Although the behavior may seem nonsensical to the observer, and although the behaver himself may be amazed and unable to explain his own behavior, nonetheless, if every conscious and unconscious influencing fact were known, the behavior would be explainable—the cause of the behavior would become apparent.

Perhaps the categorical statement "All behavior is caused," should be stated as a necessary assumption rather than as a fact. The truth of it is obvious enough when the behavior is simple: the child runs away from the snarling dog. The truth is not so apparent when the behavior is complex: the daughter gives up marriage to care for the invalid mother whom she hates. The term *necessary assumption* is used advisedly, for no other assumption can be scientifically defended. To assume that behavior does not always carry its own internal causation is to assume that behavior can be random—pure chance—or that some external force—gods or devils—intervene and use the behaver's body to work their good or evil purposes. If human behavior can be random, then psychology becomes a branch of the mathematics of probability. If human behavior can be the work of outside agents, then psychology becomes a study of the occult, if not demonology. A science of human behavior requires the assumption that effect (behavior) follows from some cause.

The cause of behavior has to lie in the relationship of the perceiver to that which is perceived. The consciousness of each person is his window to the world. There is just the "me" and the "not-me." If consciousness (the me) is taken away, then in effect the outside world (the not-me) becomes nonexistent or at least irrelevant. If the outside world is taken away, then there is nothing to be conscious about; the me becomes nonexistent or at least irrelevant. The point of these statements may be worth pondering for it leads back to the restatement of the basic idea: The cause of behavior will be found in the perceptions the behaver has of himself and of the world outside his skin.

What has been said so far may be more difficult to understand in the abstract than in the concrete. Several years ago, a student carried a small arsenal with him to the top of the bell tower of the University of Texas, and in several hours of sniping he killed ten innocent passers-by. It was not just random chance that the desire for wanton murder entered this unfortunate man's consciousness rather than some other man's consciousness. And no responsible thinker of the twentieth century would seriously believe that some external force, some demon, prompted him to commit multiple murder. His behavior, however bizarre, was caused. The cause would have to be sought in the perceptions he had of his personal universe—in the relationship of the perceiver to that which is perceived. If some very insightful psychologist were able to reconstruct the sick man's perceptions exactly, then he could define with precision the causes of the behavior.

PERCEPTION IS MEANING

A fundamental distinction must be drawn between what the sense organs bring in and what is perceived. Perception is the meaning which is attributed to the neural impulses brought to the brain. These may be outside stimulations from the eyes, ears, or nose, or internal stimulations from the stored memory or from the endocrine glands or the autonomic nervous system.

The brain is not a tape recorder or a camera or oscilloscope which with great fidelity records the sounds and sights of the external world or the sensations and emotions of the internal self. The brain is an interpreter: it strives to make sense out of the welter of sensations which it experiences. It has no built-in lie detector. As a matter of fact, it will often distort sensation to see what it wants to see, hear what it wants to hear, feel what it wants to feel. The eyes of the thirsty man on the desert pick up the shimmering heat waves and perceive them as a watery oasis. The paranoid personality hears people whispering and perceives that they are plotting against him. The young man's endocrine system prompts a sexual response to the sight of the contours of a girl's body and he perceives he is in love.

The whole perception process is analogous to a radar system. The sensory organs record the blips on the screen, but the blips take on meaning only when they are interpreted. Perception is the meaning which total consciousness interprets from the blips which the sensory system brings to the internal radar screen. The moron with 20:20 vision may get a better blip than the astigmatic genius, yet the genius will perceive much more accurately than the moron.

APPROPRIATE BEHAVIOR FOLLOWS ACCURATE PERCEPTION

Appropriateness of behavior will depend upon the accuracy of perception. If a person's perceptions correspond exactly to the reality that is in the external world, his behavior will be appropriate to the demands of that reality. His actions will appear to him and to the objective observer to be smart, correct, consistent, realistic and self-rewarding. If, on the contrary, a person's perceptions correspond only vaguely to external reality, his behavior will be inappropriate to the demands of reality. To the objective observer, if not to himself, his actions will appear to be stupid, incorrect, inconsistent, unrealistic and self-defeating.

Accuracy of perception, though positively correlated to mental ability, does not have a 1:1 relationship with intellectual prowess. There are many other influencing personality factors. The average student who perceives himself and his life situation accurately may behave much more appropriately and therefore be better able to profit from college training than the bright student whose perceptions are distorted by psychological factors not measured by past grades or by academic aptitude tests. It takes a high degree of blindness to overlook this patent fact, yet college admissions officials continue to exhibit a slavish devotion to aptitude test scores or other so-called "objective" measures. This frequently results in basing admission or retention decisions on that which is measurable, no matter how irrelevant, rather than on relevant factors which can be strongly sensed but cannot yet be measured in a quantifiable way.

The statement has been made that each person will act or behave in the way in which he sees his world. Perhaps this statement should be made stronger: Each person can *only* act on the basis of how he perceives reality. Two points deserve stress. The behaver has no alternative but to rely on reality as he perceives it. And, the reality he perceives may or may not correspond to what is objective reality. Actually, objective reality is not an absolute reality that exists independent of man. It is only the consensus of those best qualified to judge.

What is consciously experienced seems so vivid to the perceiver, he is inclined to view it as absolute reality and to react accordingly. That is understandable. The meaning that his mind makes of all the sensations coming from the external world is the only reality he can possibly know. Each person has to depend on his own perception of reality, for he has no other basis upon which to act. If he doubts the validity of his perceptions, as everyone does some of the time and as the neurotic and psychotic do much of the time, he no longer has any rationale for behaving, and he either becomes immobilized or is forced to behave without rationale, that is, irrationally. At least it will appear irrational to the outside observer; the behaver will make sense out of what he experiences even if he has to distort to do so. At the moment of action, the most bizarre behavior will appear rational to the behaver. An example from abnormal psychology: A patient who has acute guilt feelings over masturbation may interpret his own self-punishing thoughts as the voice of God telling him to cut off his offending hand. An example from everyday life: A student, whose parents in effect taught him to think of himself as inadequate, interprets one low grade on a test as complete validation of his parents' assessment of him and, on this basis alone, drops out of college.

The logic thus far has followed this line of reasoning: All

behavior is caused; the cause of behavior has to lie in the relationship of the perceiver to that which is perceived; reality for the behaver is whatever his perceptions tell him is reality; appropriateness of behavior will depend on the accuracy of perception, the correspondence of subjective reality to objective reality. If appropriate behavior is dependent on accurate perceptions, the question which next arises is, "What are the major factors which influence perception?"

DETERMINANTS OF PERCEPTION

Certainly, the sensory equipment and the complexity of the neural connections in the brain will be two primary factors. To illustrate this in a rather grim way: Blind eyes and deaf ears connected to an idiotic brain will only constitute a nonperceiving mass of protoplasm. A happier example would be the case of Helen Keller who became both blind and deaf but who had such remarkable mental potential she was able to compensate for the sensory loss of sight and hearing. In between these two extremes are to be found the prevailing facts that impairment of the sense organs makes accurate perceptions more difficult and, more important, differences in mental ability will set upper and lower limits to the level of complexity of perception. The last point is probably more apparent than it is real. Most psychological evidence points to only a fractional use of the astounding capacity of the human brain. If optimum conditions prevailed, the person with average brain power, the person with an I.Q. of 100, would be able to perceive, comprehend and remember almost any subject now taught in undergraduate college courses. There have been cases of people with average mentality earning Phi Beta Kappa honors.

Another obvious factor influencing the richness, vividness and accuracy of perception is stored knowledge accessible through memory. As folk wisdom puts it, "The more you bring to a learning situation, the more you get from it." If a person has studied English history and is well acquainted with Elizabethan England, his perception of the plays of Shakespeare will be infinitely enhanced. The sight of a digital computer would evoke only the foggiest perception in the mind of an aboriginal Australian. Those who have taken the trouble to learn something about music and have listened to a great deal of it will actually hear sounds that the uninitiated will not hear and will be moved to laughter or melancholy or joy while the musically deaf are experiencing nothing but confused noise. The important generalization to be made from these observations is that life is really lived within the confines of consciousness. If a person invests his time (capital) in the accrual of knowledge, the interest will be compounded by this knowledge, enriching every new perception so that capital and interest increase at a geometric rate. Looked at from the view that life is consciousness, the only way a man can enrich his life is to enrich the perceptions which flood through his consciousness.

A third major factor influencing perceptions is the emotional coloration of preferences, interests, prejudices, attitudes, temperament—those emotional weightings which each person gives to that which he perceives. Most of them are learned in childhood and are so incorporated into the unconscious, the adult is hardly aware of the subtle—even distorting—influence they have on his perceptions. The grown son whose beloved mother was fair finds he prefers blondes. The boy who became his father's "little man" when he played with tools records a high interest in mechanical and manipulative tasks as an adult. The daughter whose Irish immigrant parents worked hard for their middle-class status cannot see why there should be welfare programs for Negroes. Children growing up in a cocoon of love and security are shocked to find their own prevailing attitude of good will may evoke a hostile response. A young girl whose sensitive nervous constitution is rasped through the years by a nagging mother approaches each new adult experience in a state of perpetual irritation.

The last major factor influencing perceptions will be introduced at this point and developed more fully when the subject of values becomes the center of focus. This fourth factor is hard to label with a single word. It encompasses the mental picture a person has of himself, the conscious and unconscious values which he may or may not be able to spell out, and the philosophy or life view or unconscious assumptions which tend to shape any and every perception the person has.

Man has the unique and wonderful ability to look upon himself as an object, to develop a concept of himself. As a baby's needs prompt dim consciousness, he begins to separate the "self" from the "not-self" and forms at least a sketchy image of himself as a separate entity. He uses the behavior of others as a mirror, for their reaction to him reflects his image. So, when parents behave toward a child without love, the child comes to think of himself as unlovable—and his reacting behavior is often so obnoxious that in fact he does become unlovable.

In such a way, the concept a person has of what he is becomes a self-fulfilling prophesy. If a person thinks of himself as capable of learning, he is likely to keep trying until he in fact makes himself capable. If a girl develops a mixed concept of herself as both girl and boy, her behavior will reflect that ambivalence even to the point of confusion of sex role, to say nothing of exhibiting masculine interests, mannerisms, and dress. The point is, a person plays the role that his self-concept casts him to play. The young man who sees himself as the self-reliant he-man becomes a forest ranger, not a dress designer. The young lady who has been taught to conceive of herself as a charming, irresponsible hoyden is not very likely to enter a convent. A person who relishes the picture of himself as an intellectual seeks out those activities by which he will be identified as an intellectual. The young lady who sees herself as attractive will behave with implicit confidence that others will view her as attractive. The young man whose image of himself is that of the cool, objective scientist type will make an occupational choice and an educational plan consistent with this image. Of course, serious discrepancy between the concept of self and the actual reality of self will inevitably result in inappropriate behavior. The greater the discrepancy, the more inappropriate, ludicrous, strange the behavior will be.

Values are the plus or minus valences which are ascribed to almost everything which is perceivable. Values are the priorities which are given to traits, qualities, ideas, things, events. They are the weightings given to all that crosses the perceptual field. As a matter of speculation, there is some doubt if sensations without value weighting even register as perceptions in the mind. The human brain does not respond to every sensation within the range of its sensory organs. The brain will respond selectively on the basis of context or on-going organization, on the basis of need, and on the basis of that which is valued. Those with materialistic values will be attuned to any prospect for material reward. They will be able to smell money as the hungry animal smells his next dinner. People with aesthetic values will tune in on those sensations which will bring the pleasures of beauty. Persons with strong humanitarian values will see their personal welfare as part and parcel of the general welfare, and their behavior will reflect their concern for the other guy and, by progression, their concern for mankind. The man with intellectual values will organize his life to give himself maximum intellectual stimulation: within the college scene, he will be the chess player, not the football tackle. But more of this later when the relationship of values to self-concept becomes the subject of concern.

The last determinant of perception to be mentioned is philosophy, world view, what the Germans call *Weltanschauung*. Perhaps the effect of philosophy on perception can be described through examples. The Buddhist with unwavering belief in present life being a qualification for the next life is not apt to become so disturbed about existing injustices that he becomes a social revolutionary. The traditional Catholic perceives birth control measures as an attenuated form of murder while the pragmatic liberal perceives failure to impose birth control as irresponsible and even suicidal for mankind. Those who look to the state for their personal identity and immortality will perceive nationalistic wars in quite a different light than those who look inward for identity and who look upon national states as only arbitrary subdivisions of man's world. The true nonbeliever in an after life is going to perceive his sixty-plus years as his one and only opportunity and hence behave differently from the true believer in a heaven or hell.

The humanist perceives education as a means to self-fulfillment, while the technocrat perceives it as training that will result in an increased gross national product. The individualist perceives the threat of excessive population transforming man into a totalitarian robot. The believer in racial superiorities sees the Negro riots as a Communist conspiracy. The Black Nationalists see the intransigency of the Whites as proof that white men are congenital devils. So, the philosophic frame organizes and, to a large extent, predetermines how the person will perceive his own life, his relationship to others and his relationship to the world. If such philosophic positions pervade a society, the child growing up within that culture will take the philosophic premises as givens, as immutable truths, as unconscious assumptions. It takes a pluralistic society with real academic freedom in its education system to avoid built-in distortions of perception: Nazi youth had little alternative but to have Nazi perceptions.

To sum up:

1. All behavior is caused.
2. The cause of behavior has to lie in the relationship of the perceiver to that which is perceived.
3. The person has no choice but to act in the way in which he perceives reality.
4. The influencing determinants of perception are many and varied.
5. The appropriateness of behavior will depend on the accuracy of perception of reality.

This reasoning is all supportive to this contention made

in the opening paragraph: "How a person perceives his world will determine how he will respond to it. How a student perceives the college experience will determine how he will react to it, and how he will shape it to his will."

TOPICS FOR CONSIDERATION

1. Will youth perceive the world in a fundamentally different way than their parents perceive it? If so, does this make conflict between the generations inevitable?

2. Students today appear to be reacting to the college experience differently from students in the nineteen-fifties. What changes in the perceptions students have of college could account for this change in behavior?

3. Does the premise "All behavior is caused" lead to the philosophic conclusion of complete determinism? Where, if at all, does free will enter? If determinism operates, how can a man be held ultimately responsible for his actions in Heaven above or on Earth below?

4. Is there any reasonable basis for arguing against the assumption that all behavior is caused?

5. The contention was made that there is no way of establishing an absolute reality. Does this mean that reality (truth) is completely relative? If not, upon what basis can it be said that one man's perceptions are more valid than another man's perceptions?

6. When the contention is rephrased to state that perceptions determine behavior, what is the actual meaning of the charge made by some youth that "You can't trust anybody over 30"?

7. That people do, at times, distort their sensations to perceive what they want to perceive is hardly debatable. The pertinent question is, How does anyone know whether his perceptions are or are not distorted? What yardsticks of objective reality are available for measuring the distortion?

8. If appropriateness of behavior follows from accuracy of perception, why don't very bright people always have more appropriate behavior than average people? To what degree are admissions officers in colleges justified in operating on the assumption that brightness should be the primary criterion for prejudging appropriateness of behavior?

9. Colleges often require an interview with a counselor before a student may withdraw from a course or from college. In terms of the statement ". . . the behaver has no alternative but to rely on reality as he perceives it," what is the basis for such a policy of exit interview?

10. What evidence can be marshaled for or against the bold assertion that under optimal conditions the average person could handle almost any undergraduate course?

11. What weakness or invalidity, if any, can be found in the statement: "Since life is consciousness the only way a man can enrich his life is to enrich the perceptions which flood through his consciousness"?

12. If a person's values and self-concept are so crucial, should not education make a major effort to clarify them in each student's mind? What resources can a college student turn to for help in analyzing his values and in capturing his self-image?

SUGGESTED READING AND LISTENING

ALLPORT, GORDON W. *Pattern and Growth in Personality.* New York: Holt Rinehart & Winston, Inc., 1961.

FROMM, ERICH. *Man for Himself,* New York: Holt, Rinehart & Winston, Inc., 1947.

JOURARD, SIDNEY M. *Disclosing Man to Himself.* Princeton, New Jersey: D. Van Nostrand Company, Inc., 1968.

OVERSTREET, HENRY A. *The Mature Mind.* New York: W. W. Norton & Company, Inc., 1949.

SNYGG, DONALD and ARTHUR COMBS. *Individual Behavior.* Evanston, Ill.: Harper & Row, Publishers, 1959.

"The life which is unexamined is not worth living."
Socrates.

2 Choosing Values

THE MEANING OF THE WORD *value* IN PSYCHOLOGY IS LIKE its meaning in economics. It is an appraisal of worth, and just as in the marketplace, what is of great worth to some will be worthless to others. A value is the relative weighting or importance that a person ascribes to a thing, an activity, an idea, a concept.

THE FORMATION OF VALUES

American children raised in Chinese, Jewish, and Japanese homes enter and graduate from college in numbers greatly disproportionate to their percentage of the population. Why? Not because they represent superior races or chosen people; the simple fact is they value education. One man labels himself an "intellectual" and another labels himself a "practical realist." In such labeling, each is communicating a whole system or pattern of values which he holds. In exit interviews, many students say they are quitting college to devote more time to work. In one instance, that may mean the student values independence highly and is driven to cut the economic dependency strings that attach him to his parents. Or it may be that a shiny car or sharp clothes are valued more than a dull sheepskin. Still another example: One man gravitates toward being a used car salesman and another man is attracted to the ministry. Imagine the conflict of values if the two men switched roles! These are behavioral illustrations of this conclusion: Values become determinants of behavior. If a person wants to know why he acts as he does, he must analyze and develop a clear picture of his values, the mainsprings of his behavior.

Values are learned. Children learn them first from their parents, then from their peers or associates, then in a very pervasive way, from the wider society—or at least the substratum of the society which is their class.

A girl who sees her mother spending an inordinate amount of time, effort, and money in buying clothes, fixing her hair, and redoing her face, and who hears a great deal of chatter about how this woman looks dowdy and that woman is losing her husband and why age must be masked at all costs—such a daughter is more than likely to learn the values which her mother is constantly acting out. The kid in the slum school and his middle-class teacher have each learned a whole set of values, but not the same set. The street urchin's values make him perceive the cop as an enemy and being jailed as being taken as a prisoner of war. His middle-class teacher sees the police officer as the champion of law and order. The teacher's effort to organize a "Support Your Local Police" drive is scorned, sabotaged and scuttled by the kids who associate law and order with the cop's pistol. If Malcolm X had spent his youth in an upper-class private school, say as a classmate of John or Robert Kennedy, he might have joined Ralph Bunche in the United Nations or Thurgood Marshall on the Supreme Court. And at a societal level, observe how a group with an institutional set of values, such as the John Birch Society, wants to get control of the schools and every other molder of values. It is not just by chance that White Anglo-Saxon Protestant children have WASP values, that Quaker children have Quaker values, that the Mississippi white children have Southern values and that upper-class children have upper-class values. In each case, the parents want the children to value what they value, and with the decreasing influence of the home, they become more determined than ever to control what the teachers teach.

More often than not, values are learned as emotions or attitudes rather than as clear-cut ideas. Since many are picked up at a preverbal age and are more affective (feeling) than cognitive (thinking), they frequently operate at an unconscious level. This greatly adds to the difficulty of a person's analyzing, achieving insight into, and restructuring his own values. Most people will need some professional help in this sometimes agonizing, but usually fruitful, value analysis.

VALUES APPLIED TO VOCATIONAL CHOICE

There is another aspect of value choice which will be introduced in the context of this discussion and will be reconsidered when the focus is on vocational choice and educational planning. It is quite obvious that different types of occupations, and therefore different academic majors, call for different systems of values. If the worker's values coincide with those required for his particular job, he is much more likely to fit with his fellow workers, to go along with whatever occupational mystique prevails, to feel comfortable and contented—and probably he will be more successful. The reverse of this is equally true: If the values of the man and the prevailing values required by the occupation are in conflict, the man is likely to find neither success nor contentment. Since a man's job will consume some eight hours a day for thirty-plus years, it certainly behooves him to become aware of his own inner-core values and to prepare for an occupation with value demands congruent with his own.

Sometimes the negative illustrates more vividly than the positive. In the listing that follows, some traits to which people attach plus values have been mismatched with occupations which demand the contrary of these values.

Value Trait	*Mismatched Occupation*
1. Security	Actor
2. Power	Nun
3. Independence	Soldier
4. Physical activity	Bookkeeper
5. Depth competency	Receptionist
6. Regularized life	Doctor
7. Outdoor activity	Librarian
8. Social contribution	Stock speculator
9. Social contact	Researcher
10. One-upsmanship	Counselor
11. Tough-mindedness	Salvation Army
12. Precise accuracy	Teacher of feebleminded
13. Creative ideas	Typist
14. Organization	Hippie
15. Love and approval	Vice-Principal
16. Large material reward	Nurse

To get out of reverse gear and to illustrate the relationship of values to academic major, this matched listing of values with majors is also presented.

Value Trait	*Matched Academic Major*
1. Security	Public Administration
2. Power	Political Science
3. Independence	Art
4. Physical activity	Recreation
5. Depth competency	Computer Programming
6. Regularized life	Accounting
7. Outdoor activity	Forestry
8. Social contribution	Community Organization
9. Social contact	Dental Assisting
10. One-upsmanship	Law
11. Tough-mindedness	Military Science
12. Precise accuracy	Mathematics
13. Creative ideas	Humanities
14. Organization	Librarianship
15. Love and approval	Elementary Education
16. Large material reward	Business Administration

In the value analysis, which should be at the heart of the whole process of vocational choice and educational planning, the student and his counselor can work inductively or deductively. They can start with a depth exploration of the student's values and try to end with a vocational choice and an academic major consistent with the values exposed. Or they can start with the student's expressed vocational choice, extract the values required by that occupation, and then compare them with the student's values to find the degree to which they match.

VALUE CHOICE THROUGH EDUCATION

Consider again the proposition that existence is really the experiencing of perceptions. In a sense, this is saying that a person is a product of the perceptions which stream through his consciousness. If a man is what his perceptions make him, and his perceptions are influenced by his values, philosophy and self-concept, then in effect he can *choose himself* by choosing his own values and philosophy and by defining his own self-concept. This thesis is vulnerable to attack from several angles, yet it deserves all the defenses that can be marshaled, for the corollary to the thesis is that education is the means of exploring values, formulating philosophy and making the concept of self congruent wtih the reality of self. The Socratic injunction "Know thyself" and its extension *Choose thyself* must be prime goals, particularly of higher education, if education is to have significance.

In the not too distant past—in an age of psychological innocence—it was believed that knowledge, wisdom, and morality were progressive: "Upward and onward!" "Every day in every way the world grows better and better." "Where there is a will there is a way." The older generation, most notably teachers and preachers, exhorted youth to bigger, better, unqualified success. Only the ignorant are so ingenuous, so innocent, so hopeful now. No one with his eyes open claims that mankind will or can be an unqualified success. As a matter of hard fact, man must strive mightily to keep from being an absolute failure—or, in the age of the H-bomb, just to keep himself and his world all in one piece.

Even early in the twentieth century, the novelist and social philosopher H. G. Wells observed, "We are participants in a race between education and catastrophe." Those, such as teachers and students, who are privy to all the weaknesses and inadequacies of education have grave doubts about how the race will end. The citizens of educated nations still wage war, discriminate by skin pigmentation, pollute their own physical environment, and create for themselves every social problem imaginable. But after all the negatives of education are cataloged and underlined, most thinking people arrive at this conclusion: Education is not much of a hope; it is just the only hope we have.

Unending examples can be cited of educated men, or at least men with college degrees, acting foolishly, unwisely, or cruelly, giving scant heed to morals and ethics—Joseph Goebbels, the Nazi Propaganda Minister and war criminal, had a Ph.D. from a reputable German university. However, one cannot draw the reverse conclusion that uneducated men are less foolish, more wise, less cruel and more ethical. Education may simply make some scoundrels and rogues into clever scoundrels and clever rogues, yet the logic seems to dictate that with most men education, properly defined, will diminish foolish behavior, increase wisdom, and prompt men to act as moral beings.

Education, formal and informal, appears to be the only means by which a man can gain control over what he will be—the only way he can choose to be this sort of person rather than that sort of person. To the degree that he is uneducated, he is an unmodified product of his genetics and more or less a victim of an environment that just happens to be there rather than one that he has chosen.

VALUE CHOICE AND DETERMINISM

The determinism of human behavior is not unlike that of the computer; each person is initially programmed by his genetic structure. His early environment, over which he has little if any conscious control, is analogous to further programming, modifying or reinforcing the initial genetic pattern. And, as with a computer, the readout (later behavior) will be based on the input (heredity and environment). The inelegant but accurate maxim "Garbage in → Garbage out" seems to apply to human programming just as it does to machine programming.

However, anything as complex as the human psyche cannot be explained in such simplistic terms. There is more to it than that. New data keeps modifying the original genetic and environmental programming. Further, the human computer can be prompted to analyze what the consequences of its present programming will be. Other forces in the environment, education being the best example, can exercise some quality control over the input. More important, each person can and does begin to select what new data will be added. To an appreciable extent then, external controls (education) can shape and influence the internal controls over the new data which is fed into the super computer, the human mind. Thus, each person can begin to make self-conscious choices of values, can gradually build a philosophical frame to give meaningful structure to his experiences, and can, particularly with professional help, be led to intellectual and emotional analysis of the accuracy of his self-concept.

Perhaps the whole abstract idea should be approached from a slightly different angle and developed step by step. Each person is only a tiny atom on a rather small planet which is spinning through space, not really going anywhere. Man chances to be born, lives for a brief period, and dies. He comes to see the wit and wisdom of George Santayana's summing up: "There is no cure for birth or death save to enjoy the interval." Man's consciousness is the only reality he can ever know and he can experience it only moment by moment. The "self" and the "now" are reality. Everything and everyone in the past and in the future exist for him only by virtue of his consciousness. Looked at this way, past memories and images of the future are the stuff from which dreams are made—and man is the dreamer. The initial mold of his physical self and all the predispositions to later behavior are tentatively set by the genes that he inherits from a chain of ancestors reaching from his parents back to the Neanderthals. This mold keeps getting reshaped by what enters his consciousness and, as he develops, by the thought which is prompted by the conscious perceptions. Although in one sense his selection of what enters his head is also determined, in another sense his remarkable capacity to think, to see and appraise the alternative courses of action open to him, and to make choices shapes him into something approaching a free agent. He can never escape completely from his heredity, from what has happened to him in the past, nor from on-going environment. Neither can he escape from freedom. He has no recourse but to make choices—to define himself, to choose himself, even to create himself.

A negative example: It has often been observed that very young people can thank or blame their parents for the way they look. After twenty or thirty years, a person can only blame or praise himself for the way he looks. If he has churned himself into a psychological turmoil, his face will mirror the turmoil. Inner cruelty will find an exit in his eyes and will even shape his mouth. If he has been self-indulgent and always opted for the easy way, that weakness will be there in his face for all to read. If he perceives others as undeserving of respect, the disdain will show in his face. Fear will etch itself on the face like acid on glass. A mind filled with trivia will project this triviality onto the screen which is the face.

A positive example: An American boy grew up on welfare in the ghetto of a northern city. He spent most of his time playing basketball, at first because he didn't have anything else to do and later because he found he was good at it. Basketball won him a scholarship to a college where he was cheered and lionized as a star on the basketball court but was kept in his social place as a Negro. He anguished over this contradictory experience. For a while he tried to fool himself, but eventually he perceived he was being exploited. Although tempted to quit college, he decided he would exploit his exploiters. He reevaluated basketball and made it a means to the end of raising himself to the status and financial rewards of a professional. When he applied himself to his studies, he found that interest grew with achievement and achievement grew with interest. He began to see himself as an intelligent man, even an intellectual of sorts. He became a successful teacher and could have settled down to a pleasant, comfortable, middle-class life. However, his insight into the social issue of race and his developed sense of responsibility to Negroes and to the wider society forced him to assume a leadership role in the civil rights movement. He made weighted decisions that put him in constant jeopardy and which he knew would bring him a great deal of pain and little if any thanks. He was tested by fire and found it only tempered him. As he approaches middle life, he knows what his values are and is committed to them. He has sat in a jail cell and systematically constructed a philosophic frame for his life, and he has so changed his inner image of himself that it bears only a faint resemblance to the ghetto street urchin he once saw himself to be.

It is not a very comforting or flattering vision for a man to see himself as a puppet manipulated by genetic and environmental strings. Even so, complete denial of genetic determinism and environmental determinism would be to contradict truth. There is no doubt that to an appreciable degree every man is an unwitting product of the genes and early environment which he chanced to get. To some extent, he is also stuck with the values which he has consciously or unconsciously learned.

However, the case just presented rejects the bleak prospect of complete determinism. Education, formal and informal, gives the individual an element of control over what he is and what he will be. Whether through reading, through lectures, through counselling, or through thinking, if a person gains insight into the values which are motivating his behavior, he can achieve self-conscious choice. In effect, he can come to say, "O.K. that's me and I'll live with it," or he can say, "Oh, no! I reject that value and the behavior that follows from it; I'll unlearn that value and will relearn another." Higher education provides the opportunity to see the options which are open and almost forces the person to be a choice-maker. In such a way, a person can in considerable measure create himself. Ultimately, he creates himself out of his life experiences and the thought he gives to those experiences. Hopefully, continued education will provide him with the background knowledge, the thinking processes, the insights and the integrated value structure by which he can best profit from his experiences.

TOPICS FOR CONSIDERATION

1. When asked, even the college dropout will say that education is the social and financial escalator. Doesn't that attest to a high valuation of education? If so, how can his dropout behavior be explained?
2. Since man is capable of an almost infinite amount of learning, and since values are learned, why can't a person simply learn the values demanded of whatever occupation he enters? Why should he make any effort to select an occupation to fit his existing values?
3. Values analysis was characterized as "sometimes agonizing."

Why should this be true, and why should the help of a professional counselor be needed?

4. The observation was made that each group with an institutional set of values tries to capture control of those agencies in a society that mold the values of youth. Assuming this observation to be valid, how can colleges ever hope to sustain academic freedom? Should professors have the right to try to change the essential core values of society?

5. What justification can be mustered for the pessimistic statement, "Education is not much of a hope; it is just the only hope we have"?

6. Arguing by analogy is usually considered suspect. What faults, if any, can be found in the comparison made between the determinism of human behavior and the determinism of the computer?

7. Can any sound rebuttal be offered when the unwavering determinist argues that even the selection of new data by which the individual allegedly modifies himself is in itself determined by hereditary and environmental factors?

8. Education was said to be a form of quality control over the input of those experiences by which a person changes and grows. Is this quality control not violated by a cafeteria-type curriculum from which a student is given freedom to choose exactly what he pleases?

9. Is George Santayana's statement, "There is no cure for birth or death save to enjoy the interval," necessarily advice for rampant hedonism, for wine, women and song?

10. Is it not contradictory to say that a man can never escape from his heredity and his environment and then to say that he can never escape from freedom? In this context, what does *escape from freedom* mean?

11. Some negative examples were given illustrating how any evils within are registered on the person's face. Could this negative be reversed to positive; that is to say, beautiful thoughts make the face beautiful?

12. The statement has been made that education gives the individual an element of control over what he is and what he will be. Using the hypothetical case of the civil rights leader, could the radical change in his personality and character development be explained in any other way?

SUGGESTED READING AND LISTENING

BARZUN, JACQUES. "The Care and Feeding of the Mind." Record. Spoken Arts SA-713, Distinguished Teachers Series.

JACOB, PHILIP E. *Changing Values in College.* Evanston, Ill.: Harper & Row, Publishers, 1958.

RATHS, LOUIS E. "Let Us Keep Seeking to Clarify Values," *Introduction to College Life*, edited by Norman T. Bell, et al. Boston: Houghton Mifflin Company, 1966, pp. 72–75.

ROGERS, CARL. *On Becoming a Person: A Therapist's View of Psychotherapy*. Boston: Houghton Mifflin Company, 1961.

RIESMAN, DAVID. *The Lonely Crowd*. New Haven: Yale University Press, 1950.

SNYGG, DONALD, and ARTHUR COMBS. *Individual Behavior*. Evanston, Ill.: Harper & Row, Publishers, 1959.

COMMON MAN

FREEDOM

ELITE

Excellence

STANDARDS

KNOWLEDGE

EDUCATION

PARTICIPATION

DEMOCRACY

OPEN DOOR

3 Considering the Assumptions

IMAGINE FOR A MOMENT A SOCIETY SUSTAINED BY AN ECONOMY of abundance where automated machines have replaced most production workers and where cybernation has left only a few groups—perhaps the artist, the scientist and the top professional—able to find depth satisfaction or significance in what is presently defined as work. Who should be educated in such a society? Need there be universal higher education? For what should the general citizenry be educated?

In answering the last question, do not uncritically accept the facile answer "excellence." Excellence for what? Excellence to extract greater profits from the economy? Excellence to increase the efficiency of the war machine? Excellence to win the race to the moon? Excellence to enhance the reputation of the educational institution? Excellence to feed the ego of the academically able on the defeat of the less able? Or should the concern in education be for each man as a man so that the level of excellence of the entire society is raised?

Imagine for a moment, admittedly difficult, that a developing nation in South America, Africa or Asia would say to the United States, "We would like to be like you—only better. We would like to be rich, just, free, ethical, charitable, all the things you say you are. What is the secret? How can this be achieved?" Should the answer be capitalism? republicanism? democracy? individualism? Or, would the most truthful answer be universal education?

Turn now from imagination to some present and projected facts. In 1966 there were 2,168 college-level institutions in the United States enrolling 6 million full-time and part-time students. The fastest growing division of higher education, the junior college, numbered 800 public and private institutions with an enrollment exceeding 1,150,000. An average of 1 new junior college was being created each week; 52 per year. In California alone, the number of junior college students will grow from 400,000 in 1964 to 800,000 by 1970, a 100 percent increase in six years. Predictions on a national scale are almost as impressive. Projections from present population and school enrollment trends indicate that by 1970 there will be 39 million children in elementary school, 15 million youngsters in high school and 25 million youth of college age, 8 million of whom will be enrolled in college. The figure of 8 million may be conservative, for there is a percentage as well as a numerical increase of those graduating from high school and a percentage as well as a numerical increase of high school graduates matriculating in college. By 1970, 80 percent of the high school age group will graduate from high school and 70 percent of them will enter some institution of higher learning.

Although modest compared to military or space expenditures, the 1970 operational cost of higher education will be about 14 billion dollars per year. Contrasted with the 4 billion expenditure at the opening of the 1960 decade, the operational costs, exclusive of capital outlay, will have increased 250 percent in ten years. In addition, all college facilities built from the founding of Harvard in 1636 up to 1960 will have to be matched with new capital outlay in the ten-year period from 1960 to 1970 to house the 100 percent increase in college enrollment.

The message carried by these astronomical figures is simply this: Millions of young people are and will be devoting years of their lives to higher education and billions of dollars are and will be spent on this enterprise. When such a price in time and money is paid, crucial questions should be asked: Should all these people be seeking college education? Are they capable of handling this level of learning? Does a society need a college program of such magnitude? Is the product worth the price? Complete and final answers cannot be given to such questions. Instead, the assumptions and premises supporting the whole structure of higher education will be stated as explicitly as possible, followed in each case by partisan argument justifying each basic assumption. What follows then is a white paper for higher education—a case for the thesis that college education must be available at varying levels to all citizens who can profit from it.

COMPETENCE OF THE COMMON MAN

The common man has fundamental competence to learn to direct his own destiny and to participate in directing the affairs of his society. He deserves respect on the basis of this potential alone. It is quite possible that he may have a better head for wisdom than for detailed knowledge, for wisdom probably flows as much from character as it does from a vast storehouse of facts. Without expert military knowledge, he may know that major wars can only be lost, never won.

Since expertise in many subjects cannot be expected of the average citizen, great reliance on the inductive method in education may be misplaced. The need of those with average intellectual endowment may require reliance on extraction and underlining of basic principles followed by clear statements on the application of those principles to the process and problems of living. Mastery of a great array of facts may be less important than understanding the implications of such facts. Several social critics have suggested that society faces not a crisis in knowledge but a crisis in ethics. If so, it is not only absurd but dangerous to focus on knowledge for the few while the moral wisdom of the many goes undeveloped.

Faith in the essential competence of the ordinary citizen to learn is basic to the continuance of a free society. Deny this competence and the alternative is reliance upon an elite—sometimes a very strangely defined elite—that in self interest will organize the society for its own perpetuation. Every totalitarian theorist or practitioner of the left or of the right takes as his basic premise that those making up the base of the social pyramid are incompetent, not deserving of respect, and a peril to the ends of the state. The whole concept of democracy must rest on the premise that the average citizen *is* capable of learning to direct his own life and to make judgments which will enhance his own society. It is the obligation of a democracy to provide the common as well as the uncommon man with the opportunity to realize his full educational potential.

FREEDOM AS KNOWLEDGE OF CHOICES

Freedom is a function of understanding and if access to such understanding is denied or limited then freedom is denied or limited. Contrary to the emotional rantings of superpatriots, no man, American or otherwise, is born with freedom or should unthinkingly die for it. Freedom is really choice to act. If a man is physically enslaved, he has little choice to act. If a man is economically, socially, or psychologically enslaved, he has little choice to act. If a man has no knowledge, or only vague knowledge, of the alternative courses of action open to him and the consequences of each alternative, then his freedom (choice to act) has been grossly abridged. Students who have been denied exposure to any *ism* except capitalism can hardly be said to have freely chosen that economic system.

Man is not born free: he is made free by the process of education and by his own insistence. He has to learn the choices which are open to him and what the consequences of these choices will be, and by character development he must learn to make the more mature choices and to accept the consequences. If in the extreme case he chooses to die for what he thinks to be right, as many men of character have, he has learned to value his principles above his own life—he has chosen to accept the consequence of his own non-being rather than to abandon his principles. It is inconceivable to think that any truly free man would choose the extinction of life to avoid a negative aspect of life, no matter how appalling that aspect might be. To say to all of mankind in a nuclear age "Better dead than red" reflects not freedom of choice but madness.

The Negro youngster in his segregated and therefore inferior school, the high school dropout, the student unable to go to college and the student disqualified from college all suffer a loss of freedom. They are denied access to knowledge of alternative choices and the consequences of these choices. To be free in a society demands an education commensurate with the complexity of the choices required by that society.

LEVELS OF COMPETENCE REQUIRED

The level of competence required of the citizen to choose wisely among known alternatives and thereby direct his own and his society's destiny is markedly different from one generation to the next. At a time when horsepower was actually measured in horses, an elementary school education allowed survival and even progress. A high-school education was the norm as the United States moved forward technologically, and it seemed sufficient for the first half of the twentieth century. But in the 1960's and the 1970's and the 1980's the world grows and will grow more complex; hence, a higher level of integrated knowledge is needed to deal with it. Most people are aware that scientific and technological knowledge multiplies, and those who have an economic and nationalistic orientation are usually willing to support increased education on this basis alone. However, many are less willing to see that the political, social and ethical complexity of the present society has already outgrown the sophistication of the general citizenry and that terrible dangers lurk behind oversimplified answers to such complex problems.

On technological phenomena, Everyman can only echo the late President Herbert Hoover, who, when queried about Telstar, responded that he did not understand those things which were not of his generation. Of political-social issues, however, Everyman can answer thus only at his peril. He cannot shrug his shoulders on the issue of birth control. He cannot continue to breathe smog or drink polluted water. He has to solve the problem he created for himself on the issue of race or surround every Negro ghetto with barbed wire and machine guns. He will have to find some hub of significance in his life when work may no longer be satisfying. When time hangs heavy on his hands, he will need the tools for creative self-fulfillment. As cybernation brings economic abundance, he will have to develop a rationale for a different system of distribution and perhaps create a new ethic that will allow ungrudging acceptance of a guaranteed annual income even to those who do not work. He cannot afford to blind himself or be hoodwinked on ethical issues involved in foreign or domestic policy. He cannot, without rigid compartmentalization, increase in biological and psychological sophistication and remain naive in his concept of God. In short, the citizen of today and the citizen of tomorrow will progress through training in technology, only if he survives as a man through higher education in the social and behavioral sciences, in the natural sciences, and in the humanities. Specialized technological training without general education will give modern man no more survival capacity than the dinosaur.

PURPOSES OF EDUCATION

The purpose of education is to help each man experience more fully, live more broadly, perceive more keenly, and feel more deeply in order to gain self-fulfillment and the wisdom to see that his own fulfillment is inextricably tied to the general welfare. To each man on this planet, the most important life, the only life he can sense directly, is his own. There is no way ethically and only questionable ways pragmatically (IQ tests?) to judge that one man's life is more important than another's. A white, Anglo-Saxon, Protestant, male child has no more inherent right to the achievement of personal potential than the daughter of a Negro Jew. Unless one subscribes to the political philosophy that the individual exists for the enhancement of the state, it cannot be argued that the mentally gifted child has any greater right to self-fulfillment than the child of average mentality. The cosmic fate of the world, if man doesn't blow it up, is to fall into the sun. In the long meantime before that event, no elite of mentality, or nationality, or ideology, or race is likely to lead the human race to any end state of perfection. True, death awaits the individual as it does mankind, but man must be life oriented, not death-oriented. Life-orientation requires viewing life as a process, and an individual process at that. Education is an enriching aspect of the process; therefore education, whether primary, secondary or higher, should be as available to the one person as to the other.

Those who have reached middle life and have soberly watched the previous generation pass, have explored many blind alleys of purpose, have been disabused of the notion the world revolves around them, and have futilely sought some grand and mystical reason for living—in short, the intelligently disenchanted—are likely to have come to the simple, stark realization that the life process carries its own intrinsic purpose and its own intrinsic reward. Not to live it fully is the worst kind of folly. To deny another the fullest and richest life possible is to deny him a portion of his life potential and therefore to commit a most grievous act. Looked at this way, maximum education becomes a human right that cannot morally be limited to a few. Neither can it sensibly be allowed or disallowed on the basis of wealth, native ability, or conformity. In this society and in this age, punitive disqualification of students from college is not unlike ejecting the sick from the hospital.

INVESTMENT IN EDUCATION

A society can afford the kind of education it provides for its members. This is a truism which is often obscured by failure to evaluate education on the basis of its effect on a generation. The present feeble evaluation instruments may, for any one individual, reflect discouragingly little gain. But compare the material progress of nations which have had universal elementary and secondary education with those which have had education only for an aristocracy; compare the material richness of America north of the Rio Grande with America south of the Rio Grande; or compare the technological development of the U.S.S.R. with Czarist Russia. The fact is that each man does not start as Adam. One generation is the springboard for the next: if education elevates generation A, then generation B begins from a higher springboard. This has been so true it has created a severe foreign and domestic problem for the United States. Education has made the United States a *have* nation with wealth increasing geometrically over that of the poorly educated *have-not* nations. Domestically, superior education for the whites in the United States has created such a disparity between whites and Negroes that to say piously that Negroes should now have equal educational opportunity is to speak nonsense. In both cases, the variant forms of foreign and domestic colonialism have resulted in a choice between crash programs of a compensatory nature or violent upheavals by the foreign and the domestic *have-nots.*

Educators are often among the first to lose sight of the value of universal education and to espouse selectivity. On a moment to moment basis, it certainly appears more satisfying and more profitable to invest time, energy, and money on the academic elite. Unfortunately, among other evils, selectivity dries up the spring or source of intellectual wealth. The same educator who advocates selectivity will admit that it takes the stimulation of an educated home life to make native endowment flourish into full achievement. The young teacher often loses sight of the fact that the students he teaches (or disqualifies) now will become the parents of the students he will teach a generation hence.

Historically, the American taxpayer has, at least in a grumbling fashion, agreed to pay for universal education. Notably in California and increasingly in other states, the taxpayer has even voted to tax himself for something approaching universal higher education. His motivation has undoubtedly involved desire for opportunity for himself and his children. The taxpayer's support of universal education may also reflect a folk wisdom not shared by those self-touted realists who would achieve excellence in a society by concentrating on the academically virtuous. Strictly on a materialistic basis, the taxpayer may have seen that education is to a society what research and development are to an industry. It is like a giant Aladdin's lamp which magically produces the future wealth of that society. The taxpayer may have seen, better than the history professor who wants no mediocre students cluttering up his class, that American economic history was really Operation Bootstrap with universal education being the bootstrap. The taxpayer may not have missed the lesson of the post-war recovery of Germany, Japan, England, Russia, and France. The Marshall Plan notwithstanding, it was demonstrated that the wealth of a nation really resides in the education of its citizenry: If a nation has know-how, it can do what uneducated nations cannot—rise like a Phoenix out of the ashes.

Every society buys the education it can, or thinks it can afford and ends by being able to afford the kind of education it has bought. The United States can now afford top quality, universal higher education. If the national expenditure for education were even half that of the defense budget, the United States might enter a Periclean Age—might create what Lyndon Johnson termed the Great Society.

EDUCATION FOR MANHOOD

Vocational training for manpower is only one aspect of education for manhood. Although technical-vocational training cannot be minimized at present, the handwriting on the wall does predict future minimization, particularly for those skills which involve a machine-like routine. More important, a man is an economic unit only a number of hours each day and only a portion of his life. For him, for his family, for his associates, and for his society, it is essential that he be educated to be a good human being. Education has to begin with command of the symbol systems through which all learning and communication takes place. Further, one must know one's relationship to the physical world in which one lives, must understand the significant experiences of one's forebears, must comprehend the dynamics of individual and group behavior, and must be able to appreciate the pleasure intrinsic to all manifestations of beauty, if one is to reach a state of living which deserves the name manhood.

Viability, development, even survival, of a nation require maximum attention to the general education of the citizenry. In its bid for the allegiance of the uncommitted nations, the United States cannot hide its unsavory history of colonialism, its religious intolerance, its past economic exploitations, its insulting assumption of white supremacy and many other liabilities. But, it has a powerful asset: The economic system and the practice of universal education, even with their admitted failures, have created a vast middle class within the United States. This is both a source of envy and an object for emulation. For many nations, the hatred engendered by U.S. gunboat diplomacy or by the neo-colonialism of the past, the lure of communist ideology to the exploited, and in some cases the attraction of commonality of skin color, have been offset by the picture of affluence in America and by the jelling of democratic processes made possible through the breadth and stability of this middle class. Even most American Negroes, who have historically been denied the fruits of this society, aspire not to overthrow it but to become a part of it. However, there has always been the danger in the United States of settling for and rigidly defending a middle class defined only by wealth. Such a middle class is characterized by know-nothingism, by pathological fears of loss of wealth, and by rigid allegiance to reactionary political and economic dogma. It becomes crass, tasteless, and vulgar. It becomes the caricature of the Ugly American fabricated by enemies of this society and too frequently fleshed into being by members of this society.

Training can lead to manpower, and manpower can lead to wealth. The wealth should be used to finance an educational system that would become an international exemplar: a system that would create a vast, solid class with political sophistication, with an awareness and tie with the past, with critical appreciation of the Western and American heritage, and with a hunger for beauty—in short, a middle class of education, culture and taste.

EDUCATION AS A LIFE PROCESS

Education should be viewed not as a discrete phase in life but rather as an integral process throughout life. To be sure, the years of growth are the time for concentrated formal education, but that is not to say that educational need is met at the termination of high school or junior college or senior college. It is only tradition and restriction of available time that have fostered the now waning notion that education is an enterprise only for youth. Plato, who antedated the G.I. Bill by some twenty-four centuries, recommended that a period of involvement in life precede the highest and most meaningful level of education. The veterans of World War II demonstrated Plato's wisdom by achieving at a higher level in college work than the young nonveterans who often possessed greater academic aptitude. Mental agility, an advantage enjoyed perhaps more by youth, is one determinant of educational achievement. However, maturity, background information, and strength of motivation—other determinants of educational achievement—may accrue from having lived.

Labor statisticians are fond of saying that the average worker in the economy of the foreseeable future will be obliged to change his occupation five or six times in his lifetime. Will that same worker not be obliged to update his conceptualization of such a complex and changing world? As a matter of fact, knowledgeable predictions have been made that many of the worker-citizens will be completely discarded after the second or third or fourth instance of employment obsolescence. For this group—perhaps multitude—the alternatives will be either education toward a radical change of values, or existence as living refuse for the societal trash bin. If the latter alternative is allowed, such human refuse will rot the ethical fibers which hold the society together. That is already happening in the slums and ghettos of many American cities. Taxpayers will find themselves with the unhappy choice of supporting higher taxes for universal and continued education or higher taxes to contain and suppress the alienated and dispossessed.

LEARNING OUTSIDE THE CLASSROOM

Learning is not limited to the classroom. There is no magic eye which opens and closes the door to knowledge as the students enter into or exit from the classroom. As a matter of hard truth, a great deal of time has to be spent in class to disabuse students of unhealthy prejudices, attitudes, and values learned outside of class. If, for example, classes are canceled as a reward for winning a championship ball game, the students have learned an institutional value; to wit, ball games are more important than intellectual endeavors. If college sororities or fraternities can and do exclude Jews or Negroes, the history instructor, trying to teach the American heritage of equality and justice to the members of those sororities and fraternities, is talking into the wind. If student activities approaching significance are discouraged because their controversial nature may offend some part of the Establishment, the students have learned some negative (realistic?) things about academic freedom, about the power structure in our society, and about the courage of educators.

The patent fact that learning is not limited to the classroom should not just be viewed negatively or defensively. A positive perspective could be taken: Since the educational effect follows from the total atmosphere in which the student exists, the academician should abandon his posture of tolerant scorn for "student activities" and should in a conscious, calculated fashion set out to create a college milieu oriented to the intellectual, the ethical, and the cultural pursuits.

Such a baptism by total immersion may be much more necessary in the community college than in the four year liberal arts college or the university. The two-year commuter college is populated by students who still live at home, who come and go as their class schedule demands, and who often see the experience as a preparatory interlude. In sum, they have little if any *identification with the institution.* The last phrase is the key. Students will emulate that with which they identify. Therefore, the total experience in college should be designed to capture and bind their loyalty to intellectual pursuits, to wholesome fun, to the pleasures of beauty, and to ethical activism. Identification can be with values as well as with institutions; hence colleges, junior or senior, can create a climate where consciously selected values, like the prevailing winds, push students toward significant educational goals.

COMMUNITY EDUCATION

Education can come in large and small packages and the recipients can be anyone and everyone in the community. It is only convention that measures off knowledge in semester blocs, and it is only the mechanics of school finance which has in the past limited admission to those who were officially enrolled. Educational events should be open to all members of the community. Renowned speakers can be engaged to share their knowledge and wisdom. Performing artists can be hired to perform their art. Reading and listening libraries can be open to all who are interested. Orchestras can be engaged, films can be rented, popular performers can be hired. Such educational opportunities can bring enjoyment and profit to any interested citizen. They can stand alone, unconnected with any semester course, and on the basis of their educational value, they warrant general tax support. When such events—lectures, panels, debates, seminars, musical concerts, art exhibits, dramatic productions, documentary and artistic films, athletic contests and demonstrations, discussion groups, political forums, scientific conferences, technological exhibits, teach-in's—supplement the more systematic curricular offerings open to the young and the old, in the day and in the evening, then the community concept of a college begins to take form and have meaning.

TOPICS FOR CONSIDERATION

1. The uninterrupted trend in the United States has been for more and more people to get a higher and higher level of education. Would it be possible for this trend to be checked or reversed? Under what circumstances, if any, could a slowdown or sharp break in this trend occur?

2. It was suggested that universal education, more than natural resources or capitalism or individualism, accounts for the present affluence of the United States. Would it have been possible for this affluence to have been reached without an ever-expanding higher level of universal education? If universal education had prevailed but socialism had been substituted for capitalism and collectivism for individualism what then?

3. In a very real way, higher education provides the expertise (know-how) and the research for the development of the national economy. What would be a reasonable percentage of the gross

national product to be spent on higher education? If the gross national product exceeds 800 billion a year, does the 1970 projection of 14 billion for operating expenses of higher education seem excessive? minimal? optimal?

4. Is it conceivable for a society to operate as a viable democracy without a fundamental faith in the competence of the common man to direct his own life and to participate in the direction of the affairs of his state?

5. Can anyone other than experts make worthwhile judgments on such complex matters as United States foreign policy in Southeast Asia, or the devaluation of the dollar, or the value of space exploration? The average man is not likely to be an expert on anything, and certainly is not an expert on everything. Why then should he have any voice in making decisions on these most complicated issues?

6. When freedom is defined as the capacity to make choices, then the high positive correlation between freedom and level of education becomes apparent. Is there any other meaningful way to define freedom? Is freedom then a function of education or is there some way for the less educated to be as free as the well educated?

7. The point was made that the individual might make a value choice between a principle in which he believed and his own life; for example, he might choose to die so that Fascism would be defeated. Is it possible that any principle or belief is so sacred that it would be weighed against the extinction of mankind, against the obliteration of life on this planet?

8. Do citizens in a democracy have to have a high degree of general education, or could the system work like the diversified economy? Should each specialist be involved only in decisions pertaining to his area of competence, just as each cog in the economy links up to the turn of the wheels of the vast, complicated, economic machine?

9. The egalitarian position was argued that one man's life is as important (at least to that man) as any other man's life. It was concluded that the enrichment of education should be as available to the financial and intellectual *have-nots* as to the financial and intellectual *haves*. Does this argument remain valid when the enriching education is being paid for by the whole society? Shouldn't the yardstick of value be whether or not the education contributes to the aims and destiny of the national state rather than to the benefit of the individual citizen?

10. Is the statement: "A society can afford the kind of education it provides for its members," just a sophistry, just a catchy slogan, or does the logic of the statement hold up under close scrutiny?

11. Does a publicly supported college have the right, even the obligation, to insist that any student receiving the institutional sanction of a diploma complete a bloc of general education designed more for manhood than for manpower? If so, is this a serious abridgment of the individual student's freedom?

12. People say that education should prepare youth to cope with the world and in the same breath they say that the world is changing so fast that what applied last year will not apply next year. Both statements appear to be irrefutably true, but this then raises the question, When and for how long should a person be given higher education?

SUGGESTED READING AND LISTENING

FULBRIGHT, J. WILLIAM. "The University and the Requirements of Democracy," Tape No. 250. Santa Barbara, Calif.: Center for the Study of Democratic Institutions, 1966.

HUTCHINS, ROBERT. *On Education.* Santa Barbara, Calif.: Center for the Study of Democratic Institutions, 1963.

LIPPMANN, WALTER. *The Public Philosophy.* Boston: Little, Brown and Company, 1955.

MEIKLEJOHN, ALEXANDER. "Education for Freedom," Tape No. 183. Santa Barbara, Calif.: Center for the Study of Democratic Institutions.

NEWMAN, JOHN HENRY CARDINAL. "Liberal Knowledge Its Own End," *The Continuing Debate: Essays on Education for Freshmen*, edited by Leslie A. Fiedler and Jacob Vinocur. New York: St. Martin's Press, Inc., 1964, pp. 31–50.

RICKOVER, HYMAN, ROBERT M. HUTCHINS and ROSEMARY PARKS. "Education: For What and For Whom?", Tape No. 46. Santa Barbara, Calif.: Center for the Study of Democratic Institutions.

"It was a saying of his [Aristotle] that education was an ornament in prosperity and a refuge in adversity."

Diogenes Laertius

4 Functions: Counseling, General Education, and Transfer

IF COLLEGE FRESHMEN COULD BE EXPECTED TO BE EXPERTS on any subject, it would be that of education. They have spent six or seven hours per day for twelve years performing the functions of education, observing the processes of education and being the subjects who were supposed to achieve the aims of education. However, most high school graduates would admit, if pressed, that they gave about the same thought to education that they gave to the air which they breathed. It was just something to be experienced, not thought about.

The two, four, six or nine years of college education can be approached just as thoughtlessly, can be lived in just such an uncritical, uncommitted, unconscious way. Junior college students often select courses or even majors on the flimsy basis that their friends are enrolled in these courses or majors. Four-year college students frequently secure their bachelor's degree without ten minutes of depth analysis of what they are doing or why they are doing it. University students, more often than not, get their lower division education from amateur T.A.'s (teaching assistants) and are deluded into accepting the myth that university education is incomparably better than junior college or four-year college education. Even the master's degree or Ph.D. degree holder will sometimes find he has slavishly run the obstacle course prescribed without thinking out whether he was truly educating himself or whether, like

Pavlov's dog, he was simply being trained to respond to more and more complex stimuli.

No American with even a trace of the canny Yankee horse trader left in him would spend several thousand dollars on a car without knowing exactly what he was getting for his money. After thorough investigation, he would buy the car that fitted his purpose; he would insist on those features and accessories which were important to him; he would take the trouble to learn all about the product he was buying so he could use it to his fullest advantage. How often can the same be said for the investment of time and the expenditure of money in *buying* a college education? Do students insist that a counseling service be provided and then take full advantage of this vital feature? Do many students ask whether they are going to get trained or get educated? Do many students even know the difference between being trained and being educated? Do they specify an open-ended convertibility—that the options be kept open for termination or transfer at almost any point in the educational process? Do they come to full awareness and acceptance of their own handicaps and then select the education that will correct and compensate for their inadequacies? Do they demand the character- and personality-developing features of education more often found outside than inside the classroom? Do they ask for themselves and for others that the college be the intellectual and cultural center of the community? Do they insist that the prevailing attitude be one of open inquiry? of encouragement of the experimental? of frank dealing with the controversial? of expectation that knowledge frequently carries with it an obligation for commitment and advocacy?

The United States is a pluralistic society and as such has, and should have, a pluralistic system of higher education. It was previously noted that by 1970 some 80 percent of the high school age group would graduate from high school and that 70 percent of these graduates would enter an institution of higher education. All 8 million of these students should not enter the Ivy League universities, nor are the junior or community colleges the right choice for everybody. There will continue to be an enormous range of ability and background among those seeking entry into college. There will be justifiably selective colleges, snobbish colleges, easy-to-enter but hard-to-stay-in colleges, and truly open-door colleges. Within each of these groups there will still be overlapping spans of native ability and richness of background so that the man with the highest potential in a public junior college might also have the highest potential at Yale or Stanford or the University of California. A case in point: Although the University of California takes only those among the top 12 percent of graduating seniors and the junior colleges in California accept any graduate, the junior colleges actually enroll more of this top 12 percent than does the university.

The point is that in varying degrees the basic functions which a student should expect to find in a college should be roughly the same in all colleges. To be sure, the student entering Massachusetts Institute of Technology is not going to need the remedial arithmetic needed by some junior college students, but he may need some remedial humanities, as M.I.T. has come to recognize. Also, there should be no confusion about the fact that, for example, the junior college electronics technician major and the university dentistry major are both taking terminal vocation training. One simply takes longer than the other.

Every college should have the following functions:

1. The counseling function
2. The general education function
3. The transfer function
4. The vocational training function
5. The developmental function
6. The co-curricular function
7. The community service function

Each function will be presented here as though it were being discussed by professional educators with the student listening and, hopefully, gaining insight from what he hears. From the discussion the student should be able to judge whether the functions are being served in his college and in his case. Like the features in a new car, the functions of a college should be guaranteed. If the functions are not present, or are present but defective, then students should make insistent demands that the college meet its guarantees.

COUNSELING FUNCTION

Very few universities or four-year colleges have comprehensive counseling programs. They often have excellent clinics for students passing through some psychological crisis and many have a small but well-trained staff of vocational counselors for the relatively few students who have the initiative and wisdom to seek their services. Some, particularly the small, private, liberal arts colleges, have developed a faculty advisor system which provides a rather high level, yet still amateur, advisement service.

It is the new and burgeoning institution of higher education, the junior college, which has made major effort to provide professional, comprehensive counseling services to all its students. And well it might, for the critical needs and problems of junior college students are enough to make the most stout-hearted counselor blanch. Generally speaking, the community college student comes from the lower middle class and, as might be expected, he is the product of this class culturally, in level of educational background, and in past academic achievement. Of course, he may be sitting next to another student who would fit in every way at the most selective of universities, and behind him may be sitting a student whose only chance of academic survival rests on an intensive remedial reading course offered by the college.

To apologize for the nature of any college student would be like apologizing for the human race. To whom would the apology be made? College students exist, and they are going to exist in ever increasing numbers. It is impossible to reach for universal higher education and at the same time hold to old ideas of selectivity. Of course, some universities and colleges can, and should, keep upping the standards of entry as more applicants knock at their doors. One trend appears to be for the junior or community colleges to become the lower division training institutions, thereby allowing the colleges and universities to concentrate on upper division and graduate education.

At the same time, these open door colleges are, willingly or unwillingly, opening their doors wider to the young men and women that an automated economy cannot use and to the previously dispossessed who are acting out their rising level of expectation. So for many colleges—all the public junior colleges—the disparity between the high and low potential student has broadened. The ranks have been swelled by youth from the lower class as well as by greater numbers from the upper middle brackets. Such a clientele calls for professional counselors with a depth understanding of the societal forces at play; a balanced view toward adjustment vis-a-vis corrective activism; an expertise in vocational advisement and educational planning; and therapeutic skill in helping students in their search for significant values and in skirting the shoals of psychological alienation.

Counselors working with the college student from the lower strata recognize that he only half buys—and that at cognitive rather than emotional level—the prevailing myth that education will provide him the good job by which he can hope to marry the girl next door and live happily ever after in a split-level home in suburbia. He suspects he has been hoodwinked by counselors, teachers, and other moralists who have preached the rather cheap doctrine that one should study hard in order to secure the material rewards in adulthood. The counselor finds that the typical Negro, or equally disadvantaged Caucasian, has long since had his resolution and determination sapped by doubt that the American Dream is for him. From experience, the counselor is aware that a large group of students pay lip service to the idea that "education pays off," but they find this belief weak indeed as moment to moment motivation. The payoff is at the end of, not throughout the process, and every year these students demonstrate the truth of the psychological studies that show that distant goals provide puny motivational drive. The problem for the counselor, for the instructor, and most of all for the student, is to devise means by which reward or enjoyment is experienced in the process of education—means by which the pleasures of learning, of knowledge, of wisdom become intrinsic.

Out of every 100 students who begin as freshmen in the four-year colleges and universities, less than 60 will complete the requirements for the baccalaureate degree. Seventy-five percent of those enrolled in public junior colleges label themselves as transfer students, whereas less than half that number actually matriculate as juniors in a four-year college or university. This does not argue that those failing to complete the bachelor's degree or to transfer from the junior to the senior college wasted their time, but it does give measure to the awesome need for effective college guidance programs. There is good reason to suspect that failure to explore one's purpose and vain pursuit of unrealistic goals are major reasons for discouragement, failure, and dropout.

This leads to the questions of Who are doing the counseling? What do they conceive their functions to be? and How well trained and experienced are they to perform these functions? If the counseling responsibility rests with faculty advisors, any hope for professional vocational guidance flies out the window. If the responsibility rests with therapy-oriented psychologists, vocational and educational guidance is relegated to the caboose. If the counselor-student ratio is 1 to 400 or 500 or 600, then counseling becomes just a lick and a promise. Empirical evidence dictates that the counselee-counselor ratio should be no greater than 300:1. Students attending colleges staffed by poorly trained or grossly overworked counselors are being cheated.

In an end-oriented society, there is an almost unconscious thrust toward early vocational decision even when it is known that rapid technological advancement forces frequent occupational changes. Viability in occupational redirection is increased in direct proportion to the broadness of the educational base. Further, if counselors become preoccupied with helping the student find out what he wants to *do* in life, neither time nor attention will be given to explore with the student what he might want to *be* or *become* as a human being. Certainly what a person wants to do should follow from what a person wants to be, hence vocational choice should grow out of definition of self. This, of course, is not to deny that if a person knows where he wants to go it is likely that he will get there more expeditiously than if he wanders about in a random fashion. Confidence in the rightness of one's vocational decision and in the soundness of one's plan to effect this decision becomes a galvanizing prod, or to reverse the metaphor, a magnetic pull.

What is being suggested here and will be developed in Chapter 12 is that the student's attitude and the counselor's *modus operandi* should be the existential one of commitment within a frame of tentativeness. If this sounds contradictory, think of it in terms of the student who is supremely confident that he wants to work with people, not with things, yet remains unready to declare himself as social worker, psychologist, teacher, or personnel specialist.

Comprehensive vocational counseling should be integral to any college guidance program. In such counseling each student would be offered professional assistance in his exploration of who he is, what is worth the doing, and the direction of his becoming; growing out of this should be a progressive narrowing of vocational choice and a clearer definition of educational plan. Needless to say, in addition to training as value analysts and psychological catalysts, vocational counselors should have considerable knowledge in differential aptitude and differential interest testing, in securing and interpreting occupational information and in mapping detailed educational plans.

In the previous discussion of values as determinants of behavior, reference was made to the shallow commitment of many college students to any system of values. Perhaps every generation suspects the one that follows to be lacking in convictions. To be sure, the great ethical movements of the 1960's were sometimes led by dedicated youth. Yet it does appear that many of today's students vaguely sense and are confused by their weak identification with any systematic ethic. They would like to hold to something but find the complicated view of the world and man's relationship to man, slippery. Therefore, they sometimes grab out at the dangerously simply answers. Their need for the balance of general education is great and immediate, but it is hard for them to see this need clearly and they cannot meet it by rapidly synthesizing what they are learning in their various first semester classes. For that reason, frank advocacy is made for a wide ranging philosophic-psychological orientation course to help students search out some value guidelines to sustain them until time will permit pursuit at greater depth. As a matter of fact, this book was written for just such a semester course. Actually, what is envisioned is not a traditional course at all but an exploration of the basic, *nitty-gritty* questions of why a person should be educated and for what.

Instruction undeniably comes first in the hierarchy of functions of a college. However, if colleges are to open their doors to an ever enlarging segment of the population, they have a more encompassing task to perform than developing curricula on a take it or leave it basis. The counseling staff must assist prospective students to assess their own interests, abilities, traits, and ambitions. The counselor must bring two sets of data into relationship in a manner acceptable to the student as a human being: the student's attributes and the requirements of the vocation or profession for which he is seeking training—or, at a broader level, the student as he is vis-a-vis the man he has the potential to become. In addition, the counselor must stand ready to suggest alternatives when it appears that the student is failing to choose wisely.

The entire procedure must be viewed as something quite different from the usual academic sieve, and it must be manned by trained professionals who view counseling as a crucial function in a college that welcomes all students to its ranks and wants to keep them there. This procedure requires full commitment to the helping services of the student personnel department. True, there must be a grand sorting-out process but one that respects the individual's right to make some choices for himself. Learning about oneself is every bit as valuable as learning about other things and other people. Standardized tests yield helpful data; so do past academic records; and self reports of achievements, hopes, desires, and ambitions are additional variables that must be considered in assisting students in assessment of self. But the data is made meaningful by student interaction with a knowledgeable counselor who is committed to assisting each student as a person deserving of respect and who is content to play the catalyst role rather than act the junior-grade psychiatrist or punishing moralist. He simply wants to assist students in self actualization, and hopefully, he is equipped to do this. To the degree that this trained counselor is present and supported, the students are fortunate, for self assessment represents the first long step in self fulfillment, the broad goal toward which higher education is a means. The counseling function is not ancillary: it is integral.

GENERAL EDUCATION FUNCTION

At a surface level, specialized training seems the hardheaded, practical course of action. Yet some of the most respected philosophers and educators in American history (and Americans are a pragmatic people) have seen general education as the very embodiment of the pragmatic approach. They say first things must come first. They say curricular priorities can and should be established. They say a man is a man before, during, and after he is a botanist, a police officer, a psychologist, a dental technician or whatever other specialist might be named. They say specialty education is always dated, tentative, contingent upon circumstances, and of course preparatory only to a segment of a man's life. Educators insist that education lead everywhere, into every facet of life. They insist that it attempt to prepare the student as an adequate human being; as a person deserving of respect and perhaps even love; as a person mature enough to be a parent; as a responsible inhabitant of the physical world; as one whose basic animal sensuality has been sublimated into enjoyment of diverse media of beauty and, for the fortunate few, even into the creation of beauty; as a brother among brothers; and as a knowledgeable citizen in a society adrift in a sea of troubles.

Some nutritionists claim that children, like animals, would eventually, without direction, choose a diet correct for maximum health. Most educators are not that confident about cafeteria-style education. They are fearful that many prevailing but questionable values in the culture would prompt the student to prepare himself only to earn money or single-mindedly follow some other truncated goal. Hence, curriculum and instruction committees composed of professional educators are formed, and after agonizing debate, they take the responsibility for determining what range of man's knowledge will be offered and, more important, what will be required of all students who are to receive the institutional endorsement of graduation.

Any liberal arts college or university deserving of respect has the usual pattern of general education requirements for its own students which it insists the transfer-oriented student at a junior college must take during his lower division years. There is little need to champion the cause of general education for the student aspiring to the baccalaureate degree, for he cannot avoid at least exposure to the broadening effect of general education. It is that 70 to 75 percent of community college students terminating their education after one or two years of college who are most in need of the humanizing effect of general education and for whom there has to be tough-minded insistence on a balanced, comprehensive introduction to the most important areas of man's knowledge. A democratic society cannot settle for less than this, for, as Robert Hutchins said: "If we can only educate 15 percent in a way anybody would recognize as education, then we ought to reconsider universal suffrage."

There is an essential difference between education vs. training; between the value perception of a college and a training school; between the comprehensive community college and the technical institute. The training school or technical institute aims toward producing a well-honed, efficient, productive cog who will fit neatly into the economy and who will find his satisfactions in the rewards of the economy. Spokesmen for college education make the rejoinder that if economic productivity were the only aim, then the stockholders to whom the profit will accrue should pay for the training of the worker, just as they pay for the machine which he will operate. Education is an obligation of the total society because it is the total man, not just the economic man, who makes up the membership of that society. This unequivocal insistence that no part should dominate the whole—that a man is a man not just a unit of production—lies behind the resistence of many curriculum committees to establish certificate programs in vocational specialties, and explains the frequent 1:1 ratio of general to specialty education written into the graduation requirements. For the junior college, the last observation applies as much to the transfer student as to the technical-vocational student. If the Associate in Arts or Associate in Science degree calls for a minimum of sixty semester units, then no more than thirty should be in a specialty field, whether that specialty be preprofessional chemistry or prevocational electronics. In either case, the remaining thirty units should be devoted to those common elements which experience has demonstrated to be essential to preparation for manhood, for fulfillment of potential, and for self actualization.

The hammering out of minimum commonalities by curriculum committees usually creates considerable noise and brings faculty members of all persuasions running to protect their special interests. When the din subsides and the smoke clears, the pattern of general education which has emerged is almost always the same. Agreement is reached that everyone needs essential command of his own written and spoken language. There is consensus that the other basic symbol system, mathematics, has to be understood at least at the arithmetic level. Since a man's psyche is housed in a body, it becomes apparent that every person should have some knowledge of the structure and function of that body—how he can prevent abuse of it, avoid the ravages of disease, mold it into an attractive shape and give it an agility which at least for some will reach a level of beauty of motion. The wisdom of Lincoln's remark, "Fellow-citizens, we cannot escape history," and George Santayana's, "Those who cannot remember the past are condemned to repeat it," eventually prevails, and curriculum committees, if not the state legislature, mandate that the history and political institutions of the United States be taught to all. Giving rather wide choice of possible courses in each category, the remaining requirements fall within the behavioral sciences, the social sciences, the language arts, the biological and physical sciences and the humanities. Spelled out in semester units with typical course titles the usual general education pattern looks like the following:

Course	*Hours*	*Units*
Orientation and Guidance	2	1
Composition	3	3
Oral Communication	3	3
Mathematics	2	2
Health Education	2	2

Course	*Hours*	*Units*
Physical Education	2 per semester	2
American Institutions	6	6
Psychology	3	3
Literature or other language arts	3	3
Social Science	3	3
Biological or Physical Science	6	4
Humanities or Art or Music or Philosophy	3	3
		35

Proper preparation in high school will usually pare this total a bit, but even if the full 35 units of general education were taken, the student would still have a minimum of 25 units of elective courses in the academic major or vocational specialty of his choice. Usually, the elective total will be 30 units or more, for it is difficult to find a major or specialty field in which none of the general education courses, in another context, applies to that major or specialty field; for example, Economics 1A, Principles of Economics, would meet both the social science requirement and the economics requirement within the business administration major.

Thomas Jefferson made the observation, "If a nation expects to be ignorant and free, it expects what never was and never will be." Men, realizing their interrelatedness, band together into societies for their mutual benefit. Since it takes good men to make a good society, educational institutions are established and are enjoined to help youth develop into good men. Those charged with the responsibility of the education of youth know that a complex society requires many highly trained specialists, and the curricular offering reflects this. At the same time, the thoughtful educator knows that a man's work is not his whole life, that every man is a citizen, a prospective parent, a neighbor, a member of the society, a person capable of high levels of enjoyment, a unique and marvelous creature with a drive to fulfill his potential and to live as significant a life as possible. Carrying the dual, heavy responsibilities of providing for individual self-actualization and assuring full transmission of the culture, the educators pose the question What is important enough to generalize to all? In answering the question, they define the general education pattern and use the authority of the society to insist that it be followed by all who are to receive institutional endorsement.

TRANSFER FUNCTION

In discussing the transfer function, the institution of focus will be the junior college. However, the critical commentary on the equating of transfer with general education is as relevant for the university freshman as for the junior college freshman.

The junior college idea was formulated in the beginning of this century, largely by university presidents, to relieve universities of some of the burden of providing general education courses at the lower division level. The ulterior motives of achieving greater selectivity of students and more time for professors to engage in research and publication are not beyond suggestion. Whatever the motivation, in the early days junior colleges developed at the sufferance of the universities. It was, therefore, natural for the staff of the nascent two year college to have the preconception that its courses should be those accepted for transfer by senior colleges.

This function has more frequently than not continued to play the dominant role as the very junior, junior college grew into the more respected institution that has come to be called the community college. No apology need be offered for performing, perhaps too well, the function of providing education for transfer. Many community college students who have transferred to senior colleges attest to the high quality of their lower division courses. Comparative studies on grade points substantiate their testimonial and demonstrate that the transfer student does almost as well as the so-called native student. It might reasonably be expected, then, that in performing the transfer function, community colleges deserve a "well done."

However, powerful internal and external forces are brought to bear on the junior college to subordinate all other functions to that of transfer. Most faculty members are university trained, have not hammered out and internalized a junior college philosophy, and have for a reference point their own graduate education. Junior college instructors jack up their own status when they can say, "If students can make it in my course, they can make it anywhere." When counseled for courses, students ask first, "Does it transfer?" second, "What university requirement does it meet?" and finally, "What is it?" Administrators keep a hawk's eye on grade-point differentials. Parents still ask if units are discounted when transferred to the university. The board of trustees basks in the reflected glory of their products making good at the prestigious university. Senior colleges express satisfaction. The hometown newspapers point with pride to the local boy who made good. Counselors encourage able vocational-technical students to switch to transfer programs. And, the general public seems to interpret *going* to college to mean *going away* to college.

In the face of these magnetic forces, it is small wonder that the local two-year college gets its head turned in the direction of senior colleges. General education courses get confused with transfer courses; vocational-technical courses often must face the charge that they are more expensive and carry less recognition and prestige; remedial programs are barely tolerated if not openly attacked; and the community service function is often viewed as something that really goes beyond the usual responsibility of a college. So—why not just do well that which everyone seems to rank as primary and thereby please faculty, students, parents, and public?

That is exactly what happens at a significant number of junior colleges. The broad-gauge purposes of the community college are subverted. There is an unbridged chasm between philosophy and practice. Over 75 percent of the students elect transfer courses; the faculty indirectly applies the pressure to teach transfer courses; to a large extent the curriculum committee often unthinkingly surrenders its responsibility to its counterpart at the upper division college or university; the admissions and guidance office engages in voluminous correspondence with senior colleges over the transferability of courses; the chief administrators comb the campuses of the name universities for candidates with prestige degrees—and all of this despite this granite-hard fact faced by every community college: no more than one-third of its students transfer.

It isn't the legitimacy of the transfer function that is in question here. All of the community college purposes should be properly fulfilled. It is this ethos, this pervading atmosphere that pins the label of inferiority on the other programs, that is lamented. Such an outlook minimizes the needs of those who for many good and sufficient reasons are not planning to seek the baccalaureate degree. Instructors and administrators who develop the "transfer complex" lose sight of students as human beings who may benefit more from a general education course focused on societal implications than a transfer course calling for knowledge of a vast array of facts. What is it that makes teaching literature more respectable than teaching developmental reading? What is so debasing about teaching a remedial English class? And why do good vocational-technical classes have to stand the test of transferability, which, if passed, leads the instructor to complain from that point on, about the caliber of students who are enrolled?

Two points were made in passing which deserve elaboration. The first was that there is a false equating of the transfer function and the general education function. The second was that community college curriculum committees unconsciously allow the curriculum committees of upper-division colleges and universities to dictate what the offerings will be at the community colleges.

The first issue can best be clarified with an example (in this case the example is drawn from psychology but it could be selected from any general education area). The general education aim of a psychology course should be to help students understand the dynamics of individual and group behavior. The transfer aim of a psychology course is to prepare the student majoring in psychology for the next level course in psychology. It is naive, even delusional, to assume that these are common aims or even aims which overlap to any appreciable degree. This question then arises: Should the community college offer one course in psychology geared to improve human understanding and a second course including all the esoteric nomenclature, derivation of statistical formulae and other specialized information needed for the next level course that the psychology major is going to take? Note well that the distinction here is not being made between the transfer and the terminal: it is between the general and the specific. The highly specialized course in psychology does not do the transfer major in history any more good than it does the terminal student in dental assisting. So the point of absurdity is reached when a course allegedly meeting the general education needs of all the students is actually meeting, perhaps prematurely, the needs of the tiny fraction of students who will become upper division psychology majors.

The first issue leads to the second issue. Those determining curriculum in the college or university of transfer are, using the same example, hoodwinked by the members of their own psychology department into sanctioning an abstruse course in psychology as meeting the general education requirement in the behavioral sciences. The curriculum committee of the community college then reacts by saying in effect: "We have to protect our transfer students, so if psychological nonsense is classified as meeting the general education requirement at State University, then we had better give the same nonsense to all our transfer students. It would not do to present sensible material to the terminal student while foisting off nonsensical material to the potential transfer, so we will give them all the same dose of jargon and minutiae." That is an overstatement, but primarily in the insight attributed to the curriculum committee in the hypothetical quote. To put the indictment in straight language, community colleges are too willing to accept, and to accommodate their own offerings to, the curricular pattern established by the senior college. In California they now are, and in the whole United States they soon will be, the dog that gets wagged by the tail.

There is no dispute with preprofessional courses being very rigorous, very technical and very specialized. Calculus cannot be an appreciation course in mathematics, and music theory does not serve the same purpose as a course designed to develop taste and evoke pleasure in listening to serious music. Perhaps there should be highly specialized courses for the psychology major at the lower division level. The point being made is that students at junior and senior colleges deserve to have those responsible for curriculum ask themselves honest questions and then give honest answers. They should ask, Who are our students? Which of their needs can we fulfill? What needs of society should concern us? How many students will or should transfer to a higher institution? What difference in general education content, if any, should there be between a course given to the transfer student and that given to any other student? If only one-third of junior college students transfer, why should more than one-third of the curricular offering be transfer-oriented? Is it possible that the four-year colleges are wrong and that the overriding need is for the humanizing effect of general education with only subordinate need for an introduction to specialized material? Why shouldn't the community college determine what is of primary significance and value to its students and let the transfer colleges accommodate their curriculum to the transfer students who enroll, if any accommodation is to be done?

To many in the community college, the transfer function is and will be the reason for existence. The transfer function has already captured the quality teachers and endorsement of the university, state college and others in the power structure of Academe, and most dangerous, it is just too respectable and too status rewarding for community college staffs and students to resist. The attempt here is not to denigrate the transfer function but to insist that it be seen in a critical light and that, in the ordering of functions, it be put in proper perspective.

TOPICS FOR CONSIDERATION

1. The charge was made that most college freshmen have not given serious consideration to the functions, processes and aims of education even though going to school has consumed most of their waking life. Is this an unfair or valid charge? Should students be expected to question the *whys, hows* and *wherefores*? What value, if any, would critical evaluation of his education bring to the individual student?

2. *Education* and *training* are never used as synonymous terms. What are the essential distinctions in meaning between the words?

3. Cannot students at every level of college simply assume that the educators have good intentions and good sense? If this can be assumed, then would not the student be better advised to conserve his energies for following directions rather than diverting energies to critical assessment?

4. Most students and most parents of students would be for open inquiry and even for encouragement of the experimental and the controversial, but some believe knowledge will eventually result in advocacy. How palatable is open inquiry when, for example, the advocacy is for stern measures of birth control to avoid the known consequences of population explosion?

5. If almost all people are going to attend college, then should each college take its fair share of the high, middle and low ability students? What advantages, if any, are there in having a hierarchy ranging from Podunk State College to Harvard University? By the same reasoning, should or should not there be a quality gradation among the junior colleges of a state?

6. What are the relative merits of the typical junior college policy

of a comprehensive counseling service for all students as compared with the typical senior college policy of providing counseling services for those who feel a strong enough need to seek out such services?

7. Should counseling be toward realistic adjustment to the *what is*, the *status quo*, or should it sometimes, even frequently, be toward corrective activism? Instead of considering this question in the abstract, apply it to the practical problem of counseling the Negro student who complains of being hemmed in by all the barriers that form a wall around the ghetto.

8. The statement was made: "Certainly, what a person wants to do should follow from what a person wants to be, hence vocational choice should grow out of definition of self." Is this just playing with words, or is there significance in this statement?

9. It was stated that faculty members sitting on curriculum committees almost always come up with a set of general education requirements that seem to be dictated by a situational logic that makes them fairly standard. If these requirements were not imposed by external authority, would students come by the same reasoning and logic to select (self-impose) the same general education requirements?

10. The argument is often made that a student's personal freedom is curtailed if he is required to take courses which he does not want to take. The rebuttal is made that a society's responsibility to the welfare of all members is seriously blocked if each member is allowed to do just as he pleases. Are these two social values resolvable? Is freedom always in conflict with social responsibility?

11. The point was made that all too frequently there is a false equating of those courses meeting the transfer function with those courses meeting the general education function. Why should not Chemistry IA meet the general education requirement in science, or Psychology I meet the general education requirement in behavioral science, or Economics IA meet the requirement in social science?

12. The dynamics of curricular *folie en masse* was described wherein the curriculum committee of the senior college is hoodwinked into accepting highly technical courses as general education and then the curriculum committee of the junior college accepts the same specialty course as general education for its diverse students to assure transferability of the units. Is this condition as mad as it appears to be? and if so, What shock treatment might be used to check this academic psychosis?

SUGGESTED READING AND LISTENING

BARR, STRINGFELLOW. "Educational Bankruptcy," Tape No. 12. Santa Barbara, Calif.: Center for the Study of Democratic Institutions.

EDDY, EDWARD D., JR. "The Results of a Liberal Education," *Introduction to College Life*, edited by Norman T. Bell, et al. Boston: Houghton Mifflin Company, 1966, pp. 33–36.

FERRY, W. H. "Schooling vs. Education: Rx for Junior Colleges," Tape No. 191. Santa Barbara, Calif.: Center for the Study of Democratic Institutions.

KERR, CLARK. "The Multiversity: Are Its Several Souls Worth Saving?" *Harper's Magazine*, 227:37–42 (November, 1963).

LYNES, RUSSELL. "How Good Are the Junior Colleges?" *Harper's Magazine*, 233: 56–60 (November, 1966).

WHITEHEAD, ALFRED N. "The Aims of Education," *The Continuing Debate: Essays on Education for Freshmen*. New York: St. Martin's Press, Inc., 1964, pp. 219–233.

"The goal of universal education beyond the high school is no more utopian than the goal of full citizenship for all Americans, for the first is becoming prerequisite to the second. If a person is adjudged incapable of growth toward a free mind today, he has been adjudged incapable of the dignity of full citizenship in a free society. That is a judgment which no American conscious of his ideals and traditions can lightly make."

Educational Policies Commission

5 Functions: Vocational, Developmental, Co-Curricular, Community Service

VOCATIONAL TRAINING FUNCTION

IN THE MINDS OF MANY RESPONSIBLE ECONOMIC ANALYSTS, there is serious question whether cybernation may not make job-directed higher education an anachronism in the future. There is very little doubt that highly industrialized nations, such as the United States, will harness the computer to the automated machines and produce items as fast as the broken broom sticks appeared to the Sorcerer's Apprentice. This is not to say that there are many today who are ready to reject job preparation as a legitimate aim of higher education. As a matter of fact, the highly trained professional and the highly trained technician will undoubtedly remain in great demand and be overworked even when the machine has enforced leisure on the production-type worker.

Even so, the following facts should be clear to all college curriculum committees:

1. Vocational education without general education is indefensible even if it were conceded that the goal of education is only to prepare the economic man.
2. The sophistication of technology escalates so rapidly that jobs in high demand today are obsolete tomorrow.
3. Workers may gain employment mobility within broad job families if they master some commonalties of knowledge.
4. Training for most traditional trades and production-type jobs has little if any place at the college level.

5. As machines are invented to do routine tasks, production jobs diminish and service-type jobs are created.
6. Employment in the private sector of the economy has sustained and will continue to sustain a percentage decrease, and jobs in the public sector have increased and will continue to increase.
7. There is now private enterprise in the field of programmed learning and system-analysis seeking profits by providing rapid training in needed technologies. In their competition for the taxpayer's dollar, these companies will challenge the colleges that insist on education of men, not training of economic units.

The implication of these facts for the vocational training function is clear: *General education is the footing upon which specialized training is erected.* Irrespective of societal obligations to man *qua* man, general education is inextricably involved with technological or other vocational training. The specialist also has to be able to write, to speak, to listen intelligently, to co-exist with other workers, to see relationships, to understand his specialty within the context of the bigger picture, to make ethical judgment on the task he is performing, to be able to move with some ease to other positions within that job-family, to be ready to assume higher responsibilities, and in a dozen other ways to have the breadth to go with the depth of knowledge. The college should have the conviction, the will, and the vigor to insist on the long run practicality of general education as a base to purely specialized training.

A related and also cardinal point is that obsolescence in specialized training can be minimized by building each vocational category around a core of courses common in value to all specialties within that category. A good example is that of the physical science technologies. Common to industrial electronics, materials testing, engineering technology, instrumentation, and an array of other specialties are the symbol systems of technical mathematics and graphics, and the essential principles of physics. If the student has a year course in

Technical Drafting, a year course in Technical Mathematics and a year course in Technical Physics, he not only has greater flexibility of choice of specialty while in college but greater mobility, or maneuverability, after he has joined the labor force. The same core-concept applies, although not quite as neatly, in the business occupations (Introduction to Business, Economics and Accounting), in the clerical occupations (Business English, Business Mathematics and Business Machines), and perhaps even in special service occupations such as police science (Sociology, Psychology, Local Government) or dental assisting (Biology, Psychology, Office Procedures).

Production jobs in the private sector of the economy have less promise than service in either the public or private sector. The medical services such as dental assisting, dental laboratory technology, medical technology, x-ray technology, registered nursing, vocational nursing, and practical nursing are community college curricula heavy in enrollment and successful in graduate placement. Real estate, marketing, insurance, semi-professional accounting, machine shorthand, secretarial-clerical, wholesale-retail mid-management, and business data processing are examples of consistently successful two-year curricula in the business area. Police science, fire science, food service management, nursery school operation, and convalescent home management are examples of service occupations which promise to be necessary as long as people inhabit the earth. Para-professional occupations, particularly with public agencies, are beginning to swell in number and in volume. Examples include teacher aides, library aides, laboratory or scientific assistants, junior public administrators and administrative assistants.

Two seemingly conflicting educational points should be made in regard to the vocational training function. The first is that most of the vocational curricula are as demanding of learning capacity, interest, and energy as the so-called transfer curricula. Industrial electronics or computer programming are every bit as complex and difficult as history or sociology or botany. To be sure, the professional fields may grow more rigorous and demanding at advanced levels, but at the lower division level it is largely myth which separates transfer and terminal. Students poorly prepared in the tool subjects, without basic command of the symbol systems by which one learns, have no more chance of success in the two year curricula than in the transfer programs. Further, very few of the so-called terminal curricula are purely and irrevocably terminal. Secretarial students can become commercial teachers; electronic technicians can become engineers; police science majors can become criminologists, and so on.

The seeming contradiction is that neither instructors nor their students in the vocational fields should subvert their goals by striving to make their courses acceptable at the transfer college and parallel to courses presented there. If that is done, the community college purpose is not served: the upper division college then determines the content to be taught in the community college courses. For a variety of good and bad reasons, only a third or less of all students attending community colleges matriculate in the four-year colleges or universities. A much smaller fraction of those in technical, service, business, para-professional and other vocational curricula aspire to or effect transfer. To design courses for these students on the academic model is absurd. The outcome of redefining vocational courses into transfer courses is the destruction of the vocational program. Those vocational students whose life circumstances allow transfer simply switch over to academic transfer programs, and those remaining lose the feeling of direct significance and more often than not withdraw from the program and from the college. It is analogous to the seller of a very fine product pricing himself right out of the market.

If community colleges are committed to meeting the educational needs of all who enter, and if it is plain that two-thirds of the students who enter are not going to transfer to four-year colleges, then serious corrective effort is required.

This effort will call for imagination, financial support, involvement of business and industry and, most important, realistic perception of the problem and hard-headed support of the vocational training function by the students, by the instructors, by the administrators, and by the college boards of trustees.

DEVELOPMENTAL FUNCTION

Some state colleges and almost all public community colleges have the very simple and generous admissions statement that anyone who is a high school graduate or is over eighteen years old and can profit from instruction may be admitted. There are critics who jump to the conclusion that this equal opportunity policy ends by populating the colleges with the mentally retarded. Nothing could be further from the truth. The few subnormal or marginal youth who wander in are gently counseled into more realistic pursuits. The universal fact is that open-door colleges have students ranging from those with low normal ability to those who could meet the most stern admission standards of the most prestigious of universities.

However, there should be no blinking at the hard truth that from 20 to 35 percent of students entering colleges without admission barriers are in need of development in the tool subjects if they are to gain maximum profit from the content subjects. The percentage of students needing skill development will depend on the socioeconomic level of the community served and the resultant caliber of the feeder high schools. If nothing checks the present population multiplication; if cybernation radically redefines employment and unemployment patterns and attendant values thereto; if the Negro Revolution raises the aspiration level of the children of the ghetto and all the other economic casualties of the society—if all these societal forces obtain, they will coalesce to flood colleges, particularly community colleges, and make more difficult the present problem of providing developmental and remedial training to large numbers of youth.

The first struggle—and the forces are already allied and ready for the confrontation—will be to sustain financial support and philosophic commitment to this developmental function. Many budget-conscious and public relations-oriented administrators will be reluctant to acknowledge openly that a large number of students from their local high schools are poorly prepared to undertake collegiate work. Not a few academicians, resenting budgetary sharing and loss of personal status, will line up with the taxpayers' associations and deplore *wasting* money on those they term uneducable. The vocational-technical instructors, painfully aware of continued acceptance of the old myth that those who cannot think with their heads can think with their hands, will give small welcome to the disadvantaged students for fear they will, without proper preparation, be shunted off to their programs. Already, some argue that those youth should be sent to area vocational schools rather than to the comprehensive colleges. That is a euphemistic way of arguing for cheap, short-term training which at best will give employment without significance and at worst will mock newly found aspirations by training those presently deprived for future obsolescence. The defenders of the developmental function will be that small, but hopefully tough, band of humanistic egalitarians who argue that full education for all is the pragmatic means to elevating the whole society and is the only ethical and democratic position that remains tenable.

The referent, or what is being talked about, in all this discussion of the developmental function, is the symbol system by which thinking and learning occur. To say the obvious, communication, and hence the learning process, can only take place via the use of words and numbers. The student has to have essential command of the structure of his language and, to a lesser degree, must have fundamental understanding of arithmetic processes if he is to progress, for no subject can be taught without at least moderate command of the symbol systems. To speak of this 20 percent, this 30 percent, this 40 percent of students as if they were all deficient in the same category is an oversimplification. The fact is that among these students, reading, composition and mathematical competency is distributed along a continuum from low to middling high. A student may be low in one skill and quite high in another. Some can have their academic sins washed away with a baptismal sprinkle: others will need total immersion and may need to be held under for quite a spell.

For the most severe victim of environmental deprivation, remedial work is possible only if he, like the member of Alcoholics Anonymous, recognizes and accepts the fact of his handicap. The task will begin with nonsentimental but empathetic counseling, for the student will probably have had a history of performing below grade level; will have had the stigma of segregation into slow learner groups; will have developed an emotion bordering on hate for teachers, principals and all associated with schools; and most damaging, will have come to view himself as a failure. On the positive side, the counselor will know that each person, at least by his own perceptual definition, seeks self-enhancement. Even the case-hardened ghetto victim will have some forlorn hopes and some tentative twinges of desire to "get ahead," and will have come to believe that in our society the road to financial success winds through some college campus. Since college represents a discrete break from the high school, he may feel that a new leaf has been turned and that perhaps things will be different this time.

In working with such a student, the counselor will know from past experience that increased maturity, the imminence of the hard choices of the adult world, the attitudinal change that comes with going to school by choice rather than by compulsion, the status pressures from the peer group, and the institutional commitment to give this person not a sink or swim chance but a well programmed chance to improve himself—all are factors the counselor will be able to use in the opening motivational and planning sessions. The counselor will convince, cajole, insist that the student deficient in the tool subjects take a semester or, if necessary, a year crash program to secure the hammer, saw, and nails by which he can build his own educational edifice.

The basic ingredients of this curricular crash program are several. Of central importance is developmental reading, and evidence proves that reading rate, vocabulary, and reading comprehension can be elevated to at least the floor level competency required for profiting from all but the most rigorous content courses. Of course, the student in the reading laboratory must have the help of a specialist, must be in a class limited to fifteen to twenty students to allow for tutorial help, and must be presented with interesting, challenging materials.

Parallel with the reading program should be a concrete approach to teach the student how to think about and organize what he wants to write and how to write it effectively. For students who have been constant losers in the game of grammar, another attempt to learn writing via the abstraction of grammar is not worth the effort. Vocabulary should be studied, for word meaning is essential for conceptualization. Spelling and punctuation are also important, but they should not be allowed to become obstacles to attempts to write. The instructor's main concern is to teach the student to organize an idea into a logical whole and then to get that concept down on a piece of paper in such a fashion, however primitive, as to be understandable to the reader. Since people think in chunks bigger than sentences, writing exercises should deal with a whole concept and should not be limited to interminable attempts to write the perfect atomistic sentence. Remedial composition courses which never get past the sentence are as absurd as the character in Albert Camus' *The Plague* who spent his whole life trying to write the perfect opening sentence to an otherwise unwritten book.

A third segment of the crash program should be a course in oral communication which concentrates on organization of thought. Here, students should be trained to learn, in a self-conscious way, through their ears, possibly even as a partial substitute for learning through their eyes. As with developmental reading, there is already good evidence to show that students can be taught listening skills and that this newly sensitized medium of learning can be used with great profit in all subsequent content courses.

Closely related to organized thinking in composition and in oral communication should be a course in garden variety logic, or what might be called an introduction to thinking. This has no history of experimentation as do reading, composition, and speech, yet it seems apparent that such qualities of thinking as objectivity, marshaling of evidence, clarity of basic thesis, distinguishing of assumptions from proof, sequential ordering of premises, subordination of detail to major point, and the building of transitions or conjunctions from one concept to the next—all of these essentials to clear thinking should be learnable, and the content used in teaching them should have high intrinsic interest. Certainly the obvious pitfalls in thinking could be pointed out with great value to the student. It may be that the English or speech instructor, or perhaps a specialist in learning theory, would be better than the professional logician in presenting such a course.

A standard part of developmental programs for the more marginal student is a review, or sometimes an introduction, of fundamental arithmetic processes. Beginning evidence seems to indicate that basic rules of arithmetic, if not their derivation, can be learned in a programmed fashion, perhaps through teaching machines. For the nontransfer students not entering the scientific or business technologies, the mathematical demands of twentieth century living are probably no more than the command of basic arithmetic necessary to figure income tax. Nonetheless, awareness of the marvels of today's science, and at the same time the dispelling of attitudes of overawe toward scientific "miracles," requires that citizens develop an appreciation of mathematics. Perhaps this could be without technical understanding of mathematical derivations, just as the concert music listener develops an appreciation for music without being able to read musical scores. The point being made here is that attitude toward mathematics as well as fundamental arithmetic processes must be a part of the developmental course.

To recapitulate, the academically impoverished student whose skill level is marginal for college-level enterprises should be dunked into this fount of symbol systems and, in the cases of flagrant deficiency, should be held there for the first academic year. The following chart is a sample curriculum.

Course	*Hours Per Semester* First	Second	*Units Per Year*
Developmental Reading	3	3	4
Vocabulary Building	2	2	4
Fundamentals of Composition	4	4	6
Oral Communication	3	3	6
Introduction to Logic for Clear Thinking	3	—	3
Basic Mathematics	2	—	2
Group Vocational Guidance	2	—	1
Elective Courses	—	6	6
	19	18	32

CO-CURRICULAR FUNCTION

Students enroll in colleges for reasons too diverse, vague, and subtle for present perceptual testing devices to measure. Their day-by-day behavior demonstrates that they are not in college just to earn a diploma or prepare for a job. All students probably expect to find profit, if not personal gratification and pleasure, in the more formal instructional program. Most, no doubt, expect to enjoy a new freedom and a fellowship offered by the campus community. And, although they may not be too articulate about this, the great majority hope to arrive at new levels of maturity, to perceive themselves more accurately, to exercise more discrete judgments: they seek an expanded, more effective, and more acceptable self. These motives deserve profound respect and should command vigorous support.

Establishment of a college does not automatically create a collegiate atmosphere, the breathing of which contributes to the personal growth of the students. That atmosphere is generated when the college becomes an academic community characterized by mutual respect among its members, commitment to academic freedom and academic responsibility, and common goals enjoying the active support of the governing board, the administration, the faculty and the students. To enlarge the metaphor, the atmosphere will be sterile and stagnant unless the breeze of dialogue circulates among the various components of the academic community. It will be fresh, gusty, and occasionally cyclonic if those recurring virtues—serious thought and ethical involvement—bring about an unleashing of the winds of change. Whether the term atmosphere, climate, milieu, or total environment is used to describe the pervasive condition, it is clear that the co-curriculum—that which happens outside the formal classroom—is part and parcel of that condition and is essential to the attainment of the broadest aims of higher education.

The co-curricular function is more than just dances, football games and student elections. Students today are not going to be content with a social program in which boy meets girl and conventional adult-approved "fun" has been prearranged. Although student-body budgets still reflect the anachronism, the day is coming when students will refuse to spend 40, 50, or 60 percent of their student-body money to pay for a small group of athletes to play interminably repetitive and sometimes harmful games before smaller and smaller crowds in pallid imitation of the contests of professional gladiators.

Even the naive student will soon be disenchanted with a

student government carefully set up and controlled by administration so that college students merely "play" at self direction. It is flagrantly disrespectful and ultimately dangerous to fail to include students in the decision-making process when their own welfare is at stake. The time is passing when the college can act as parent substitute and when students will accept the role of youngsters who are incompetent to participate in decisions affecting their interests. College students are not children, clients, or patients: they are participating members of the academic community with certain rights, prerogatives, and responsibilities. Once this perception of the student is shared by governing board, administration, faculty and student, then the co-curricular function will not be a puerile appendage to, but rather a core function in, the total college experience.

COMMUNITY SERVICE FUNCTION

The arguments have been made and are repeated here that education is a lifelong process, not just a preparatory period for the young; that education can be a single event and does not have to come in a semester package; and that the recipients of education can and should be everyone in the community. Having said this, a realistic note need also be struck: expanded services greatly increase the cost of the educational enterprise; therefore communities willing to accept the expanded functions of the college must have the means and the willingness to pay for them.

The most obvious and least costly service the college can provide to the community is to make the facilities of the college available to authorized groups or to the public at large when such use is not in conflict with the instructional program. That is done to an appreciable degree in every college and in some cases (for example the eighty community colleges in California) has the sanction of state law. The California Civic

Center Act even authorizes a five-cent property tax override on the legal limit to provide funds for the provision of educational and recreational services and facilities to the community. That is mentioned at this point to underline the necessity of finding an additional financial base to pay for community services. Operation and maintenance of facilities cost money, and if the total income is not increased, it becomes a matter of robbing Peter to pay Paul. Money for building, operating, and maintaining facilities which are loaned to the community has to be taken from available money budgeted for funding the other major functions of the community college. When adequate additional money is made available, then the auditorium, the little theatre, the lecture halls, the music rooms, the art gallery, the science museum, the planetarium and observatory, the swimming pool, the tennis courts, the conference rooms, the library, the listening rooms, the kitchen and dining hall—all of the marvelous facilities and equipment of the modern campus—can be used to make the college the educational, cultural, recreational, and social center of the community. And, of course, such generous use of the facilities ties the community to the college with the invisible but unbreakable bonds of identification.

A second community service (which the junior colleges, particularly, have provided with increasing emphasis in recent years) is that of presenting cultural events or, more broadly, of becoming the cultural center—the nexus—of intellectual life of the community. The fact is that such cultural, political, artistic, scientific, musical, cinematic, athletic, dramatic, literary, and technological events are necessary enrichments to the standard curriculum. Opening them to the public simply increases the beneficiaries, adds excitement and enthusiasm, and as policy allows, provides some subsidization of the cultural events program. The educational value of affording regular students or the public the opportunity to see and hear the intellectual and cultural giants of the times is hardly contestable. The debatable questions are, Who should pay for it? and How ambitious should the program be? They are related questions, for the scope and quality of the program is only limited by the amount of money that can be secured to finance it.

A third community service is the wholesale extension of the educational program to the community: it is both Mohammed going to the mountain and the mountain going to Mohammed. It looks beyond the classroom and campus and proposes to diagnose and then prescribe for the educational needs of all the individuals and groups within the community that the college serves. It is bold in concept and expensive in money and in time, talent, and energies of the professional staff. It would organize, staff, and operate the workshops, institutes, seminars, special lectures, and in-service training which a survey would reveal are needed by the industry, unions, businesses, and professions within the community. It would not only open the college library to the public, young and old, but would provide research, bibliographical, and reference services. It would use instructors and students to staff a speakers and performance bureau and put them on call to any organization which felt it could profit from their special talents. It would undertake to supply professional counseling to noncollege youth and adults in the community searching for answers to personal, vocational, and educational problems. It would establish and operate on a full or partial scale an educational FM radio station and, in concert with other colleges, would provide daily educational television programs. Finally, it would set up a faculty consulting service where specialists in every discipline would be available to individuals or groups to help solve problems within the scope of their professional competence. These are all commendable services and are to greater or lesser degrees provided by some colleges. The optimistic and forward-looking are confident these services will soon be as commonplace as the offering of standard college courses.

A fourth subdivision of the community service function

is that of recreation programs which will contribute to the health and physical well-being of the members of the community. Certainly the physical education facilities of the college should be made available when such programs do not interfere with the instructional use for which the facilities were constructed. Critics of this expanded service point out that there is no overriding reason why recreation should become the responsibility of the college. The objection is also made that recreation direction is a profession quite apart from that of education and to put it under the aegis of education would require hiring professionals in this field and adding them to the staff. Again the dispute is not with the need for or value of recreational services but rather with the inevitable drain on financial resources that a year-round recreation program would entail.

The fifth and last of the tasks most frequently subsumed under the community service function is that of providing research and development toward the solution of community problems. Proponents of this service argue that it will provide the maximum opportunity for integration of the college with the community it serves. They see staff members involved in research and planning; serving on coordination councils; conducting studies, surveys and polls; providing workshops and institutes; and offering advisory and consulting assistance in their special areas of competence. This, of course, is not without precedent, for university professors have more and more made their teaching secondary to that type of consulting. This function would change the complexion of the community college as a teaching institution. Instructors with full teaching loads cannot assume additional burdens, even if paid for it, without diminishing their effectiveness as instructors. Expansion of this service would therefore require an equivalent expansion of the professional staff. Ambitious and expensive service can be added only if new, generous sources of revenue can be found. Those with bold imagination and optimism would rest their case for the exciting innovations in community services by reiteration of the premise: "Every society buys the education it can, or thinks it can, afford and ends by being able to afford the kind of education it has bought."

TOPICS FOR CONSIDERATION

1. Would it not be consistent with a free enterprise economy for colleges to accept responsibility only for that aspect of education of value to the total society? Why should it pay for training that will profit a company or an individual? Should a college agree to bear the expenses of training television repairmen needed by Acme Television Repair Company? Should colleges agree to bear the expenses of training men for the vocation of dentistry?

2. It takes considerable knowledge of technology and the labor market to guess accurately which jobs will or will not become obsolete. How can the student, or even his more knowledgeable counselor, hedge on his wager of time and money against possible loss due to technological obsolescence?

3. What evidence can be mustered to support the general contention that employment in the public sector and in the service occupations is more promising than employment in the private sector and in production occupations?

4. What is wrong, if anything, with the popular notion that students with less academic ability should be counseled into fields requiring hand skills, such as machine shorthand or industrial electronics or piano playing?

5. Can a college really be a college if 20 to 35 percent of its students are deficient in the tool subjects? Is a policy of providing developmental training an investment in a poor risk, sending good money after bad? Should not the whole enterprise of education be based on society reaping maximum dividends from its investment?

6. Are the colleges simply letting the elementary and high schools off the hook when they accept students who are not up to standard in oral and written communication, reading, and arithmetic? What would happen if the colleges categorically refused to accept any students with tool subject deficiencies?

7. The proposal was made for what might be called a vestibule year at the open-door college during which those students who are below college standards in the tool subjects would be required to take intensive remedial work. An alternate proposal would be to forget about deficiencies, allow any student to take whatever courses he pleased, and operate on a sink or swim basis—a policy of freedom to flunk. Are either of these policies feasible? fair? to the interest of the individual? to the interest of the society?

8. The University of California, Harvard University, and several others have experimented with admission of some students, particularly Negroes, who were substandard in academic requirements but who were judged to have compensating personality qualities, such as drive and confidence. The results indicate the students have done quite well. Could it be that admission to college has been based on criteria which were measurable rather than criteria which were relevant?

9. It is demonstrable that ghetto schools have given such inferior education that many, if not most, high school graduates from such schools need developmental training in the tool subjects to improve their prospects for success in college level work. Should that training be a responsibility of the college, should some other training agency undertake it, or should colleges have a policy of equal but not compensatory opportunity for all college applicants?

10. The statement is made: "The co-curricular function is certainly more than just dances, football games, and student elections." What should the dimensions of this function be? What do students expect and want the co-curricular program to be?

11. When college budgets are limited, as they almost always are, money expended on the community service function has to be subtracted from money needed for some other function. Does this mean that only surplus money should be spent on community services? Are there some community services that deserve higher budgetary priority than some aspects of the other functions mentioned?

12. It may be that societies can eventually afford the kind of education for which they are willing to pay. Even so, not even affluent societies appear willing to spend on education what they spend on military defense. How then should the priority of functions be ordered? If some functions have to be reduced or eliminated, which should they be?

SUGGESTED READING AND LISTENING

CARSON, RUTH. "Two Year Community Colleges," *Parents Magazine*, 39:66–67 (April, 1964).

FERRY, W. H. "The College: Expectations and Implications," Tape No. 39. Santa Barbara, Calif.: Center for the Study of Democratic Institutions.

HUBBARD, JOHN. "The Junior College: Giant American, Giant Job," *C.T.A. Journal*, 66:34–37 (March, 1966).

MERLO, FRANK P. "Higher Education for All?" *Saturday Review*, 47:50–52 (Dec. 19, 1964).

PART 2

Societal Considerations

IN THE PAST, HIGHER EDUCATION IN AMERICA WAS SEEN largely as a means of improving the graduate's position in life: one went to college to "get ahead." That is still true, but there is a new awareness that one person can't "get ahead" unless the whole society "gets ahead." To paraphrase a biblical quotation: What would it profit a man to gain the whole world if the whole world were atomic ash? As John Donne put it, ". . . any man's death diminishes me, because I am involved in mankind;" and he who is involved in mankind must educate himself to deal with that which threatens mankind. So when the student asks, "Who am I?" he has to answer, "I'm a unique creature but tied by a Gordian knot to my fellow man." When the student asks, "What am I doing here?" he has to answer, "I am trying to better myself but find I cannot without working for the betterment of others." And when the student asks, "What is worth studying?" he has to answer, "Those things that enhance me as a unique creature but in the context of those things that will enhance the world of which I am a part."

Part 2 will introduce some of the social and psychological problems that will dominate the lives of those living in the last third of the twentieth century. Chapter 6 will deal with the population explosion. Chapter 7 will explore the cybernation revolution. Chapter 8 will describe the revolution of rising expectations. Chapter 9 will treat the psychosocial problem of alienation. Chapter 10 will measure the dimensions of the credibility and generation gap. Chapter 11 will summarize other ethical crises to be faced and weathered. These six chapters are not presented as an abstract study of social problems. The issues will be defined and the major implications will be drawn in order to convince the student that these problems will grow to overwhelming proportions during the days of his life—and that he had better educate himself to try to solve them.

". . . it is futile to expect a hungry and squalid population to be anything but violent and gross."

Thomas Huxley

6 The Population Explosion

COLLEGE FRESHMEN OF THE LATE 1960'S WILL BE APPROACHING age fifty at the turn from the twentieth to the twenty-first century. They will have long since become the generation in power and they will have inherited from past generations some problems of monumental proportions. Long before the year 2000, they will have had to defuse the population bomb or it will be ticking off a count-down toward disaster. Unfortunately, this generation will not have an opportunity to avoid all the harsh consequences of the population explosion. Some of the effects are already beginning to pain, and others, not yet felt, are irreversible. At best, they may be able to gradually restore the ecological balance and prevent complete catastrophe.

THE THEORETICAL EXPLANATION

It is not from lack of warning that man finds himself in such dire straits. As early as 1798, the Presbyterian minister Thomas Robert Malthus warned that population increases by geometric ratio while food production increases by arithmetic ratio. To illustrate: An arithmetic progression of 2 for thirty years would be 1, 3, 5, 7, 9, etc., to 61. A geometric progression of 2 for thirty years would be 1, 2, 4, 8, 16, etc., to 1,073,741,824. Altough the population increase is not as terrifying as that, it is still overwhelming.

In approximate figures, the world population in 1830 was one billion. It took one hundred years to bring the total to two billion. But in the thirty years from 1930 to 1960, a third billion was added. The fourth billion will be added in fifteen years and the fifth in only ten years. By the end of this century, the world population will be six to seven billion people. The increase from the present onward will be astronomical, for, as can be seen from these figures, the first doubling took one hundred years; the second doubling will take only forty-five years; the third doubling will occur in twenty-three years; the fourth in fifteen years, and so on to absurdity and to doom. By these trends, the population of California will grow in the second century of its existence as a state to 1.5 billion. That is two and one-half times the present population of China. This unbelievable figure demonstrates the "dismal theorem" of Malthus: No matter what the technological advances may be, the means of subsistence cannot keep pace with the increase in population.

Man has existed on Earth for several million years and other animals have been here even longer. Why, then, didn't this mathematical tragedy manifest itself long ago? With animals, the limitation of plant food and the fact that the strong eat the weak has kept the ecological equation in balance. Man, however, can seemingly outsmart nature. First he devised means to kill potential predators, then he forced the land to yield an increasing abundance, and most recently and most important, he developed a medical technology that greatly postponed death. The problem is not that more people are being conceived but that less of them are dying. Death control has operated while birth control has not. Man in his cleverness has upset the balance of nature, and he is now about to pay for his offense against natural law.

THE STATISTICAL EVIDENCE

Actually, the birth rate in the Western world has decreased within the last one hundred years. In 1860, the birth rate in the United States was 38 per 1000. By 1900, it had dropped to 30 per 1000, and in the depression years of the 1930's, a low of 16.6 per 1000 was reached. Since then, the rate has climbed back to 22 per 1000 and has remained fairly constant. These figures are for the U.S. population taken as a whole. The rate for the rural population is higher than for the urban, and the lower economic and less educated classes tend to have larger families. Even though the death rate among American Negroes is higher than among whites, the birth rate is high enough to result in a net gain. In 1960, 1 in 10 Americans was a Negro. Now it is 1 in nine, and if nothing changes the birth to death ratio in 10 years every eighth American will be a Negro. Even now, 1 out of 6 children in the public schools is a Negro. In the underdeveloped countries, the rate of birth is much higher. For example, in Guatemala the rate per 1000 is 48.7 and in Ghana the registered births (many go unregistered) are 52.4 per 1000.

The significant factor, however, is that throughout the whole world, the death rate has gone down. In the United States, where medical advancement has been spectacular, the percent of male babies who died during the first year of life dropped from 18% in 1900, to 10% in 1920, to 5% in 1940 and to 3% in 1960. Degenerative diseases and accidents are now the leading causes of death in the United States and in other highly developed countries. The contrasting figures of births and deaths in the U.S. are 22 per 1000 population for births as opposed to 9.6 deaths per 1000 population. Further, the Western sanitation, hygiene, and medical practices which account for the much lower death rate have been made routine and simple allowing them to be exported wholesale to every country on earth. So even in underdeveloped countries, death rates have been cut in half while birth rates (except in countries where contraception is widely practiced or abortion is legal) have remained about as high as ever. This disbalance accounts for a population increase of 1.7% per year in the U.S. and the U.S.S.R., a 2.3% increase in India, and a 3% increase in poor countries such as Egypt, Ceylon, and many

South and Central American countries. A 1% increase per year results in a doubling of the population in seventy years, whereas a 3% increase per year means a doubling in twenty-three years. It is like compounding interest with a vengeance.

SOME DIRE PREDICTIONS

The underdeveloped countries account for 80% of the population explosion. A few decades ago, less than half of the babies born in underdeveloped countries lived to reach the child-bearing age. Today, 80 out of 100 grow to the age where they can reproduce. The result, of course, is that a large part of the population of poor countries is very young. Actually, some 40% to 45% of the people are under fifteen years and are, therefore, only consumers, not producers. These nonproducers have to be provided with food, clothing, and education while the country tries to increase production at a faster rate than it increases population. With a yearly population increase of 3%, production of food has to increase 3% annually or the people simply move from perpetual hunger to starvation. The dilemma is even worse than it seems: an economic maxim holds that $3 must be invested annually to produce $1 of income. Countries with a 3% population growth must invest 9% of current income to maintain the same standard of living. To improve the living standard by 1%, they must invest 12% of current income, and to improve it by 5%, they must invest 24% of current income. For most countries, it is like running on a treadmill which is moving faster than the runner. Many countries are falling behind even now; their per capita income and their per capita food consumption is diminishing. If this is the case when the world population is 3 billion plus, imagine the conditions in 1975 when the population is 4 billion, in 1985 (5 billion), or in 2000 (6 to 7 billion).

Actually, famine will strike long before that. Population and food production experts attached to the United Nations predict that China, India, Pakistan, Egypt, Iran, and Turkey will have famines of serious proportions in the early 1970's, and before 1980 the famine will have spread to Central Africa and to much of Latin America. Many of these countries already have endemic malnutrition, and it is just another step to famine affecting possibly a billion people. It is difficult for diet-conscious, overfed Americans to believe the food and population statisticians when they flatly state that the greatest disaster in the history of the world is just around the corner. Right now, 25% of the people in the world are in danger of actual starvation, 50% are seriously undernourished, 15% have adequate caloric intake, and a small, fortunate 10% are well fed. It should be noted for later reference that most of the 25% whose diet is adequate or rich are Caucasians. There will be a tie between skin color and starvation, which adds a further ominous note to an already appalling situation.

POLITICAL CONSEQUENCES

The population explosion is as terrorizing as the nuclear explosion, and the latter may grow out of the consequences of the former. Each person sees only his own little corner of the world, so it is not surprising when Americans take the insular view that the problem of population should be the exclusive concern of India and China and other centers of proliferation. There are two serious blind spots in this perception of the problem. The first is that the world organism cannot have a cancerous explosion of cells in one part without affecting all other parts. The second is that the United States itself is beginning to experience the negative consequences of overpopulation.

In 1967, the population of the United States passed the 200 million mark. Even at the present 1.7% annual growth rate, the U.S. population will grow to 330 million by the year 2000. The educator, who has had to struggle with a doubling of college facilities and staff within the past decade; the physical environmentalist, already losing the battle against smog, erosion and pollution; the city planner, trying to stem the sprawl of megalopolis; the naturalist, fighting to keep some physical refuge for plants and animals and some psychological refuge for man; the foreign aid specialist, who has seen the food reserves of the U.S. siphoned off into the bottomless pit of world hunger; the military high command, charged with the responsibility of protecting the welfare of the *haves* and viewing the endemic insurgency of the multiplying *have-nots* —each of these looks at the prospect before him and is appalled.

A political consequence which looms large for the Western *have* nations is the issue of foreign aid to Asian, African and Latin American *have-not* nations. Western death control was miraculously successful; feeding the millions who were spared to reproduce additional millions first grew burdensome and now appears to be a hopeless and self-defeating task. To give hungry nations food without giving them the means of producing their own food only postpones starvation and allows further proliferation during the postponement. Remember that increasing the standard of living by 5% in India would take 24% of India's current income. Since India needs every rupee for rice and other necessities, it cannot invest 24% of income in fertilization and insecticide plants, in steel mills and cotton gins, and in export industry. A Western power, such as the United States, gives generously of its surplus foods but has second thoughts about giving the means of production, for that would be like a business financing its own competitor. In the case of India, some 18 billion dollars in aid will be needed in the next twelve years, 14 billion to pay interest on past aid debts and 4 billion for new aid programs. It is more than doubtful if such aid will be forthcoming for India; the spectre of famine is so close that the foredoomed have to be abandoned. Stanford University Professor Paul Ehrlich suggested in 1967 that the U.S. stop shipping food to such countries as India ". . . where dispassionate analysis indicates that the unbalance between food and population is hopeless . . ." and reserve its aid for those that it might save.

Except for political advantage, the *have* nations do not give their treasure away. The United Nations target of 1% of gross national product (GNP) to be given by the developed countries to the underdeveloped countries has never been reached. In the case of the U.S., the contribution decreased from .87% of GNP in 1961, to .72% in 1965, to .62% in 1966 to .55% in 1967 and to .27% in 1968. The more militant *have-not* nations claim that the rich nations owe aid for past exploitation and call on the poor to battle the rich in a new class struggle. Ironically, Communist Russia and Capitalist America may find themselves lining up as allies against the hungry—and largely colored—nations of the world.

Other political implications of the population explosion are more subtle than famine and the militancy of the have-not nations but just as dangerous. Delineation of a few of these should make the point.

Massive populations may smother participatory democracy. Active participation in the democratic process is most feasible when the group of people is relatively small and when the problem at hand is actually solvable by the people involved. The student disturbances of the 1960's were attempts, some within the law and some outside it, at participatory democracy. They were active bids for involvement in the use of political power. Many of the activists had lost all faith in representative democracy and, in desperation, took the issue "to the streets." They were attempting to communicate both their outrage and their proposed solution, not by petitions to college presidents or to boards of regents, but often by painful acts of affirmation. When, after jolting penalties and even jail sentences, this too appeared to fail, the students were often bitterly disenchanted and opted out: "Stop the world. I want to get off."

These group dynamics, whether applied to student unrest, civil rights demonstrations, peace rallies, or even riots, seem closely tied to the proposition that in a mass society, he who controls the mass media controls the masses. In the perception of the protesters of the 1960's, the Establishment controlled the mass media; therefore any attempt to communicate a different message to the people's representatives (congressmen, mayors, boards of regents) was fruitless.

Vast numbers may pose an even more serious challenge to the democratic process. Handling people takes organization; handling lots of people takes bureaucratic controls; handling crowds of people takes regimentation; and handling vast hordes of people takes the absolute power of totalitarianism. Clubs, classes, small groups of any sort, are organized. College registrations are bureaucratically controlled. Armies are regimented. Nations, in the crisis of war or famine or any disaster, are subjected to totalitarian controls. Is there any escape, or is the progression one of control, bureaucracy, regimentation, totalitarianism?

After some critical level of the inevitable bureaucracy is passed, the individual is devalued for the sake of the smooth running of the system. The individual case can hardly be given consideration when, say in the question of admission to a multiversity, there are literally thousands, if not tens of thousands, of cases. It is difficult for the college instructor to remain interested in each student if students are funneled at him like a subway crowd. It is difficult for the students in such a crowd to keep from feeling like impersonal numbers, I.B.M. cards. During the 1964 Free Speech Movement confrontation at the University of California, Berkeley, students wore placards shaped like I.B.M. cards which read "I am a U.C. student. Do not bend, spindle or mutilate."

PSYCHOLOGICAL CONSEQUENCES

The psychological consequences are as stern and unyielding as the political effects of uncontrolled population. One of the reasons why flies and ants can be slaughtered without a twinge of remorse, is that there are so many of them. Value placed on life seems to be in reverse proportion to the amount of it. Chairman Mao Tse Tung could threaten, as an American president could not, to unleash the dogs of war, for as Mao pointed out, if China sustained 300 million nuclear casualties, there would still be 400 million Chinese. An excessive amount of life cheapens it almost as an overproduction of goods causes a drop in price. Both human dignity and individualism are early victims of the crush of population. Dignity, decorum, and self respect are hard to maintain when there is no privacy—no refuge from the constant friction of human contact. When day by day life in the crowded, decaying, sordid, degrading urban slums is contemplated with any imagination, the resultant question is not "Why are there riots?" but rather "Why aren't there more riots?" When people live like bees in a hive, the friction will cause mounting frustration, the frustration will cause mounting aggression, and the aggression will explode first chaotically and then systematically. The dynamics of violence which apply to the urban slum will also apply on an infinitely larger scale to the starving nations of Asia, Africa and Latin America.

To feel significant, a person must see himself as a special creature sharing some characteristics with others, yet, at the same time, sharply delineated from others: different, distinguishable, unique. Tight control of vast numbers militates against a tolerance for individualism. Army commanders do not smile indulgently at oddballs; they put them in the brig. Freeway-driving or subway-commuting or queuing up for college registration, or milling in a crowd more often than not induces a feeling of insignificance, of aloneness. The search of the beatniks, the hippies, the flower children, for a flamboyant individuality may be a defiant reaction to being mass produced, a revulsion against the anonymity of being another in a multitude of look-alikes. Alienation was not found in the nineteeth century small town. It is a psychological disease that grew, and continues to grow, with the twentieth-century megalopolis.

A feeling of ethical responsibility requires the corresponding feeling of control over what happens. The survivors of an earthquake do not feel morally or ethically responsible for the deaths of the victims. When vastness of population creates a social system over which the individual has little control, he is not likely to feel ethically responsible for the actions of that society. The individual American could hardly be expected to feel a strong moral responsibility when the famines of the 1970's begin to take their toll. He cannot escape being brutalized by knowing that millions are dying of hunger while he is eating. Yet, he can easily apply soothing balm to his conscience: "What can I do? I don't have any say in running the world."

EDUCATIONAL CONSEQUENCES

A great demand creates a seller's market where the price keeps going up. A flood of young people asking for admission to college tempts colleges to keep raising the admission and retention standards. This has already occurred in the prestige colleges and the state universities, and it presents an increasing threat to the open-door community colleges. At the same time that the need for collegiate education is becoming most crucial, there is a gathering alliance of taxpayers' associations, budget-conscious politicians and (strange bedfellows) faculty members who demand a higher selectivity in college admissions and a ruthless weeding out of those who do not perform at some arbitrarily determined standard.

Although it is a very profitable investment for the society, there is no gainsaying the fact that higher education is expensive. When the costs go up with increased enrollment, there is great pressure to find cheaper ways to get by. The developmental or remedial function is immediately threatened. The community service function becomes a target for curtailment. The student personnel services are charged with being an unnecessary frill. Even the core function of education and training is subjected to drastic economy measures. Class sizes go up. The large lecture is substituted for the small discussion. The 50 percent of students who by definition fall below average are dismissed or encouraged to withdraw. T.V. education is lauded as the panacea. "Operation Cutback" becomes the order of the day.

CONCLUDING REMARKS

The solutions—if there are solutions—to societal problems will be developmental. It is useless for a tiny group of specialists to discover curative steps unless, through general education, the large group is persuaded to take those steps. As for the population explosion, results of the possible courses of action are obvious: If society does nothing, the harsh natural solutions of famine, pollution, and war will bring the death rate in line with the birth rate. The much more pleasant alternative would be to bring the birth rate into line with the death rate. But that will take depth study of the psychological, religious, and physiological obstacles to birth control and an education of the people to really want depopulation.

As the concern shifts from a scarcity of food for all the mouths (the population problem) to distribution of a superabundance of goods (the cybernation problem), problem two will appear to solve problem one. Such is not the case. To demonstrate to believers in the miracles of technology that no amount of production could keep pace with the present growth rate in population, one last statistical projection will be quoted. Philip Hauser, University of Chicago demographer, has calculated that, if the present rate of population increase were to continue for 1700 years, the weight of all the people would be greater than the total mass of the Earth.

TOPICS FOR CONSIDERATION

1. The present world population will grow from 3 billion plus to 6 to 7 billion within the lifetime of most readers of this book. The U.S. population will grow from 200 million to 330 million during that period. How will these facts affect the lives of the people? What will be the economic effects of the worldwide population explosion upon Americans? What political consequences for the U.S. are likely to follow from widespread famine?

2. The U.S. military follows a policy of deterrence and counter-insurgency. Nuclear deterrence is directed primarily at Russia and secondarily at China. Against whom is the counter-insurgency effort directed? Whose insurgency will be countered? Why is the U.S. committed to the quelling of insurgency? Who gains and who loses when insurgency is militarily checkmated?

3. Democracy began in small Greek city-states and flourished in the agrarian America of the eighteenth and nineteenth centuries. Does population impose any limits on participatory democracy? on representative democracy? What kind of democracy, if any, will be possible in the year 2000 when the U.S. population will be 330 millions?

4. It was suggested that valuation of life is dependent on how much there is of it. Are there any ways in which respect for, and high valuation of, the individual could be maintained in the face of vast numbers of people? When the individual is devalued, is there a tendency for the individual's loss to accrue to the state? Are the individual aims subordinated to the group aims?

5. Is there a direct correlation between numbers of people and rigidity of control? Is the progression from organization to bureaucracy to regimentation to totalitarianism? Is there any escape from the relationship of numbers to rigidity of institutional controls?

6. In reference to colleges, it was implied that big is bad; that a large student body destroys personal concern for the individual and brings irritating bureaucratic controls. Are there ways of keeping big from being bad? Can small universes be created within large universes so that students can feel as though they belong, are respected, and have significance?

7. The Catholic Church is often blamed for the population explosion because of its traditional opposition to birth control.

However, Catholic France has no more of a population problem than Protestant England. Although Catholic Latin America is a potential famine area, so are Buddhist Southeast Asia, Hindu India, and Communist China. Even so, considering the gravity of the problem, how tolerant can the prospective victims be to any group whose policy contributes to their victimization?

8. Japan found that contraception alone was not successful in reducing Japan's alarming excess of births over deaths. As a second and more effective measure, Japan legalized and encouraged abortions. Would such a radical measure be acceptable in the United States? What groups would be for legal abortion? What groups would be against it? What would be the major arguments of each?

9. Assume for a moment that the psychologists are correct in saying that men and women conceive and have children because, at an unconscious and instinctual level, they feel procreation to be a means of self-perpetuation, a form of eternal life. Are the schools and colleges justified in mustering an attack upon those unconscious attitudes by forcing the students to look closely at the consequences, to explore their instinctual feelings about reproduction, and to face up squarely to the moral problem involved?

10. The evil effects of overpopulation will be felt in varying degrees by all members of a society. Does this fact justify a social institution like a public college in requiring sex education of all its students? Should a health education instructor be permitted to advocate contraception or even legal abortion?

11. Assume some students are genuinely concerned about the disastrous effects of the population explosion. For what occupations might they prepare to put them on the front lines of this battle?

12. If the problem of population is as grave as this discussion makes it out to be, should every college student be obliged to study its full dimensions and to consider whatever alternatives may be open? In what specific ways can the college help the student to come to a full understanding of this problem?

SUGGESTED READING AND LISTENING

BATES, MARSTON. "Expanding Population in a Shrinking World," *Reading for an Age of Change*. No. 4, New York, Public Affairs Pamphlets, 1963.

DEEVEY, EDWARD S., JR. "The Human Population," *Scientific American*, 203:48, 194–198 (September, 1960).

HUXLEY, ALDOUS. "The Politics of Ecology." Tape No. 29. Santa Barbara, Calif.: Center for the Study of Democratic Institutions, 1963.

———. "Tangents of Technology," Tape No. 7. Santa Barbara, Calif.: Center for the Study of Democratic Institutions.

HUXLEY, JULIAN. "World Population," *Scientific American*, 194:22+ (March, 1956).

NUVEEN, JOHN. "The Facts of Life," *Christian Century*, 83:983–986 (August 10, 1966).

STEWARD, MAXWELL S. "A New Look at our Crowded World," Pamphlet No. 393. New York, Public Affairs Pamphlets, 1966.

UDALL, STEWART. "Our Perilous Population Implosion," *Saturday Review*, 50:10–13 (Sept. 2, 1967).

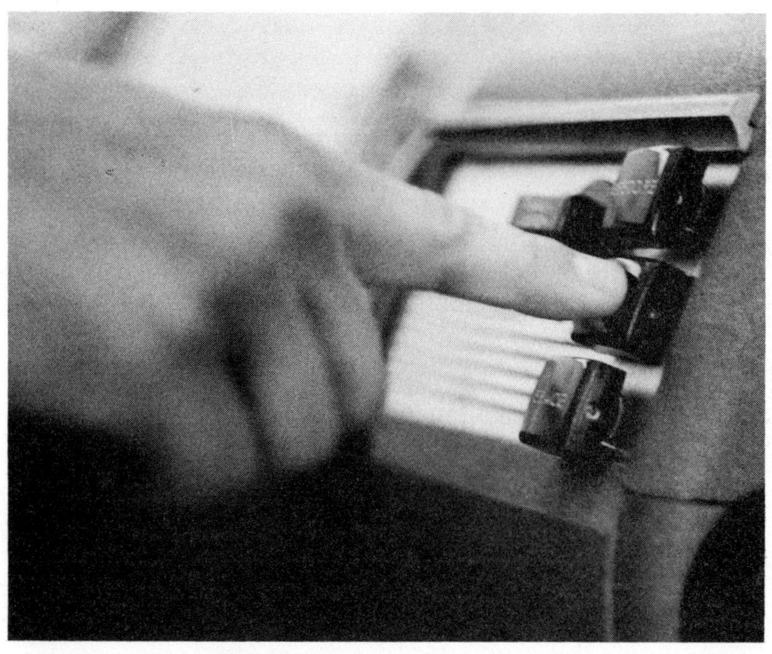

"The image of the automation engineer may not excite the imagination as does the image of the astronaut, but the fate of mankind in the foreseeable future will depend more on what we do manipulating machines here on earth than on how we do hurling them through the heavens."

Adlai Stevenson

7 Cybernation

WITH REMARKABLE VISION OF THINGS TO COME, ARISTOTLE wrote, "When looms weave by themselves, man's slavery will end." Looms do weave by themselves, and man could be emancipated from onerous work, but it may be that man does not know how to deal with his new freedom. Further, there is the frightening possibility that man has been made subject to a new master, the machine. Put in straightforward terms, the thesis to be developed here is simply this: Linking the cybernetic computer with the automated machine (cybernation) can result in vastly increased production with greatly reduced manpower. It is possible to create an economy of abundance, but it would involve radical psychological changes. Man must educate himself to these changes or be the victim of them.

The first computer, the Univac, was assembled in 1951. The silent revolution of cybernation was under way by 1956. The 1000 primitive computers of 1956 have been replaced by 30,000 sophisticated computers, and by 1976, U.S. science, business, government, education, research, and industry will be using close to 100,000 of these seemingly magical machines. Within a decade, the multibillion-dollar computer development industry has used its own machines to calculate ways to make the computers ten times smaller, one hundred times faster, and one thousand times less expensive to operate. The generation of computers which were capable of 20 billion computations per hour has been superseded by a new generation capable of 20 trillion computations per hour, and by 1976 the third generation of computers will attain 400 trillion computations per hour. These astronomical figures, taken from a history-prognostication by David Sarnoff, historian and history-maker in the electronic industry, are used to introduce the scale to be used in any thinking about the cybernation revolution. Cybernation is not just another step in technological development, just as the H-bomb was not just a bigger bang in the military arsenal. Both are qualitatively different from that which preceded them, and the magnitude of their effect can only be measured by those with elastic imagination.

THE PRODUCTIVE MIRACLE OF CYBERNATION

Even after one decade, the effect of cybernation has been staggering, and those technologists and social thinkers who are at the frontier of this new science warn the world that it has not seen anything yet. Farming may be a good beginning example, for in that field the automation has barely been linked to the cybernetics. Even so, in 1949, 1 out of every 15 workers worked on the land; by 1966 the ratio had dropped to 1 out of 27 workers. At the same time, production had increased to feed the existing population better, to feed 20 million additional Americans, to help feed a war-ravaged world and to keep millions in the underdeveloped countries from starving. A specific illustration is that of a tomato-picking machine used in California which in its developmental stage did the work of 40 to 60 men. In 1965, there were 261 of these $25,000 machines, and it was projected that by the following year there would be 700 machines improved to do the work of 80 men each, thereby displacing 56,000 farm workers.

Facts from several industrial studies made during the early 1960's provide evidence to support the generalizations which will follow.

Steel industry: With 50 percent of production potential

going unused, output was up 20 percent while employment was reduced by 17,000 steelworkers.

Chemical industry: Production rose 27 percent while employment fell 3 percent.

Telephone companies: Volume was increased 50 percent with only a 10 percent increase in employment. The brain of the long distance and direct dialing system is a computer called the "line marker." American Telephone and Telegraph Company estimates it would take all the women in the present labor force plus 20 percent more to do by hand the work the line markers now do.

General Electric Corporation: Output was increased 8 percent while the payroll went down 25 percent.

Automobile industry: The Buick plant in Flint, Michigan, turned out the same number of cars it did six years earlier with about half the number of workers. In 1962, Chrysler Corporation was able to make 60 million dollars from its production at the same time it laid off 30,000 workers. From 1955 to 1961 auto employment actually dropped by 132,000 workers.

Elevators: In New York City alone the installation of automated elevators displaced 40,000 elevator operators.

General: The muscle power of one man can produce about 48 kilowatt-hours of useful work per year. The 750 billion kilowatt-hours of electricity generated yearly in the U.S. provides the equivalent of 85 slaves for every citizen in the population. One man-hour of work today produces an amount equal to three man-hours of work 60-odd years ago. If the 60-hour work week of 1900 still prevailed, the present total of goods and services would only take 40 million workers, and 30 million workers would be unemployed. Even in the automation, not cybernation, decade of the 1950's, the index of manufacturing output increased from 75 to 110 with a manufacturing work force stabilized at roughly 12 million workers; since then the index has gone higher and the work force has declined.

The claim made by Norbert Wiener, Donald Michael, Gerard Piel, W. H. Ferry, Robert Theobald, Jacques Ellul, and an impressive number of other serious thinkers is that automated machines, controlled by cybernetic devices such as the computer, can make the economy produce not just affluence for many but affluence for all. Any task which can be systematized can be automated and then cybernated: since almost all physical labor can be systematized, almost all physical labor can be subjected to cybernation. These theorists boldly assert that the cybernation revolution is qualitatively different from the industrial revolution. It is not just that machines replace some men: the whole process can be design-engineered to operate itself.

Cybernation engineers say that it is now possible to construct a cybernated bakery so that grain delivered to the silo will not be touched by human hands until it emerges as bread from the oven and that one plant operated by one man could supply the needs of all of Southern California. No twentieth century Luddites will be able to destroy these machines nor even effect a moratorium on cybernation. Once machines have been created to do the work, there is no going back to "the good old days," for the old days were not so good, not so competitive with foreign manufacturing, not so profitable for the owners, not so affluent, not so convenient, and not so leisurely. The technologically advanced nations have the means, and the immediate prospect appears to be that they will inevitably break free from the age-old economy of scarcity and enter into an economy of abundance. However, some heavy prices will have to be paid.

THE EFFECT ON EMPLOYMENT

The inroads of cybernation on employment have been obscured since 1964 by the nonproductive use of manpower in the Vietnam War. An analysis of employment made by Gerard

Piel in 1961, before escalation of the war, is instructive for the issue under discussion. Only twenty-five million workers did productive work in the sense of making consumable goods from the raw materials which they had extracted. Twelve million people advertised, packaged, and distributed the goods which the twenty-five million produced. Another 12 million provided the financial, clerical and service functions. Some 5.5 million much maligned bureaucrats operated the national, state and local governments. Two million people were household employees and another two million were teachers and other professionals. Before proceeding, the subtotal should be noted: 25 million people were producing all the goods while the other 33.5 million consumer-workers produced nothing. The nonproductive workers, who made up only 30 percent of the labor force in 1900, represented 60 percent of the labor force in the 1960's. An additional 2.5 million people in the armed forces neither produced nor distributed any goods. One million civilian employees of the Department of Defense were needed to keep the military under arms. And, 2.5 million workers in industry were engaged in one aspect or another of producing the arms. When Mr. Piel made this breakdown, there were nearly six million people unemployed. Since that time, unemployment has gone down as the total military effort has gone up. But neither the nuclear arms race nor the fuses of counter-insurgency wars can go on indefinitely. In the not-so-long run, nations will either blow each other into oblivion or find some means to coexist. If total peace broke out this moment, twelve to fifteen million Americans would be unemployed and GNP would be in excess of 800 billion dollars. That would be catastrophic unemployment.

Less noticeable, but inexorable, is the accretion of the technologically unemployed. The 40 percent of the labor force now engaged in actual production will be halved again so that within a decade the actual extraction of materials and manufacture of finished goods will engage only 20 percent of the potential labor force. John I. Snyder, Jr., President of U.S.

Industries, claimed that cybernation eliminates 40,000 jobs per week. Labor Secretary Willard Wirtz stated it was not that high; that the loss was only 35,000 per week. The more conservative figure multiplies out to a net loss of 1,820,000 jobs per year. But the situation is twice as bad as that, for twenty years after the post-war baby boom there are two million more youngsters each year entering the labor market.

The increased unemployment gets hidden in several ways. During the administration of President Johnson, much of the employment slack was taken up by the Vietnam War. Some adjustment to decreased employment is made by later entry into the labor market by youngsters and earlier leaving by older workers. Some of the unemployment is masked as underemployment reflected by the fact that 40 million Americans live below the poverty line while others are wallowing in affluence. Some unemployment is camouflaged by the labor statistics which report only the four or five million who are actively seeking work, not the other three or four million (the old, the uneducated, the Negroes) who have given up the unequal struggle and do not even list themselves as unemployed. Willard Wirtz also commented that even unsophisticated machines now have skills equivalent to a high school diploma, which makes tough competition for the 30 percent of all students who are high school dropouts.

Much of the unemployment cannot be hidden. The first casualties of cybernation are those who do tasks which are unskilled or semiskilled, for these operations can easily be routinized and then mechanized. Other casualties, usually older workers who feel incapable of relearning, are those whose skilled jobs have become obsolete. In the United States, unlike in some highly industrialized European countries, unemployment in general often reaches 5 or 6 percent of the total labor force. The Negro unemployment rate ordinarily is twice as high. Unemployment among the seventeen-to-twenty-one-year-old group who escape the forced employment of the draft stands at about 15 percent. The unemployment rate for Negro teenagers again doubles to an average of 30 percent, and in the heart of the ghetto unemployment among the young dispossessed reaches 50, 60, even 75 percent.

Technological unemployment and increased population combine to make a net need for approximately four million new jobs per year. Generation of new jobs in the private sector has almost ceased except in the service occupations: in the five-year period 1957–1962, of the 4.3 million jobs created, only 200,000 were provided by private industry through its own efforts. The more recent inroads of cybernation into the service occupations lead to the prediction that no significant job creation will occur in the private sector in the coming years. One can look in vain to the private sector, particularly the production segment, for jobs for the undereducated, for the Negroes and other disadvantaged minorities, and for the old.

The last group, those past 45 years, are going to be increasingly hurt by the effects of cybernation. The Bureau of Labor Statistics estimates that 50 percent of the jobs to be held ten years from now do not exist today. This pace of change makes it difficult enough for the young to prepare themselves for future employment; it virtually excludes the middle-aged who do not have a broad educational base from which to make a new start. To call loss of a job due to technological obsolescence "a temporary employment dislocation" is a false optimism belied by the facts. To be sure, some middle-aged workers replaced by machines do retrain themselves. Some find lesser or part-time jobs. Many are reduced to penury, which to save face, they call "retirement." One year-long study of meat workers laid off by Armour and Company showed that 42 percent of the machine operators, service workers, and laborers had been unable to find work.

The conclusions reached by responsible analysts of these dreary statistics on unemployment contradict the political promises and slogans and run counter to the whole structure of values upholding the institutions of work, wages, profits, and property: Full-employment is an outmoded objective. An economy of abundance is possible with many people making no direct contribution to the economy. A large segment of the present population are already casualties of the cybernation revolution, and their material and psychological needs must be met by means other than gainful employment.

DISADVANTAGES OF CYBERNATION

Other things being equal, it would appear that any society with the capacity to produce a veritable cornucopia of goods and services and the desire to consume these goods and services would do so—and with dispatch. However, other things are not equal, and although the movement is toward this ancient goal of man, it is often by fits and starts and is accompanied by a great deal of pain, particularly the pain of discarding outmoded but cherished ideas.

The United States could build—really unleash—a cybernated economy that would provide affluence to all its citizens. However, since cybernation would create technological unemployment for many, equitable distribution of goods must be made to those who do work and to those who do not work. The employed cannot bring themselves to share the rewards with the unemployed, so cybernation has only brought a lower standard of living to the poor Negro, the poor white, the under-class. This has occurred coincidental with a rising level of expectation leading to the sequential dynamics of anger, desperation, disorder, and riots. Technological unemployment has given leisure time to those least prepared to use it, for meaningful use of leisure takes education. Hanging around the pool hall or "TV-ing it" are a meaningless killing of time, not meaningful leisure. The older workers forced to premature retirement are too frequently unprepared to do anything but wait for death. The high school dropouts and other youngsters not as skilled as the machines too frequently can only find trouble to fill their vacant hours.

ADVANTAGES OF CYBERNATION

Cybernation provides the potentiality for a technological society to actually move to an economy of abundance. That was well expressed by U Thant, Secretary General of the United Nations: "The truth, the central stupendous truth about developed countries today is that they have—in anything but the shortest run—the kind and scale of resources they decide to have. . . . It is no longer resources that limit decisions. It is the decision that makes the resources. This is the fundamental revolutionary change—perhaps the most revolutionary mankind has ever known." People can be made to want to consume the goods and services. Invention being the mother of necessity, if the goods and services can be made available people will learn to need them. The only direction open is forward—to an ever bigger, ever more productive link-up of more complex automated machines controlled by more sophisticated computers.

And why not? Automated machines can relieve men from a lifetime of drudgery—from spending eight hours a day, year in and year out, doing unpleasant, routine tasks which have no significance. Cybernated machines can supervise the automated machines so that the worker is no longer an appendage to or custodian of the machine. If production can be accomplished largely without men, then leisure becomes the way of life for most men. For the managers of the economy, cybernation is a means of greatly boosting output while cutting costs. Reduction of unit cost of production makes U.S. exports competitive even in markets where overpopulation makes cost of labor very cheap. As a matter of economic fact, an expanding productivity is necessary in a capitalistic economy, for any drop in gross national product can trigger off a recession or even a depression. Substitution of machines for workers in production allows the diversion of workers into service occupations, and it is self-evident that increased service makes life more convenient and pleasant. Finally, as any foreman or personnel manager will attest, machines are more efficient than men, make fewer mistakes, can work 24 hours a day, do not complain, and never strike.

ECONOMIC IMPLICATIONS OF CYBERNATION

Imagine that after bitter and bloody wars between the Catholics and the Protestants over which road leads to heaven both groups discovered that all roads lead to heaven. Imagine that after cold and hot wars between the capitalists and the communists over the better way to divide the scarce and limited goods both groups discovered that the goods do not have to be scarce—or even limited. In both oversimplifications, the life and death issue is suddenly found to be irrelevant. Both the theory of capitalism and the theory of communism assume an economy of scarcity. The communist proclaims that a dictatorship of the proletariat must take over the means of production to assure an equitable distribution of the scarce goods. The capitalist reasons that there must be differential reward in order to motivate the more energetic and able to accumulate property (capital) to invest to make the wheels of the economy hum. What happens to at least a portion of the theoretical superstructure of both capitalism and communism if the assumption of perpetual scarcity is disproved? if in fact there comes to be an economy of abundance?

The twentieth-century capitalist has already come to realize that some key concepts must be redefined. The importance of property was devalued by the machine, which in turn is being replaced by the idea, the design. Design is the key factor in productivity. The new engineers and managers contribute brains, not capital, and are rewarded for their intellectual contribution by stock certificates symbolizing the property they created. The research and development (R & D) departments are now the creative centers from which productivity emanates. Gerard Piel sums up the shift of centrality in this statement: "Most profitable manufacturing enterprises are those that show a shrinking ratio of plant to output and a rising ratio of instrumentation to plant."

There is a serious threat in the technologically advanced societies that the machines can produce much more than the distribution system is geared to parcel out. Even now, the main function of work for many seems to be not to produce but to provide a means of distributing the goods. Wages can be paid to people who work and the wages can be spent on the consumption of the abundance the machines turn out. There must be consumers for this abundance and there must be a way to provide wages or an equivalent means of purchasing goods in a relatively workless society. This dilemma has driven economists of both left and right persuasion to advocate some form of guaranteed annual salary to all citizens —whether they work or not. If full employment is an impossible goal, and therefore to be abandoned, and if work and wages are redefined beyond all recognition, then profit can no longer have the old meaning. Economic motivation has to spring from something other than getting a lot of that which is scarce. The whole economic rationale has to be restructured to fit the reality of the new facts.

As was pointed out before, the productive miracle of cybernation cannot counterbalance the population explosion. Cybernation can mitigate the effects of this problem in the short run, but it cannot eliminate them in either the long or the short run. Cybernation, in a manner of speaking, procreates itself, so the machines of the technological West could reproduce machines which would allow the underdeveloped countries to skip the industrial revolution and move directly into the cybernation revolution. For political advantage, the U.S. and the U.S.S.R. do have limited aid programs by which entire factories, automated means of production, are given to those uncommitted nations which might be enticed to one camp or the other. The U.S. faces an unhappy choice: It can either provide *have-not* nations with the means of production to compete with its own exports, or face the loss of these nations to an insurgency from the left, a national liberation front of one sort or the other. An advantageous *quid pro quo* might be generous gifts of cybernated means of production made dependent on tangible evidence of stern programs of birth control.

Four economic implications with direct relevance for vocational choice and educational planning should be repeated.

1. When less manpower produces more goods, there will inevitably be later entry into and earlier exit from the labor market.
2. The people most severely handicapped by the environment the society has inflicted on them will probably never work in the traditional sense of the word.
3. The present shift of employment from production to services will continue and will accelerate.
4. With more governmental services for an enlarged population and reduced manpower for production, the public sector of the economy will create more new jobs than the private sector. Already, there is pressure for the government to become the employer of last resort: even the hard-core unemployed should be provided a means of earning an income by the government.

PSYCHOLOGICAL IMPLICATIONS

Work has always been a hub of significance around which man's life has turned. A man's work defined him. To the question, "What are you?" the answer was, "I'm a teacher," or "I'm a plumber," or "I'm a drill-press operator," or "I'm just a housewife," or "Man, I ain't nothing. We're on relief." The machine has set this psychological balance-wheel wobbling, for as early as the introduction of the production line, the worker began to feel as if he were only an appendage of the machine and just as replaceable. Now the machine—the machine-controlled machine—threatens to rob many people of the central significance of their lives. Americans, particularly those in the lower-middle and upper-lower classes, are dominated by the Protestant ethic that work equals good and idleness equals bad. For these groups, as well as for the economically depressed, work has been psychologically linked with manhood—so much so that unemployed men tend even to doubt their masculinity and sometimes move to sexual promiscuity or even to bloody riots to prove it.

All may regret it, many may decry it, and some may blind themselves to the reality of it; nonetheless, the present constellation of values associated with work will simply have to change. Within the foreseeable future (for some right now), many people will have to find their life significance in activities that have nothing to do with work. If work is what keeps them psychologically glued together, they are going to come unglued, for there will not be work for all even if it is doled out in smaller and smaller portions. Old values must be unlearned and new values must be learned. Work will have to be redefined, or put another way, significance will have to be attached to activities not now labeled as work. People will have to learn (as most of the rich have done so easily) to graciously accept income without work. And those who do work must learn not to resent their neighbors who do not work, just as they have long since learned to accept the leisure of the rich. The citizens of the immediate future must learn to accept the fact that the income-through-job link has been cracked, if not broken, and that a new economic system, not yet named much less understood, is being ushered in willy-nilly.

If, as the government experts claim, 50 percent of the jobs a decade hence are not yet known, psychological rigidity about occupational choice will come to be looked upon as a mental illness. It is estimated that many industrial and clerical workers may have to retool themselves for changing jobs four or five or six times in a work-life. This occupational instability will require considerable psychological bounce, hence education in attitude will be as important as training in skills.

Cybernation will bring varying degrees of leisure. There will be the unemployed; the low-salaried, short-week production worker; the higher-salaried, short-week skilled worker; and the overworked professionals. Ironically, leisure will come to those least prepared to handle it. Intelligent use of leisure must become one of the central values of a cybernated economy. Educational institutions will be obliged to do more than preach leisure; they will have to teach for leisure—create the interests and teach the skills by which people can perform well the activities they consider to be pleasurable and significant.

A final but paramount psychological implication is the threat of subordination of man to the machine. Computers can store more facts, assemble them more logically, handle complexities faster, and in the view of many, are more competent to make decisions than man. This is bruising to the human ego. More important, it may deal most men out of the decision-making process. It may mean that those who feed the data into the computer, program its manipulation of the data, and interpret the output of the computer will become the new elite, the only ones qualified to govern. Much of the decision-making of the Pentagon, of big government, of big business is already being done by computers. The President of the United States had to be artificially interposed in an otherwise computerized system for decision on firing of nuclear intercontinental ballistic missiles. The biggest threat to democracy may not be communism, fascism or any other "ism." It may be that good and evil genie of technology, the computer. Certainly, if man at large is going to maintain his place in democratic decision-making, he must education himself to say "Yes" to the machine working for him and to say "No" to the machine controlling him.

OCCUPATIONAL AND EDUCATIONAL IMPLICATIONS

Occupationally, the posture of the college student today must be one of tentativeness. A few, particularly in the professions, can find an occupational lodestar upon which they can set a narrow and undeviating course. For many, it would be most unrealistic to prepare in depth for some narrow occupation which may become obsolescent before they enter it and probably will become obsolete before they voluntarily leave it. The question is how to prepare for predictable change, and the answer is that a broad educational base is the only means of assuring viability—of having the key to many doors that open into opportunity.

The firm grounding in general education (the language and mathematical symbol systems, natural science, behavorial science, social science, humanities) does more than increase the occupational options. It is necessary for understanding the society well enough to make the crucial decisions—to make cybernation the tool of man, not man the pawn in a chess game played by machines. When work has been devalued as *the* reason for living, then education must become preparation for other and perhaps more valid reasons for living. This is not to say that vocational training should not be an important part of education. It is simply to draw the conclusion from the evidence presented that there is a new urgency to search for meaning, significance, and ego satisfaction, independent of and unrelated to occupational career.

TOPICS FOR CONSIDERATION

1. No one contests the present potential of technological societies to produce an economy of abundance. If such abundance is possible and desired, then what barriers block men from achieving it? Are the barriers immovable economic facts? If so, what are they?

2. Assume for the purpose of discussion that man is kept in the bondage of scarcity by dearly held but obsolete economic ideas. Do those who are better informed have an obligation to break this bondage, to disabuse people of the economic unreality upon which they are basing their behavior? What if the public, fearful of economic heresy, objects to a college professor pointing out the fallacy of old doctrines?

3. Most employment experts agree that cybernation causes a loss of 35,000+ jobs a week at the same time as an additional 35,000+ young people try to enter the labor market each week.

What factors counterbalance or hide this alarming condition of unemployment?

4. A forty-five-year-old, semiskilled or unskilled worker who is replaced by a machine is likely never to be employed again particularly if he is a Negro. His son who drops out of school after the ninth grade is almost doomed to join him in the ranks of the hard-core unemployed. What obligation, if any, does society have toward these casualties? What will happen to the society if it disclaims responsibility for these unemployables?

5. If the Bureau of Labor Statistics estimates that 50 percent of all jobs a decade hence do not exist today, then how can college students best prepare themselves for employment? Can educational preparation stop with a college degree?

6. Two contradictory forces were described as being categorically true. It was stated that cybernation could not be checked. It was also stated that most men could not bring themselves to accept the consequences of cybernation. What happens in a society when the inevitable hits squarely against the unacceptable?

7. It was stated that the theories of capitalism and communism are both based on the continuance of an economy of scarcity. It was suggested that if, in fact, an economy of abundance obtained, then much of the doctrine of both capitalism and communism becomes irrelevant. Is it possible that much of the controversy is without substance? Can anyone living through the cold and hot wars between these two ideologies afford not to have a well-considered opinion on the preceding question?

8. The production explosion of cybernation cannot keep pace with the population explosion. If foreign aid took the form of gifts of cybernated factories, some of the miseries of the *have-not* nations could be materially reduced. Would it be to the advantage of the *have* nations to make such gifts contingent on the establishment of birth control programs? Can anyone facing the population disasters of the late twentieth century afford not to have a well-considered opinion on the above question?

9. If late entry into the labor market will be one of the effects of cybernation, will there be a marked increase in the number of young people going to college and going for longer periods? Should longer college experiences be accompanied by later marriage or should the society either subsidize earlier marriage or relax its restrictions on premarital sexual experience?

10. One of the aims of education has always been to increase

the significance, the meaningfulness, of a person's life. In the past, the meaning has been associated with preparation for work. When, for many, work will not provide this feeling of significance, what substitutes does education have to offer? What new significance can higher education inject into the lives of those who cannot find meaning in their work?

11. It is all very well to say that man should make the machine work for him and not be controlled by it. The question is how can man, particularly political man, keep himself in the decision-making process? Should he make decisions himself if, in fact, the machine is capable of handling all the data more completely, logically, and rationally?

12. The old advice about the necessity for students to choose their *life work* is challenged. Is it possible for students to prepare themselves for occupations not yet known? What does the concept of tentativeness imply about the duration and pattern of higher education?

SUGGESTED READING AND LISTENING

DIEBOLD, JOHN, et al. "The New Computerized Age," *Saturday Review*, 49:15–25+ (July 23, 1966).

FERRY, W. H. "Technology; Toxic or Tonic?" Tape No. 266. Santa Barbara, Calif.: Center for the Study of Democratic Institutions.

———, et al. *The Triple Revolution*, Santa Barbara, Calif.: The Ad Hoc Committee on the Triple Revolution, 1964.

MICHAEL, DONALD. *Cybernation: The Silent Conquest*. Santa Barbara, Calif.: Center for the Study of Democratic Institutions, 1962.

PIEL, GERARD. *Consumers of Abundance*. Santa Barbara, Calif.: Center for the Study of Democratic Institutions, 1961.

———, et al. "The Bleak Outlook: Jobs and Machines," Tape No. 78. Santa Barbara, Calif.: Center for the Study of Democratic Institutions.

SARNOFF, DAVID. *The Social Impact of Computers*. Santa Barbara, Calif.: Forces of Change Discussion Program, 1965.

SEABORG, GLENN T. "The Cybernetic Age: An Optimist's View," *Saturday Review*, 50:21–23 (July 15, 1967).

THEOBALD, ROBERT. "Cybernation and the Fulfillment of Man," *Liberation* (March, 1965).

"I can't lose by rioting. Done lost. Been lost. Gonna be lost some more."

Negro gang leader

8 The Revolution of Rising Expectations

ON THE EVE OF THE RUSSIAN REVOLUTION, PRINCE KROPOTKIN wrote, "The hopeless don't revolt, because revolution is an act of hope." In 1967, a Negro gang leader in Oakland, California, was quoted by *Newsweek* as saying, "I can't lose by rioting. Done lost. Been lost. Gonna be lost some more. I'm sayin' to the Man: 'You includin' me in this game or not?' And I know his answer, so I'm gettin' ready to get basic."

Whether it be prompted by hope or whether it be prompted by despair, a revolution of rising expectations is occurring throughout the world. It is best dramatized by the "Negro Revolution" in the United States. However, it extends beyond the Negro to what Michael Harrington called "The Other America," the more than forty million poor and dispossessed who make up the underclass in this country. On a world scale, it includes those hundreds of millions of people who constitute the 75 percent who are inadequately fed.

Certainly, the generation now being educated to assume power will have to face the ethical, economic, and political issues involved in this worldwide revolution of rising expectations. Even before they are well into their higher education, many men will be sent to remote countries to fight in what some call wars to preserve freedom and others call wars to counter the insurgency of the *have-nots*. Some may not be touched by these distant wars, but no one in the generation coming to power will be able to escape the effects of the domestic revolution, the so-called Negro Revolution. The issue has been drawn, the ethical choices have been made clear, the polarization echoes the words of the chant "Which side you on, boy? Which side you on?" The thesis to be developed in this chapter will be narrowed to the domestic confrontation and can be expressed thus: If the generation coming to power has the will and has the courage—and if it hurries—it may be able to avert the ethical, political and international catastrophe of nationwide, violent, racial conflict.

SOME DISTRESSING FACTS

A decade after the 1954 Supreme Court decision that touched off the civil rights movement and a year after the passage of the last of the conscience-soothing civil rights acts, President Lyndon Johnson felt obliged to say, "In far too many ways, American Negroes have been another nation: deprived of freedom, crippled by hatred, the doors of opportunity closed to hope." In 1967, 40 percent of black Americans as opposed to 14 percent of white Americans lived below the poverty line, and as Judge Wade McCree of riot-torn Detroit pointed out, "Many Negroes are poor because they are Negroes. No whites are poor because they are white."

The pre-Civil War voting rule that a Negro represented three-fifths of a man manifests itself a century later in some facts which, ironically, show a devaluation. The median income of Negro families is only a little over 50 percent of that of white families ($3,839 vs. $6,858). Unemployment among Negroes is double that of whites. Twice as many Negro babies die in infancy. Life expectancy for the American Negro is five years less than the life span of the American white. Half of America's Negroes live in substandard housing. The substandard schools which go with the housing are so poor that over half the Negro men taking the army's minimum ability test fail it. One in four Negro men aged twenty-five or over has finished high school (one in two for whites); only one in twenty adult Negroes is a college graduate (one in ten for whites). Although Negroes make up 11 percent of the population, 22 percent of the American soldiers killed in Vietnam were Negro. Today, if the society actually valued the Negro as three-fifths of a citizen, his lot would be measurably improved.

The rate of unemployment among adult Negroes has been at a depression level for the last 35 years. When the unemployment rate for whites is at 5%, the rate for Negroes is at 10%. When the white rate hits the recession level of 6% or 7%, the Negro rate is 12% to 14%. Unemployment that would be called a national disaster if it obtained among whites is called a social problem for black citizens. The unemployment rate for young Negroes, those most prone to riot, is again double that of their white peers, topping the 25% to 30% level. In the heart of the ghetto, unemployment among those who get their education not in schools but in the streets runs as high as 75%. Of employed Negroes, 75% are in menial jobs. Negroes constitute 11% of the labor force but hold only 6% of the nation's professional and technical positions, 3% of managerial posts, and 6% of jobs in skilled trades. Despite their liberal protestations, the labor unions, particularly those in the construction industry, have been every bit as discriminatory as the most bigoted employers. The factor on the horizon which makes these wretched employment statistics more ominous is that routine, semiskilled and menial jobs are the first to be eliminated by cybernation. So the Negro complaint that he is the last to be hired and the first to be fired will grow louder—and more bitter.

The defeat of a Federal Fair Housing Bill by the Ninetieth Congress (resurrected later and passed in an emasculated form to assuage national guilt following the assassination of Rev. Dr. Martin Luther King, Jr.) was probably an accurate reflection of majority sentiments and without question was in line with the trend toward increased housing segregation. During and since World War II, the rural, southern Negro has migrated in great waves to the northern, and southern cities. Coincidentally, and partially because of the Negro influx, the white city-dweller has migrated to the suburbs. More than half of the white city workers now live in suburban homes which were, to a large degree, insured if not subsidized by Federal Housing grants. When an urban neighborhood reaches a certain degree of blackness, then there is a further flight of the whites. The inner cities have been increasingly abandoned to the Negroes who then share less and less community life with the whites. Washington, D.C., which had 35% Negroes in 1950, passed the 50% mark by 1960, and in 1967 Stokely Carmichael, Black Power spokesman, could in truth say to fellow Negroes, "This is our town. Our town." The Negro population in New York is 15%; in Philadelphia, 26%; in Detroit, 29%; in Newark, 35%. In 1967 University of Chicago Urban Expert Philip M. Hauser predicted that by 1970 Negroes would equal or exceed the white population in a dozen major cities. Thus Sociologist Daniel Moynihan could conclude, "The present generation of Negro youth, growing up in the urban ghetto, has less personal contact with the white world than any generation in the history of the Negro American."

As the Negro is locked into the ghetto, racial segregation of the schools increases. Actually, there were more children in segregated schools in 1967 than there were in 1954, the date the Supreme Court ruled that the separate but equal clause was a contradiction in terms. What happened in Washington, D.C., represents a dramatic example. Prior to the 1954 Supreme Court decision, 51% of the pupils enrolled in the Washington schools were Negro. The vigorous push for desegregation increased the white flight to the suburbs so that by 1967 Negroes constituted 90% of school enrollment and present trends predict this will reach 95% by 1969.

San Diego, California, at the opposite end of the country, has some 40,000 Negroes representing about 6% of the general population but about 9% of the school population. All but a handful live in southeast San Diego, which has a densely populated black core in an old, deteriorating section of the city and some lower middle-class tracts on the fringes from which the whites have fled as the more able Negro escapes from the hard-core ghetto. Elementary schools in the center of southeast San Diego have racial balances that the Federal Courts would rule illegal in Alabama or Mississippi. For example, the racial distribution at Johnson Elementary School is 91% Negro, 4% Mexican, 2% other nonwhite, and about 4% white. Stockton Elementary has 91% Negro, 7% Mexican, about 1% Oriental, and about 1% white. At the junior high level, Gompers has 70% Negro, 14% Mexican, 6% other nonwhite, and 10% white, while Mann Junior High School just across the gerrymandered border has 3% Negro, 6% Mexican, 1% Oriental, and 90% white. Lincoln High School, which had about 12% Negro in 1958, before a redistricting occurred, now has 69% Negro, 16% Mexican, about 6% Oriental and other nonwhite, and 9% white. Crawford High School, which lies just outside the Negro school districts, has 11 Negro students out of an enrollment of 3,372.

The account of what happened in Washington, D.C., and what happened in San Diego could be replicated in most of the major cities of the United States. These facts bear out the bitter verdict made by Morris Hauser, Chairman of the University of Chicago Center for Urban Studies, "We're making sure the next generation of Negro children will be as unprepared as this generation."

PHASE TWO OF THE CONFRONTATION

The nonviolent civil rights movement, heroic chapter that it might have been, no longer offers much hope in solving what Gunner Myrdal called "The American Dilemma". The nonviolent solution was defeated by the police and judicial power of the white Establishment.

Leaders such as the late Dr. Martin Luther King, James Farmer, and Bayard Rustin, whose small victories came at exorbitant prices to themselves and their followers, became the moderates. They found their message of nonviolence less and less heeded by the ghetto dwellers and appealing mostly to those who actually gained from the civil rights movement, the black bourgeoisie. In recent years, they have been importuned by those who previously jailed them to try to put out the fires of racial violence. The Black Nationalism of Malcolm X, which always touched a responsive chord in most Negroes, has become the gospel of the young Negro militants. This doctrine made the objectives of the civil rights movement sound like Uncle Tom begging for leftovers. No one has expressed better than Dr. King the failure of the civil rights movement to get the white majority to transcend decency of treatment and arrive at equality of treatment: "White America was ready to demand that the Negro should be spared the lash of brutality and coarse degradation, but it had never been truly committed to helping him out of his poverty, exploitation, or all forms of discrimination. . . . To stay murder is not the same thing as to ordain brotherhood."

The militancy and the brashness of the spokesmen for Black Power pushed many whites toward the camp of segregation and white supremacy. Such polarization has taken place that bloody riots, bordering on guerrilla warfare, have become annual spectaculars for the summer TV audience, and repression, Nazi-style, is openly discussed. Julian Bond, formerly SNCC's director of publicity and now a member of the Georgia legislature, sounds this warning: "The country is too violent to be changed by nonviolent methods. I don't feel the white system has reason or desire to make fundamental changes. So where does that leave the future? Either continued riots in the city with the countryside following suit, producing either repression or determination to do something about it. I'm afraid the white system will adopt repression." Harvard Professor G. Franklin Edwards is not much more hopeful:

"The conventional leaders of the past won't be accepted by the militants and the militants are too rigid to deal with the white community." If no representative black leadership can evolve to work within the existing political system, then the possibility of bridging the gap between the blacks and the whites becomes bleak indeed.

For the Negro, there is really no return to the pre-1954 status quo nor even a retreat to the level of the civil rights struggle. As is usually the case, the militants have moved the moderates in their direction. It was the Rev. Dr. King, not Rap Brown nor Stokely Carmichael, who a year before his assassination told White America it had the choice of integrating the Negroes as full members in the society or putting them in concentration camps. The new Negro psychology, which found articulate Black Power spokesmen, is one of pride, not shame, in being black. Many American Negroes both envy and identify with the black leadership in the emerging African states. The extremists eschew any form of integration with what they diagnose as the psychotic white society. They are as segregationist as their counterparts, the White Supremacists. Even the older and more servile Negroes say with the marvelous accuracy of folk language that "they are sick and tired of being sick and tired" and although they will not join any riot neither will they ever go back to the old caste status. For the Negro, the direction is inexorably forward and although blacks and whites recognize that 22 million blacks cannot defeat the immense physical and economic power of the 178 million whites, both groups realize that the society could break up on the rock hard issue of race.

Several factors are acting to speed the tempo of this confrontation. Cybernation threatens increased unemployment and thereby embitters the antagonism between the poor whites and the poor blacks. The economic gap between the whites and the blacks widens. The Negro high school dropout earns one-third less than the white high school dropout. The Negro high school graduate earns an average $4,500 per year in comparison with the $6,400 earned by white high school graduates. This discrepancy by skin pigmentation even continues when the educational qualifications are equalized: in 1967, the median income for white college graduates was $9,023, for black college graduates $5,928. The impact of this inequity is felt more keenly as the notable success of some Negroes, the TV vision of affluence, and the Negro sacrifices in the Vietnam War open the door to new aspirations and new expectations.

A second factor is the snail's pace of desegregation of schools in the South and the marked increase of *de facto* school segregation in the North and West. Negro parents who have more or less accepted their own bad fortune show a rising fury over the failure of the public schools to give their children even an equal educational opportunity, not to speak of the needed compensatory opportunity. The federal, state and local legislative actions perceived by the whites as protection of their property values and the quality of their neighborhood schools, are perceived by Negroes as insulting barriers to their escape from the ghettos, a condemnation of their children to inferiority, and in general a "white backlash" which they have no intention of tolerating. So—both the glimmer of hope and the pall of despair make desperate men willing to take desperate chances.

THE ISSUE PASSES TO THE NEW GENERATION

When faced with a seemingly intractable problem, members of a society are usually quick to counsel patience and to say that the only solution lies with education. Perhaps this is true in regard to the issue of race in the United States. It certainly appears that the present generation in power is going to pass the issue on to the next generation unsolved. There are some grounds for hope that those experiencing their higher education in the 1960's and, if not too late, the 1970's, may be better qualified to come to some accommodation. Those who sustained the mauling of the depression years and managed to gain the comfortable affluence of the middle class do not look kindly on any rocking of the boat. After the 1967 riot in Newark, Mayor Hugh Addonizio told President Johnson's riot commission, "It is a delusion to presume that the self-interest of middle-class Americans links them with the needs of the poor in the cities. . . . Affluent Americans are gripped more by the need to buy a vacation home, a sports car for their college-bound son, and a second color television set than they are with sharing their affluence with the poor."

The generation now in power grew up in a social order where Negro inferiority was assumed and was accepted by almost all whites and most blacks. Stepin Fetchit, not Sydney Poitier, was the Negro depicted by the great image-maker, the movies. Even mature whites of good will, as was often demonstrated in the civil rights movement, found communication with the Negro difficult due to an almost unconscious assumption of the right to tell the Negro what to do and how to do it. And for many whites intellectually dedicated to racial equality, there remains unexpressed fear, a hang-up, in the sexual area. Since they balk at the ultimate integration of interracial marriage, they do not know at what point short of racial mixture they can take a tenable stand.

The generation coming to power are not victims of these environmental forces, and at least in years, have more of the education alleged to be the cure for such a social problem. The champions of ethics, particularly of the human rights struggle during the decade which began with the presidency of John Kennedy, were the young. Perhaps their ethics have not yet been eroded by repeated compromises, by the pervasiveness of hypocrisy, by the inevitable disenchantment of the years. At any rate, the palpable failure of the older generation to deal effectively with the racial issue leaves no alternative but for the younger generation to grapple with it.

ETHICAL, POLITICAL, ECONOMIC AND INTERNATIONAL RAMIFICATIONS

From time to time, societies reach what might be called ethical crossroads. For the United States, the issue of slavery was one, and a century later, the issue of racial justice is another. Such crossroads, such crises, put the whole basis for ethical behavior in jeopardy. The U.S. is fast approaching such an either-or situation. At a rational level, the white majority will have to move toward racial justice or admit that it makes a self-conscious choice for the advantages of racial injustice. If it opts for the latter, then much of the framework of secular and religious law becomes sham. Of course, neither individuals nor groups always operate at a rational level, so a third alternative of perceptual distortion, of irrationality, is admittedly open. Many Germans during the Nazi period and many South Africans and Rhodesians in the recent past found this irrational escape hatch. The price of this route, however, is the abandonment of sanity, or at least a near-psychotic compartmentalization of mind in which one segment espouses Judeo-Christian morality and democratic ethics and the other segment feeds on hate and takes sadistic pleasure in witnessing the pain of others.

Politically, the issue of human rights has subjected the social cement of constitutional law to an earthquake jolt. The white apologist has asked, "Why don't you Negroes appreciate the civil rights acts we have given you?" and the more sophisticated Negro has answered, "Since skin color has nothing to do with citizenship, why are civil rights acts even necessary? Does the constitution not already guarantee equality before the law to all citizens?" The police, the courts, perhaps the majority of the people give number one priority to the value of law and order. The Black Nationalists dismiss this as the white man's law, which the black man had no hand in making, and the white man's order, which sustains the white man's position of superiority. The more intellectual black or white civil rights worker argues that laws are made by men and when the laws and police powers are used to contravene the higher law of justice—and when all legislative and judiciary means of redress are exhausted—then civil disobedience is the only ethical recourse open. By such reasoning dogs, tear gas, billy clubs, and jail sentences have been used on demonstrators, and by such reasoning civil disobedience has become endemic throughout the United States. On the brighter side, it may be a sign of political health that Americans have challenged the law and order that sustained racial injustice, whereas the Germans under the Nazis failed to challenge the law and order that was even more palpably evil.

Probably the most important resource in any economy is human intelligence. Even nations with minimal natural resources, Japan and Israel are excellent cases in point, have found that an educated citizenry actually creates economic resources. The economic history of the United States is the prime demonstration that when natural resources are developed by trained intelligence, unprecedented richness is the result. The U.S. taught this lesson to the rest of the world, yet oddly failed to apply it to its own Negro minority. By the society's failure to educate the Negro properly, the U.S. economy not only loses billions in productivity but also gets saddled with at least millions in welfare benefits to keep the unemployed Negro alive. Economic Analyst Sylvia Porter made this calculation of the productivity loss: "If both Negro unemployment and productivity could be suddenly 'equalized' at the level of today's white citizens, the rise in GNP would be an astounding $27 billion—a gain of four percent in our yearly output of goods and services." To pay 27 billion dollars, not once but every year, for the luxury of racial discrimination violates common sense as well as economic sense.

As the Declaration of Independence points out, every society must have "a decent respect for the opinion of mankind." It is important for the United States to maintain a posture of moral and ethical responsibility in its relationship to the rest of the world. As a matter of history, the Johnson Administration's posture of the U.S. fighting for freedom and human dignity in South Vietnam was compromised if not made absurd by the frequent race riots (guerrilla warfare) that erupted in the ghettos of Los Angeles, New York, Detroit, Cleveland, and other American cities. The fact is that the Caucasians are a rather small minority of the world's population. Most of the people of the world are of a darker hue, and there tends to be some identification by color. To many of the yellow, the brown and the black, the behavior of white America only differs in degree, not in kind, from the almost universally condemned apartheid of the whites in South Africa and Rhodesia.

RELATIONSHIP TO HIGHER EDUCATION

An issue as complex as the revolution of rising expectations, domestic or foreign, cannot be solved simply by realizing that something is awry and then willing that it be set straight. It is much more difficult than that. Proposed solutions are not in short supply, but the generations which will have to live out whatever solution is applied had better make more than a superficial study of the alternatives that are open and the effects which will follow from each.

There are those, mostly whites, who counsel gradualism and say that it will take generations to bring the Negro to a level acceptable for integration. Not many Negroes will buy this solution and, as the rioting has demonstrated to all but the most obtuse, some Negroes will burn the American cities down during the waiting period. One of the crippling disillusionments among Negroes in the civil rights demonstrations was the mounting evidence that most people could not be shamed into ethical behavior: the Negro came to feel that to prick the conscience of many whites would take a jackhammer. From the time he is first called "nigger," the Negro in the ghetto begins to sense that the human psyche, a man's character and personality, can be maimed just as his body can be murdered. Even the staunchest advocate of nonviolence cannot watch this happening to his children without experiencing hatred and fury. One of the shoals upon which the civil rights movement foundered was the gradualism of the white liberals. Even Martin Luther King was accused of just putting out fires so the whites never really got scorched.

Apartheid, white or Muslim style, has appeal to the extremists in either camp. The white segregationist would like a complete separation with a wall built around the ghetto. Step one, however, calls for step two: disenfranchisement of the Negro. If the Negro is concentrated in racial enclaves *and* is given the vote, then he becomes a political force with tremendous bargaining power. This is already occurring in the urban centers of the North and West and in the towns and counties of the Black Belt of the South. Some diehard southern and northern segregationists are beginning to have some second thoughts. The Black Muslims ask for what Abraham Lincoln once proposed: physical separation of the Negroes into an independent colony in South America or Africa. The Muslims want it to be New York State or some prosperous tenth of continental United States. Most Americans, black and white, consider this preposterous on two counts: (1) The Muslims have no rational economic plan to make such a separation work. (2) A nation within a nation has a potential for more trouble than the blacks unintegrated but dispersed among the whites—the metaphorical two nations of which Lyndon Johnson spoke.

Dramatic and overdrawn as it may sound, the possibility of "a final solution" a la Hitler has to be considered. It should be remembered before quick dismissal of this thought that Germany was a highly civilized, Christian nation and that the six million Jews murdered by the Nazis were not as distinguishable nor as threatening as the Negroes. In the 1960's, National Guard or Federal troops were put on alert each summer as the riot season approached. Los Angeles police have a 20-ton armored personnel carrier complete with a 30-calibre machine gun, tear-gas bombs, and a siren whose wail can stun rioters.

In November, 1967, *Newsweek* put out a special issue on "The Negro in America" in which this ominous statement appeared: "Talk of repression in one form or another is widespread today. Radicals mutter about black rebels being shunted into concentration camps—and their conversation reflects a real element of fear, not just agitators' hokum. There are advocates of garrisoning the ghettos and of limiting freedom of speech in the face of clear and present danger. 'What is remarkable,' says Political Scientist James Q. Wilson, 'is that there has not yet emerged a [Joe] McCarthy of race: a figure with a mass audience . . . who would say boldly and demagogically what millions of people are already thinking.' "

None of the alternatives suggested thus far appear very palatable. It is not likely that serious attacks on the problem will receive universal applause. Most sophisticated thinkers recognize that the much feared and maligned Black Power Movement is probably a necessary phase to reknit the divided Negro community, to build Negro morale, to make white America aware and properly fearful of what goes on in the minds of black America, to help both black and white to reevaluate old notions of Negro inferiority, and to dramatize the urgency of massive measures for righting old wrongs. Even though Black Power may be a necessary part of the solution, it will be hard for whites to accept. Further, the crash programs, not for equal, but for compensatory opportunities in education, employment, and housing, will have to be directed by Negroes, for the black man no longer wants to be rescued by the white man. Sacrificial help from, without control by, White America may be a necessary part of the solution, but that again will be hard for whites to accept.

The intent of the above discussion is not to propose solutions but to make clear that if the educated do not intervene on the side of rational, nonviolent solution, then the noneducated black and the noneducated white will move, and very soon, to violent "solutions." To repeat an important point made earlier: higher education does not always lead to ethical behavior, but it increases the chances thereof. If it doesn't raise the whole standard of ethical behavior, then education is practically worthless for the civil rights issue, for the revolution of rising expectations is essentially a crisis in ethics. If the crisis is to be met, the generation coming to power will have to make itself fully aware of the problem, peer deeply into all factors involved, extract rational solutions and become active in effecting these solutions.

TOPICS FOR CONSIDERATION

1. The contention is made that no one in the generation coming to power will be able to escape the effects of the Negro Revolution; that all the obscuring qualifications and reservations have been chipped away, and that each must face the naked question "Which side you on, boy? Which side you on?" Is this an oversimplification? If so, what would be a more accurate description of the issue left as a legacy by the previous generations?

2. A universally accepted assumption in psychology is that all behavior is caused. By the statistics quoted in the section, "Some Distressing Facts," it would appear that as a group American Negroes experience about half as much of the good and twice as much of the bad as white Americans. What causes this? What constellation of factors in human behavior accounts for this inequitable distribution of good and bad fortune?

3. It would appear that cybernation has and will continue to cut like a scythe through the ranks of menial and semiskilled jobs held by some 75 per cent of employed Negroes. Considering this, was the picketing and demonstrating of the civil rights organizations against job discrimination a painful and fruitless enterprise—the fighting of a battle already lost?

4. The Supreme Court ruled that in regard to schools *separate* by

definition is *not equal.* To a slight degree, the ruling worked for the desegregation of the schools in the South but in the North the white flight to the suburbs and the ghettoizing of the Negroes nullified the Supreme Court ruling. Is there any way to beat this? Should school integration be abandoned as a lost cause and the corrective thrust be applied from some different angle? What about the Black Power proposal to have black children in schools staffed by black teachers and administrators and controlled by black boards of trustees?

5. The statement was made that the ethical issue is now so clear-cut that if the white majority decides in favor of the advantages of racial injustice there will be no way of hiding what has happened. Will this, as is contended, put the whole basis for ethical behavior in jeopardy? In what ways, if any, will it make sham of much of secular and religious law?

6. It is quite apparent that Negro Americans as a group do not have the same perception of law and order as do most white Americans. What accounts for this marked difference in perception? What predictions can be made about the future behavior of each group that will follow from their respective perceptions?

7. One of the political effects of the civil rights movement and the whole confrontation over the racial issue has been a questioning of the sacredness of law and a gathering hostility to the order imposed by the police. Civil disobedience has become one of the political options resorted to by protestants. By what reasoning, if any, can this be justified? Does endemic civil disobedience indicate that less drastic means of political change are no longer open?

8. Gradualism, apartheid, and annihilation are three possible ways of dealing with the racial issue in the United States. Each of these alternatives has its spokesmen and its group of advocates. Under what circumstances might each of these three options become the prevailing policy of those in power? What other courses of action are open, and under what circumstances might each be adopted as national policy?

9. Who should be participants in decisions on policies affecting the explosive racial issue? Does a citizen who has not seriously studied the issue or given much thought to the possible solutions have much of a right to be involved in the decision-making process?

10. Is there any reason to believe that by virtue of education people will arrive at more rational solutions to an emotionally

charged issue such as race? If so, what aspects of education are likely to lead them to more rational solutions? Does the society have the right to insist that all citizens prepare themselves to participate in decisions on crucial issues?

11. Many college students are genuinely concerned about the racial crisis in the United States. What actions, off and on the campus, might these students take to give expression to their concern? Should they involve themselves while still in college? What forms should this involvement take?

12. Assume that some students came to feel that the domestic revolution of rising expectation was of such overriding importance that they wanted to devote their careers to it. How could they best educate themselves for such a career? What major should they follow and what courses should they take?

SUGGESTED READING AND LISTENING

JOHNSON, LYNDON B., et al. "The Negro As An American." Santa Barbara, Calif., Center for the Study of Democratic Institutions.

KAHN, TOM. *The Economics of Equality*. New York: League for Industrial Democracy, 1964.

KING, MARTIN LUTHER, HARRY GOLDEN, et al. "Toward Civil Rights Now," *Progressive*, Madison, Wis., 1964.

LYFORD, JOSEPH P. "A Walk on the West Side," Tape No. 69. Santa Barbara, Calif.: Center for the Study of Democratic Institutions.

"The Negro in America: What Must be Done," *Newsweek*, 70:18–44 (November 20, 1967).

RUSTIN, BAYARD. "The Negro Revolution," Tape No. 128. Santa Barbara, Calif.: Center for the Study of Democratic Institutions.

STERN, SOL. "America's Black Guerrillas," *Ramparts* 6: 24–27 (September, 1967).

THOMAS, TREVOR, ed. "The Fire This Time," Tape No. 307. Santa Barbara, Calif.: Center for the Study of Democratic Institutions.

"What we dare not face is not total extinction, but total meaninglessness."

David Riesman

9 Alienation

SOME SOCIAL PROBLEMS CAN BE REDUCED TO THE NUMBERS of the statistician. The obvious social issues can be described by almost anyone willing to gather and write down the facts. The complex problems that have a tangle of roots and branches call for the analysis of a social scientist. That which resides within the inner recesses of man requires at one level the clinical insight of the psychologist and at that higher level, capturing all subtlety and nuances, the intuitive wisdom of the poet, the literary artist. So it is with alienation. An attempt will be made here to describe this existential nausea—what Sören Kierkegaard called "the sickness unto death"—psychological alienation. Even as this description is attempted, the reader is referred to the deeper understanding of alienation that can be found in Franz Kafka's *The Trial*, Fëdor Dostoevski's *Crime and Punishment*, Albert Camus' *The Stranger*, George Orwell's *1984*, Aldous Huxley's *Brave New World*, or Ralph Ellison's *Invisible Man*.

ALIENATION DEFINED

Alienation is man's sense of estrangement from the world—the world which to some degree he made and to some degree he inherited. As the word suggests, it is the member of a society feeling like an alien in his own culture. Alienation is man's sense of estrangement from others: it is seeing other people as things and reacting toward them with emotional neutrality. Most important, alienation is man's sense of estrangement from himself: it is perceiving himself as a thing and experiencing an emotional deadness even in his reaction toward himself. The deeply alienated have a weak sense of self and, being unable to clearly differentiate self from not-self, have only a tenuous grip on reality. Even at a less than psychotic level, the alienated person is desperately troubled over the simple yet complex question, "Who am I?"

Alienation is then man's emotional detachment first from others and then from himself. Alienation is a feeling of loss of self, of depersonalization, of rootlessness, of utter loneliness, of loss of beliefs and values; a feeling that nothing is really significant; a feeling that nothing has any real meaning. This is not a philosophic conclusion about life such as Shakespeare had Macbeth voice at the moment of his personal denouement: ". . . it is a tale /Told by an idiot, full of sound and fury,/ signifying nothing." It is, rather, a pervasive emotional reaction that touches every moment of life with a dead hand.

Alienation is a man's feeling that he is drifting in a world that has little meaning for him and over which he exercises little, if any, control. Friedrich Nietzsche put it this way: "He who has a *why* to live can bear with almost any *how*." But to varying degrees the alienated cannot see or feel much *why* to living; therefore, their *how* of living can become what appears to be senseless, and in its senselessness, very dangerous to themselves and to others.

Finally, alienation is characterized by non-concern and uninvolvement. It is experiencing the world while encapsulated in an emotional vacuum. It is the detached acceptance of horrors, of human suffering, of murder, of mass killing, of the prospect of nuclear war, as if they were occurring in a dream, or as if they were only shadow images on a TV screen. Historically, alienation was personified by the "good German" who knew that the Jews were being taken off to the gas chambers of Auschwitz or Dachau or Buchenwald but somehow disconnected himself emotionally from what his mind told him, so that he felt nothing. In 1968, there was an element of this same severance of knowledge and emotion in the behavior of millions who, while having their pre-dinner drink, watched the latest bloody battle in Vietnam on TV, and after noting the kill-ratio as they might check the baseball scores, went unperturbed to their dinners. There is also an element of this divorcement of emotion from knowledge in the willingness of some intellectuals to treat the unthinkable as if it were a reasonable option: to debate the pros and cons of a nuclear war to decide the supremacy of capitalism over communism, or vice versa.

SOME OBVIOUS TYPES OF ALIENATION

At a pathological level, alienation manifests itself in various forms of schizophrenia, in anxiety neuroses, in depressive states, in some psychopathic personality syndromes, and in suicide. The incidence of alienated forms of psychosis and the frequency of self-destruction are both on the rise. One in twenty Americans will sometime in his life be hospitalized as a psychotic, and psychiatrists agree that a second in twenty should be hospitalized. One in five Americans will suffer symptoms of neurosis severe enough to require the help of a psychiatrist, clinical psychologist, or professional psychotherapist of some sort. The suicide rate in the United States is only exceeded by that found in the Scandinavian countries and Japan. This is not to say that all psychosis, all neurosis, all psychopathic personality, all suicide, follows directly from alienation. Yet, there are signs of alienation in the unhappy lives of most of these unfortunate people, and for many, the pathological symptoms represent either a giving up of the unequal struggle or a desperate and bizarre striking out at that which torments them.

Again, without saying that all crime is a direct expression of alienation, it is fair to say that most serious crime develops within a setting of alienation. In two of the world's most affluent nations, Britain and the United States, the crime rate has during recent years had an annual increase of 10 to 12 percent. The rise in violent crime has been much steeper than the rise in crimes against property; a greater percentage of the crime is committed by youth; and, as could be surmised from the ratio of crimes of violence to crimes against property, the increased rate cuts across all the social classes. The prisons are not full of Jean Valjeans who were caught stealing bread to fill their empty bellies. In 1963, the arrests of youth under 18 increased by 4 percent generally but by 15 percent in suburban areas. For grave crimes such as homicide, forcible rape, robbery, aggravated assault, burglary, larceny, and auto theft, those under eighteen accounted for 46 percent of all arrests; in the suburbs the rate was 51 percent. Criminal behavior, like all other behavior, is caused. The act leading to the arrest of some youngster is not random. It is the culmination of years of subtle influence of the attitudes and values of the parents and, by progression, the attitudes and values of the entire society. Robert Coles, in a *New Republic* article entitled "Youth: Opportunity to be What?" said this to parents who complain their ungrateful children have betrayed them:

> If we are at present appalled at a soaring, reckless criminality in our middle-class children, it is likely we are really appalled at what has happened to ourselves, because much of what horrifies us is our own assumptions and actions come to expression and perpetuation by those who know us best and are our most eager followers.

There is danger of loss of meaning when one word is used to describe too much. So it is with the word *alienation.* If the whole spectrum of mental illness and the whole gamut of crime are subsumed under alienation, then the word collapses beneath the weight of too much meaning. Even so, there is one horrifying type of criminal whose behavior reflects the very essence of alienation. Reference is made here to the people who commit senseless acts of violence for "kicks"; for example, Perry Smith and Dick Hickock, whose alienation was described by Truman Capote in the novel-biography *In Cold Blood.* Such people—their acts fill the daily tabloid papers—are so emotionally turned off they must resort to dangerous excitement, wanton violence, bestial sexuality in order to feel anything. The depths of such human depravity seem to be bottomless as was demonstrated by the horrors of the Nazi madness. In the United States the cumulative impact of the assassination of President John F. Kennedy, Rev. Dr. Martin Luther King Jr. and Senator Robert F. Kennedy, to say nothing of the murder of scores of black and white civil rights workers, has raised serious question regarding the sickness of the whole society.

To double the darkness of this depressing picture, the social dynamics would predict more, not less, of both group and individual violence growing out of alienation. Those factors making for present alienation will be exacerbated by the loss of human feeling in the lonely crowd and by the boredom of a generation in transition from an economy of work to an economy of very little work. The evidence is already at hand that vacant lives get filled with depravity, riots and crime. British poet Sir Herbert Reed wrote, "The Nazi Party, for example, in its early days was largely recruited from the bored . . . from the street corner society of listless hooligans." He went on to predict that the boredom and ennui in the decades ahead will make the suburban towns as dangerous as the city slums and will make it difficult to find a safe place to live.

A third alienated group, almost as clinical as the mentally ill or those who manifest their alienation in criminal behavior, is the growing army of old people who are idle, lonely, and no longer attached by any strong bond to family. They make up a clinical group in the sense that they have been well studied, and it has been shown that the dynamics of their alienation and the symptoms which they exhibit follow a common pattern. They grew up in an era in which the family was home base, the port which offered safety in life's storms, the source of psychological solidarity. During their early and middle years, everybody perceived work as the hub of a person's life, and therefore, work gave meaning and significance to that life. For many, and the number will be vastly increasing, the psychological foundation stones of family and work are wobbly, crumbling, even disappearing.

There is irony in the fact that medical modernity has added many years of life which industrial and other forms of modernity have voided. Man lives longer, but unless he has prepared himself for it, he has less to fill the days of his years. For the semiskilled and unskilled worker, for the lower middle and lower classes, the age of onset of this form of alienation is not the traditional retirement age of sixty-five or even sixty. They may begin to suffer from feelings of purposelessness, to lose the centrality which work gave their lives, to feel like aliens or strangers among their educated children—they may begin to experience the alienation of age while in their early fifties or even in their forties. The point is stressed here because present signs point to a life expectancy of seventy or more years with an exit age from work at fifty or below, except for those in professional and managerial positions. For many—those least prepared for purposeful use of leisure—there will be no exit age from work since they will never have entered it. The present trend is toward a vastly increased number entering the emotional and mental vacuum now called the alienation of age.

MORE SUBTLE FORMS OF ALIENATION

Henry Thoreau, critical observer of the mid-nineteenth century industrial revolution, sadly noted, "The mass of men lead lives of quiet desperation." Existential nausea has always afflicted the rich: the industrial revolution, now multiplying many times into the cybernation revolution, has converted it into a common disease. There is a nebulous quality about this form of alienation which makes it hard to diagnose and to give statistics on its incidence or frequency. Yet few would deny that it is endemic in the United States and in other technologically developed nations.

The afflicted are the people (millions?) who find the truncated tasks which make up their jobs to be trivial, monotonous and degrading; who have no compelling interests or competencies outside the job; who may lavish upon their children, or wives, or husbands, material things in compensation for being incapable of giving real love and serious attention; who cannot find or develop much meaning in their lives, and who cannot bear to think about this. They find escape by stupifying themselves with alcohol: There are over four million compulsive alcoholics in the United States. They help themselves through the emptiness of the day and the anguish of the night with drugs and other chemicals. They blank out their problems of family relationship by sitting mesmerized watching anything and everything that comes across the TV screen—"TV-ing it" as the Negro expression goes. They are the compulsive pleasure-seekers, the promiscuous adventurers in sexual alliances, the people who cannot bear ten minutes of solitude, who cannot stand their own company, who must have something—anything—to divert them from their inner-core feelings of failure as full human beings.

Joseph P. Lyford, describing life in a Negro slum, said, ". . . in my neighborhood an adult is a dead child." Social philosopher Hannah Arendt observed that evil is commonplace and that most of those who commit evil are "asleep." Certainly among the casualties of this society are those who are truly emotionally dead, the people who have blocked off feelings of love, affection, brotherhood, anger, outrage, concern, interest. These people have almost unconsciously committed psychological suicide. The number who have thus died in their heads and hearts before dying in their bodies remains indeterminate. Of much greater concern is the pervasiveness of emotional blunting—what Joseph Lyford calls auto-anaesthesia, or a self-induced cutting off of any perception of a painful evil. To extend Hannah Arendt's point, not only those who commit evil but also those who live with it and accept it must be "asleep."

Not many Germans actually inflicted torment on the concentration camp victims, but millions of Germans blinded themselves to the evil. Not many South African or Rhodesian whites take sadistic pleasure in the pain of the blacks, yet they countenance it. Not many, if any, Americans actually want the destruction of children and the continual waste and loss of human life that is occurring in the city and rural slums. Analyzing the American example in his book *The Airtight Cage*, Joseph P. Lyford came to what he called "this tidal fact":

> We are, practically speaking, unconscious of what is going on. We seem to have pushed whatever knowledge we have about "the process" into a part of our minds that is not directly connected with our emotions or our motor mechanisms. The knowledge is there, but it is lodged in such a fashion that it does not affect our behavior, and when we are presented evidence of what is going on, we respond to it the way we do to an act of violence on television or the movies. We have the so-called vicarious experiences in which crime is relayed to us stripped of all its meaning because it is presented as an image of crime, not as a crime itelf.[1]

There is such a paradox as being alienated on the outside without being alienated on the inside. The treatment by the popular media notwithstanding, this paradox may describe many of the hippies, the intellectual beatniks, the rebels with and without causes, the self-styled anarchists—those people, usually young of mind, who reject the prevailing values of the society and cannot or have not found any tenable alternatives.

[1]From Joseph P. Lyford, *The Airtight Cage* (Evanston, Illinois, Harper and Row, Publishers, 1966).

However flamboyant they may be in their outward alienation from the culture, inside, where they really live, they are still psychologically concerned. The males may have long hair, beards, and beads which distinguish them from the buttoned-down men in the grey-flannel suits; yet much of their behavior, particularly that of the hippies and the political radicals, reveals that they are "involved in mankind," that they fit theologian Paul Tillich's definition of religion: they have "ultimate concern."

These young men and women may have a gut-level disenchantment with the values and mores of the society and even suffer a period of hopelessness. However, their fundamental, perhaps unconscious, assumptions are that life should be good, should be ethical, should be beautiful. They simply "drop out" (in the case of the hippies) or move to outraged activism (in the case of the radicals) when they hit rock-bottom disappointment that elements in society keep life from corresponding to their basic assumptions. If the hippies, and all other groups of this kind, are neither emotionally nor ethically dead, then they are not truly alienated. In a stumbling fashion they may even be creating the value structure of the society of the future.

Although not often decried in the popular press, the many gullible conformists may be more seriously alienated than those few who deviate widely from the norm. Their whole approach to life comes to be what Erich Fromm called *the other orientation*: "I am as you desire me to be." They will undoubtedly have the outer shell of what the image-makers project as the ideal, but when the outer shell is penetrated by some hard-rock event or by some moment of insight, it is discovered—they discover—that they are hollow on the inside. They are the patsies—the insipid victims of the pervasive and insidious consumer orientation of an economy which creates the needs to fit the production more than it creates the production to fit the needs. With its subtle soft sell and with its hypnotically repetitive hard sell, it tells people what to value, what to want, what to be. It woos the individual into believing that he will be successful, rich, and happy if he smells right, if he smokes the right cigarette, if he can attract and display as his property an equally stereotyped sex object, if he shapes himself to be the advertiser's manikin. He is bombarded from every angle—flattered, urged, cajoled. But the values peddled to which he eventually succumbs do not meet his deep human needs. In attempting to achieve the aims which serve the purposes of others, the person becomes alienated from himself—sells out unwittingly and is himself the sacrifice before the graven image of the commercial myth.

ALIENATION AND HIGHER EDUCATION

The devaluation of the individual and the movement toward lock-step conformity that are fall-out from the population explosion are causes of alienation. When the job is no longer there to define the man and before new meaning replaces the life meaning once provided by the job, alienation flourishes. Black Power may buoy up black men, but unless it brings them a real stake in the society they will grow more alienated, this time as a group, in which case the individual may find himself in the camaraderie of guerrilla bands. The generation and credibility gaps, to be discussed next, are also contributing factors to alienation. With each issue, and with the amalgam of all issues, it comes to what was said before: "Education is not much of a hope, it is just the only hope we have."

For the society, higher education has many essential objectives. Although the individual may intellectually agree to and identify with these societal objectives, his basic motivation is subjective: it is the maintenance and enhancement of his total self, the pursuit of happiness as he perceives it. The pursuit of happiness is, in essence, a search for meaning: "The life which is unexamined is not worth living." Involvement in life, commitment to beliefs and values, willingness to make the struggle even when the game is bruising, all carry a common reward. They make the person feel alive. They define the person so he knows who he is. They give meaning and significance to his life. To be sure, retreat from time to time is necessary for wound licking and for thinking things over and perhaps for taking a new direction. Such periods of detachment are probably essential for regaining strength and regrouping for continued or new commitment and involvement.

Higher education should not be a two-year or four-year or eight-year period of detachment in which the student *prepares for life*. Higher education is part of life. The student can tune himself in or tune himself out of the intellectual dialogue and the action which follows from it just as he can tune himself in or tune himself out at any other point in his life. If he tunes himself in, he is almost bound to discover that meaning and significance are qualities of the mind. If he opens his mind and trains it for an active mental life, he will find no end of things which can absorb his interest and give him a lifetime inoculation against the nausea of alienation.

TOPICS FOR CONSIDERATION

1. Psychologists keep saying that many people agonize over the question, "Who am I?" It would seem that anyone except the amnesic and mentally defective should be able to give a straightforward answer to this question. Are the psychologists being naive or are they capturing the subtle in the starkly simple? Other than by giving his name, how does a person say who he is? define himself?

2. The suicide rate in Western nations went down during the war as it does during most periods of national crisis. Also, people suffering from hunger rarely commit suicide. What accounts for these facts? Would it not seem reasonable to expect those experiencing severe hardships to destroy themselves?

3. The charge is made that the intellectual, the academician, is often willing to treat the unthinkable as if it were a reasonable

option. Is this an unfair allegation? Does it represent a commendable willingness to look at both sides of any problem? Is there an element of alienation in acting as if every problem had two defensible sides?

4. The inference is made that the crime rate, particularly that of youth, is like a thermometer registering the illness of the society. What is the nature of this illness? Does it imply an environmental determinism? Will increasing the number and the effectiveness of the police act as a counter determinant?

5. If medical science and the cybernation of work combine to give most people twenty or even thirty years of retirement, what should the age pattern of higher education become? What kind of education should be offered to prepare people for the many years of retirement?

6. Is Henry Thoreau's statement "The mass of men lead lives of quiet desperation" a poetical exaggeration? Put in nonpoetical specifics, what did Thoreau mean by this statement? If a person really thought about it, would the lives of the people about whom he had intimate, personal knowledge bear out Thoreau's depressing observation?

7. Very little distinction is drawn between the inflicting of evil and the countenancing of evil inflicted. There obviously is a difference between committing a crime and being an accessory to the fact. In terms of societal evils, for example apartheid or extermination of the Jews, could the active be pursued without the silent consent of the passive? How does this apply to the issue of racial injustice in the United States?

8. The writer Joseph Lyford, on the subject of Negro slums, contends that there is a mass loss of grip on reality; that people distort their perceptions or turn off their perceptions so they do not have to feel the pain of what their sense organs are bringing in. Is this special pleading by a man with a biased view on a current issue, or is there a tidal truth in what he says?

9. Some responsible social analysts and almost all writers in the popular press have labeled the hippies, the intellectual beatniks, and the radical activists as obvious cases of alienation. Rebuttal of this popular view is based on the contention that many of the hippies and members of other such groups "are involved in mankind," "have ultimate concern." Which side has the better of the argument? How should these nonconforming groups be

appraised? What should the larger society's reaction be toward them?

10. It is rather easy to sense in a global way that alienation is linked to such issues as population, cybernation, and the Negro Revolution. In what specific ways does each of these have a causal relationship to alienation?

11. The words of psychiatrist Vicktor Frankl are echoed in the conclusion that the pursuit of happiness is, in essence, a search for meaning. If this were accepted as a prime objective of higher education, then what would be the nature of this education? What sort of subjects would be studied? Should this content or an approximation of it be made mandatory for all students?

12. Some students will be appalled by the gravity and pervasiveness of alienation in this society and would like to devote their careers to combating it. For what occupations might they prepare themselves at a professional level? at a para-professional level?

SUGGESTED READING AND LISTENING

CAMUS, ALBERT. *The Stranger.* New York: Alfred A. Knopf, Inc., 1946.

COLES, ROBERT. "Youth: Opportunity to be What?" *New Republic*, 151:59–64 (November 7, 1964).

ELLISON, RALPH. *Invisible Man.* New York: Random House, Inc., 1952.

FROMM, ERICH. "Alienation Under Capitalism," *Man Alone*, edited by Eric and Mary Josephson. New York: Dell Publishing Co., Inc.

GABOR, DENNIS. "Fighting Existential Nausea," *Technology and Human Values*, Santa Barbara, California: Center for the Study of Democratic Institutions, 1966.

HUXLEY, ALDOUS. *Brave New World.* Evanston, Ill.: Harper & Row, Publishers, 1932.

KAFKA, FRANZ. *The Trial.* New York: Alfred A. Knopf, Inc., 1957.

LYFORD, JOSEPH P. *The Airtight Cage.* Evanston, Ill.: Harper & Row, Publishers, 1966.

MARMOR, JUDD. "The Crisis of Identity in a Workless World," Tape

No. 187. Santa Barbara, California: Center for the Study of Democratic Institutions.

ORWELL, GEORGE. *1984*. New York: The New American Library, Inc., 1954.

RIESMAN, DAVID. *The Lonely Crowd*. New Haven: Yale University Press, 1950.

———. "The Changing American Character," *The Humanities in Contemporary Life*, edited by Robert F. Davidson and others. New York: Holt, Rinehart & Winston, Inc., 1960.

WEIS, FREDERICK. "Self-Alienation: Dynamics and Therapy," *Man Alone*, edited by Eric and Mary Josephson. New York: Dell Publishing Co., Inc.

"You can't trust anyone over thirty."
"Tell it like it is."

Slogans of the '60's

10 The Generation and the Credibility Gaps

> Look at you, brainwashing a whole generation of kids into getting a revolving charge account and buying junk. (Who's a junkie?) Look at you needing a couple of stiff drinks before you have the guts to talk with another human being. Look at you, making it with your neighbor's wife just to prove that you are really alive. Look at you, screwing up the land and the water and the air for profit, and calling this nowhere scene the Great Society: And you are going to tell us how to live? C'mon, man, you've got to be kidding![1]

HOPEFULLY, MOST YOUTH ARE NOT SO BITTER AND MOST of the older generation are not deserving of such articulate wrath. Nonetheless, the young character used by J. L. Simmons and Barry Winograd in *It's Happening* captures in one outburst the larger than life dimensions of the generation and the credibility gaps.

Trust and communication are the sand and cement that mortar a society together. Each generation has to pass on the cultural heritage to the next, and to do it, there must be wide, connected channels of communication and reasonable belief in and acceptance of that which is communicated. In the process of growing, the child looks to his parents and elders for verification of his very shaky perceptions. This perceptual dependency on others continues to some degree throughout

[1]"Inheritor: Man of the Year: The Man and Woman Twenty-five and Under," *Time Magazine*, 89:18–23 (January 6, 1967).

life but is most marked from birth through post-adolescence. If youth comes only to turn to youth to check its perceptions, the result may be the group distortion of reality so chillingly described by William Golding in *Lord of the Flies*. A society is in trouble when the natural separation becomes a gap so wide the generations cannot be heard across it, or, if heard, are mutually distrusted. Education as the transmittal of cold facts might continue to flourish; education as the transmittal of the cherished wisdom distilled from past experience would not.

If, in fact, the past generation has been gulled into believing the undressed emperor is clothed in gorgeous raiment, then it is healthy for the younger generation to shout out that despite what the older people say the emperor is naked. Some members of the older generation, in more measured tones, are voicing their own alarm. Harvard Professor David Riesman said, "The generational gap is wider than I've ever seen it in my lifetime." Walter Lippmann, Dean of American pundits, wrote, "It is a bad and dangerous situation when a great power in this anarchic world finds itself without leadership which it fully trusts and in which it has confidence." Leslie Paul, British writer, said: "The relations of the generations may become the central social issue of the next fifty years, as the relations between the classes have been for the past half-century."

WIDENING OF THE GENERATION GAP

To expect no gap to exist between the generations would be to expect what never was and never will be. Each generation tends to have its perceptions rooted in the conscious and unconscious assumptions that were current during its formative years. An example: Many of the parents of today's college students are hag-ridden by the fears of financial insecurity that they overlearned as children of the depression. The students, who often grew up as display objects of their parents' new affluence, came to have the same feeling about the world's goods as they might about air: material things come as part of life's deal. Parents perceive their children's cavalier attitude toward money, material things, and security, as an ungrateful betrayal of the sacrifices they made for them. The children perceive their parents' anxiety as proof of their sell-out to materialism. Pop-rock Singer Spanky McFarlane told a *Newsweek* interviewer, "My parents disowned me when I started singing. Now they are terribly proud of me. Of course, this doesn't mean that they like me; they like my success. They're materialists, just like everybody else."

Another example: The generation that cut their political eyeteeth on the Cold War Doctrine of John Foster Dulles and were witness to the national hysteria of the McCarthy Period are likely to divide the world into the Red camp and the Red, White and Blue camp, attributing supernatural cleverness to those in the Red camp and suspecting those who take a less simplistic view (college professors and other intellectuals) of being either misguided eggheads or subversives. Their children, to whom Dulles or McCarthy are merely names in a history book, realize that technological changes have made much of communist doctrine irrelevant, and they cannot see it as "a clear and present danger." They fail to see domestic communism as sufficient threat to justify rulings against leftist speakers on campus or any other form of repeal by college authorities of the First Amendment's guarantee of free speech.

Still another example: Those who were born into a world that everyone knew would go on forever, despite having lived to see the coming of the A-Bomb and H-Bomb, have difficulty understanding the "now-orientation" of those who grew up with the prospect that civilization might be blown up tomorrow. People with different time-orientations are likely to set different life paces and life styles for themselves. Further, the psychological evidence points to assumptions about time being picked up by osmosis (unconsciously learned) during childhood.

During the late nineteenth century and first quarter of the twentieth century, when many second generation American youth had parents who could not speak English and who were culturally tied to Europe, the generation gap was severe but quite different from that found today. The children had to translate for their parents and interpret the new culture to them. Often the children felt ashamed of their parents, yet felt guilty about this shame as well as about their rejection of their parents' values and style of life. A parallel to this facet of the generational problem grows out of children outstripping their parents in education. Almost all American parents want their children to get a better education than they had. Nonetheless, when the educated child begins to correct the parents' grammar or to point out the naivete of some of the parents' religious beliefs, or to dismiss the parents' unsophisticated political views, the parents would be more than human if they did not resent it. The wide differences in educational level between children and parents tend to create a divorcement. It is difficult to have a real companionship, even a close emotional relationship, when the children's perceptions of the world are much more complex than those held by the parents and when the parents' pride and the children's shame have established barriers to communication. This generational breach becomes very evident in lower-middle and lower-class families as universal higher education widens the distance between the new and the old generation. If Negro education spurts forward, the same mixture of blessing and pain will be felt—has already been felt in the cases of Negro children who have had a first-class education.

It is really not surprising that the generation gap has become more pronounced and has generated more of a problem now than in the past. As previously illustrated, the generation gap is really a discrepancy in the way people perceive the world. Since behavior follows from perception, those who see the world one way are going to act consistent with that perception, and those who perceive it in quite a different way are going to behave differently. The two variables involved in this psychological truism are *the people* and *the world.* The basic nature of people may not have changed much, but the irrefutable, stark fact is that the world has changed so radically that those whose perceptions are rooted in the assumptions of the 1920's or 1930's are not seeing the same world as those whose perceptions are rooted in the assumptions of the 1950's or 1960's. Never has the world changed more in such a short period, and the trend predicts an even faster rate of future change. The generation now leveling the criticism of the generation gap will have to exercise great mental agility to keep abreast of the changing world, or within a decade or so they will be the target for the same criticism.

Of course, a chronological gap in years does not necessarily bring a generational gap in perceptions. Those people who really give thought to the changing world alter their perceptions to fit new realities. By reverse token, there are many people young in years whose perceptions due to various environmental forces are rooted in the assumptions of the nineteenth century. Some parents and teachers try to bridge the gap by being one with youth; a mother may dress, talk and act as if she were her daughter's sister. More often than not, this simply looks like arrested development, for youth certainly do not want their elders to emulate them. As the attraction of President John Kennedy demonstrated, many youth wanted to find someone approaching a hero figure with whom to identify. Now, most young people even eschew this and would be glad to settle for the abandonment of adult double standards and for insight into and correction of what they consider adult hypocrisy. They demand, as youth has always demanded, that those calling themselves mature give up some of their own egocentricity to pay attention to the more forgivable egocentricity of youth.

SOME EFFECTS OF THE GENERATION GAP

On Parents' Day of the fall quarter, 1967, the *Stanford Daily* printed this stinging message: "We would say Welcome Parents, but on the contemporary university campus one does not fraternize with the enemy. During the eight hours that you will be guests of the university, many speakers will be telling you what Stanford life is like. Strangely, the only group you will not hear from is the group that is living it—the students."

This message may be journalistic overstatement, yet it depicts very accurately the effect of the generation gap on parents and children. When parents are looked upon as the enemy, children can neither fraternize nor communicate with them. People share their perceptions of what is reality by means of communication, and when they can no longer talk to each other, their world is no longer shared. The result is a psychological divorcement even though some of the outer forms of parent-child relationship, such as financial support or sleeping and boarding at home, may continue. True, the college years have always been a time for the cutting of the psychological umbilical cord, yet it need not be so painful nor so destructive to later, more adult relationships. When the communication link between parents and children gets uncoupled, there is usually a desperate need to tie on to some substitute, and for youth the handiest and most mutually supportive is the peer group. This attachment is not bad in itself. In fact, within limits, it is natural and necessary, but beyond these limits it can produce the same bad effect as an incestuous marriage: an accentuation of the weakness of youth or even the piling up of youth's virtues to the point where they become vices.

Good, bad, or indifferent, the generalized concept which young people develop about the adult world is mostly based on the concept they have of their parents. When college students chant the slogan "you can't trust anyone over thirty," they are not saying, "You can't trust anyone over thirty, except my parents." The meaning is closer to, "You can't trust anyone like my parents who are over thirty." Since youth often has little faith in the word of the older generation, disputes between college students and college authorities can quickly escalate. When dialogue is impossible, confrontation is inevitable. If the administrative officers or the trustees of the college are cut off from real communication with the students, they are likely to see student protest as a basic challenge to their authority and overuse the power with which they are vested, thereby proving the students' claim about people over thirty. The intent of this discussion is not to make whipping boys out of either parents or college officials but rather to describe the dynamics of the generation gap applied to student-college relationships.

Still another effect of the generation gap in the college situation is the unnecessary barrier to learning experienced by those students who transfer their distrust and other negative feelings from their parents to their instructors. Although learning may be possible without some positive identification of the learner with the teacher, it is not likely. Learning is an emotional as well as an intellectual process. The student whose mind gets turned off like a faucet upon contact with any adult authority figure has defeated himself, probably unconsciously, in the struggle to learn. University of California Psychologist Barbara Kirk and others have demonstrated that even among the very able, hostility toward parents can have a causal relationship with poor or failing academic performance. The generation gap which keeps Generation B from perceiving life situations in essentially the same way and with similar attitudes and values as perceived by Generation A will also spark hostility between Generation B and Generation A. Doing poorly in college or dropping out can be a revengeful way of expressing this hostility. To hurt self in order to hurt others is not rational, but a great deal of human behavior is irrational.

The forces in the ethical confrontations over civil rights

and the Vietnam War during the decade of the 1960's often lined up on the basis of generation. The civil rights workers, black and white, who were jeered, beaten, jailed, and even murdered were, with some notable exceptions, young people. The massive and sometimes violent demonstrations against the U.S. military involvement in Vietnam also involved young people. It was largely protesting college students and men and women in their twenties who were clubbed and beaten by the Los Angeles police in the now historic anti-Vietnam War demonstration at Century City Plaza. Even apolitical youth who were never personally involved in demonstrations were indirectly touched by what appeared to be an overreaction by institutional authority. They could not help but see that the police power of the state was being used against their contemporaries, and that knowledge contributed to the *we vs. they* feeling. Draft resistance to the Vietnam War has no parallel in modern times, and again this has pitted youth against the authority of the generation in power. When General Lewis Hershey, septuagenarian Selective Service Director, issued orders that war protestants would be drafted immediately, that science and technology students should have deferment priority over arts and humanities students, and that terminal junior college students should not be given deferments, even some of the students who would benefit showed evidence of guilt, of betrayal, and of generational disgust. Those who were targets for the reprisal reacted with increased fury and intransigence.

Of course, youth do not compose a monolithic group with a common perception and a common reaction. Some are rabid segregationists and pro-Vietnam War and would like to see all draft protestants jailed. Those in the opposite camp have already been described. Most young people are probably moderates who feel both sympathy and guilt toward the plight of the Negro and are as confused as many of their elders about the murky ethics of the Vietnam War. They see the draft as something to be avoided, but they will serve if they are called. Even so, the greater involvement of youth in the ethical issues of the times has made many feel that the older generation will not only countenance evil but will be quick to use the harsh police power at its command to maintain this evil. For the many who personally or vicariously had their innocence beaten out of them by a police truncheon, the generation gap is a bitter reality, not an idle phrase.

EVIDENCE OF THE CREDIBILITY GAP

In October, 1967, the Gallup Poll reported that 70 percent of its sample thought that the Johnson Administration was not giving the people the facts about the war in Vietnam. Put in less euphemistic terms, 70 percent of the citizens suspected that their government was lying to them by omission or commission. Whether the people were right or wrong in their distrust is beside the point. The distrust itself is the pertinent fact. Social Philosopher Walter Lippmann wrote of his deep concern: "The polls are a mere indication and do not describe the quality and depth of feeling of having been misled and having been had. In our times there has been no parallel in any other war in respect to any other President."

A credibility gap of such mammoth proportions assumes the qualities of a constitutional crisis. The whole theory of democracy is based upon an essential trust between those who govern and those who are governed. It is not likely that law and order will be highly respected when most of the people do not believe what is said by those who make the laws and keep the order. Such distrust is much more destructive to law and order than the behavior of those who practice civil disobedience, accepting the risk of openly challenging the morality and constitutionality of certain laws. At an even deeper level, the poisoning of credibility begins to destroy man's psychological basis for operation. Man's sense of reality is shaky at best. If he finds he cannot believe even what authority figures tell him, then he is in the same predicament as the paranoid personality who is suspicious of everybody, rejects what is commonly accepted as reality, and therefore bases his behavior on what he thinks to be reality no matter how distorted that may be.

The erosion of political credibility evidenced by the Gallup Poll example could not have been an isolated social phenomenon. It has a history behind it. It developed in a milieu where increasingly truth was neither given nor even expected. The nineteenth century business slogan was *caveat emptor*, let the buyer beware. In twentieth century advertising, the overriding aim is to sell the product, not tell the truth about it. The public does not expect, much less demand, that advertising even approximate honesty. The overwhelming evidence of causal relationship between cigarette smoking and lung cancer has been known for years, yet no one is surprised that the advertisers for the tobacco industry have been successful in increasing the desirability and the sale of cigarettes. The public has been much more amazed at the single-handed success of Ralph Nader as the consumer's champion in auto safety, in food processing, and in drug controls. Advertising, particularly the inescapable TV advertising, has been so honestly dishonest that it endeared itself to the arbiters of "camp" and became part of the "camp scene"; it was perceived as a rather lovable caricature of itself.

What has obtained in the advertising of things has also obtained in the advertising of people or institutions. The public relations firm has made it unnecessary for a person or a corporation or an institution to make a good reputation; they can buy one. For a price, the public relations experts will create in the public's mind whatever image the buyer wants. If one image is not satisfactory, then another image can be substituted: thus the media can announce the appearance of "The New Nixon" or "Johnson's New Look." Public relations has come to be such an accepted part of the ethos that image-making is viewed as a respectable and dignified profession—the cosmetic surgery that covers the sags and blemishes of personality and character.

Educator Robert Hutchins once suggested that the late Henry R. Luce, founder-editor of *Time* and *Life*, had two to twenty-five times the influence on American character as the University of Chicago. He continued, "I might even say that Mr. Luce and his magazines have more effect on the American character than the whole educational system put together."

W. H. Ferry, in his article "Masscomm as Guru," attests to the power for good or evil in the mass communication media and makes the indictment that it is masscomm's knowledge that its bread is buttered on the side of money that makes it abrogate its responsibilities under the First Amendment. Mr. Ferry wrote:

> Thus I agree with the Rt. Hon. W. F. Deedes, M.P., who recently said of television "It has within its power to decide what kind of people we become. Nothing less." I would only make the statement retroactive and extend it to the rest of masscomm. It seems to me beyond argument that masscomm is a chief contributor, though not the only one, to the social and cultural malaise lying on us all. This is so because masscomm is a major beneficiary. It can make more money not meeting its responsibilities than by doing so.[2]

It is common knowledge—and probably inevitable—that masscomm is either owned by or derives its revenues from the economic Establishment. Such being the case, it is not going to bite itself nor the hand that feeds it. Realizing this, the people do not expect to get even the approximate truth from most of the media. The commercial motive of masscomm results in such a built-in credibility gap that schools and colleges feel obliged to teach the young not to believe a good deal of what masscomm puts before their eyes or dins into their ears.

No doubt governments have always found it to their

[2]W. H. Ferry and Harry S. Ashmore, *Mass Communication* (Santa Barbara, California, Center for the Study of Democratic Institutions, 1966). Reprinted with permission.

interest to be secretive sometimes, to be devious, to be dissembling, even to tell boldface lies. Without a worldwide communication system and without an educated populace, the rulers could with impunity follow the cynical advice of Machiavelli to *The Prince*. Today, such behavior, though it continues, stretches credibility to the breaking point. When men in high places, veritable symbols of veracity, are caught lying, people ask, "If such men cannot be trusted to tell the truth, then who can?" Illustrations from recent American history underline the point. Political credibility was jolted when President Dwight Eisenhower denied and then recanted his denial that the U-2 photographic reconnaissance plane had violated Russian air space. The gap was widened dramatically when Ambassador Adlai Stevenson, knowingly or unknowingly, lied to the U.N. Assembly about the American involvement in the Bay of Pigs fiasco. The gnawing doubt left as a legacy by the Warren Report on the assassination of President Kennedy, the alleged complicity of the C.I.A. in everything from bribing the National Student Association to political murder, the obscure account of what actually happened in the Bay of Tonkin incident used to justify the escalation of the Vietnam War—these and many other factors put the presidency under a cloud of distrust and disbelief. This crisis in credibility became so acute during the Johnson Administration that Columnist Murray Kempton felt obliged to comment regarding the "Pueblo Incident" of 1968, "It is painful and embarrassing to me both as a person and a citizen to say so, but I cannot believe anything my government says about the Pueblo."

BRIDGING THE GAPS

Awareness of a problem is at least the first step to solving it. Such awareness does not necessarily activate people to take the second step toward solution of the problem, but the second step cannot be taken before the first. Groups within the college community, the young in years and the young in spirit, have by their insistence helped the society to take the first step, to come to an awareness of the generation gap and its companion, the credibility gap.

The professional moralists act as if the separating issues between the generations are psychedelic drugs and pre-marital sex. An historic recounting of the dramatic confrontations during the last decade usually shows youth to have been on the side of respect for the individual, civil liberties, peace, the brotherhood of man—the verities of the Judeo-Christian and the democratic heritage. Men such as Michael Schwerner, James Cheney and Andrew Goodman died in Mississippi for the freedom and equality of other men—the ultimate in idealism. The many recent battles between the police and college students have been fought on the issues of freedom of speech, democratic involvement in decision making, the influence of the military-industrial complex on the college, inequities in the draft, and peace. Youth's opposition and resistance to the Vietnam War may prove to have been an error in geopolitical strategy, but it can hardly be faulted in the realm of morality. Harold Taylor, former president of Sarah Lawrence College, summed up youth's stand in this statement: "The student has become the most powerful invisible force in the reform of education—and, indirectly, in the reform of American society." At what *Newsweek* called a Berkeley anti-commencement, former University of Chicago President Robert Hutchins told a rump group of the 1968 University of California graduating class, "You have awakened the conscience of America. You have changed the course of history. You have made peace in Vietnam inevitable."

Perhaps Dr. Taylor and Dr. Hutchins are right in saying that youth has already set forces in motion toward those reforms, those second steps, that will begin to close the generation and credibility gaps. On college campuses some students are saying in louder and firmer voices, "No dissembling. No equivocating. No hiding behind smoke screens of scientific objectivity. No eternally suspended judgments. No temporizing with profitable evil. Tell it like it is."

It would be indulging in callow romanticism to fantasy a "children's crusade" in which youth led their parents to a new understanding of them and to a rededication to the eternal verities. The younger generation are not such unblemished heroes, and the older generation are not such double-dyed villains. Nonetheless, the members of the academic community can probably do more than any other single group in bridging the gaps. Youth are becoming more and more insistent that their education be relevant. If it is not, they leave: A study at the University of California, Berkeley, showed that over half of the very able students who enter that university do not stay long enough to graduate. Educators have been shaken by the repeated outbursts of student discontent first dramatized by the 1964 Free Speech Movement at Berkeley and escalating by 1968 to violent insurrecton at Columbia University in New York and the Sorbonne in Paris. They are reappraising curriculum, teaching method, student role in decision making, and the nature of student activities. The most forward of them are involving the students in the reappraisal. Those who do not may find they have merely substituted new irrelevancies for old ones.

The nub of the matter is communication. The young cannot be older and the older cannot be young, but if the differences between them are ever to be bridged, it will be through communication. Hopefully, communication can be honed as an effective weapon in the classroom, in the exchange between the student and the instructor, and then be used in the home and on all other battlegrounds where the generations are in eyeball-to-eyeball confrontation. The same prescription is the specific for credibility. People of all ages have to be taught to say politely but firmly, "I don't believe you. You are lying to me and perhaps to yourself on the following counts. I am plenty willing to listen to you, but tell it to me like it is or you will be wasting your breath and my time."

TOPICS FOR CONSIDERATION

1. The generation gap is spoken of as if it pervaded the whole society, as if it applied in every family situation. Are there some families where generational differences are simply inconsequential? If so, are the children in such families affected by generational combat in other arenas?

2. Imagine a hypothetical situation where the generation gap kept eroding away until a Grand Canyon separated the middle-aged parents from their late-adolescent children. What would be the ultimate psychological effects of such a complete severance? Is Leslie Paul being an alarmist when he writes, "The relations of the generations may become the central social issue of the next fifty years, as the relations between the classes have been for the past half-century"?

3. The observation is made that whereas the disaffected hippies may eschew materialism and turn their backs on the goods of the world, the young disaffected Negroes certainly do not. Does this mean the hippies are truly ascetics who have freed themselves from dependency by the abnegation of the things of this world, or are they parasites who feed off the affluence of the earlier generation? Might they show the way to those whom cybernation may relegate to a life of enforced leisure?

4. Mention was made that a person's time-orientation would be a determinant of his life pace and his life style. What is meant by time-orientation and how would it affect life pace and life style? Is there any reason to believe that the younger generation has a qualitatively different time-orientation than the older generation?

5. It was implied that children whose perceptions are rooted in the assumptions current during the youth of their parents may have avoided a generation gap problem only to fall victim to a worse problem. It was also implied that parents who keep young by emulating their children may not have a generation gap problem but do have a maturity problem. Does this mean that the generation gap may be a natural, unavoidable, and even healthy aspect of the maturation process? If so, why does it now seem that by falling into the gap people take a painful psychological pratfall?

6. The generation gap is constantly referred to as a discrepancy in perceptions leading to a problem in communication. If this is an accurate definition, then how could the college contribute toward reducing the discrepancies in perceptions and toward im-

proving the flow of communications? Would this require an almost psychotherapeutic approach? Would the parents also have to be *treated*, or could it be restricted to the students?

7. The contention is made that the dynamics of college dropout often include the element of revenge on parents toward whom a great deal of conscious or unconscious hostility is felt. Since this is like cutting off one's nose to spite one's face, is it reasonable to accept this as an explanation other than in cases of serious psychological disturbance?

8. The source of greatest alarm about the credibility gap seems to be that the poisoning of belief and confidence begins to destroy man's psychological basis for operation. Does advertising really loosen man's grip on reality? Does the public relations treatment actually undermine reality? Are the mass media seriously guilty of contributing to the irreality of their readers' or viewers' perceptions?

9. It was stated that advertising is so palpably false and that propaganda in all forms creates such serious mischief that colleges present courses in which the student is taught to discount much of what he reads, hears and even sees. Should colleges undertake this task as an obligation? Is this a sensible way to deal with the credibility gap? If not, what effort should the college make toward bridging the credibility gap?

10. W. H. Ferry questions whether masscomm can ever be a truly free agent and exemplar in free speech since it is either owned by or is a beneficiary of the economic Establishment. Could this same doubt be raised about colleges? Can professors be assured of academic freedom when their message runs counter to the interests of those who contribute most heavily to the cost of education? Should not he who pays the piper be allowed to call the tune? If so, then is not academic freedom just window dressing? a pleasant sounding but hollow concept?

11. It was observed in the section "Bridging the Gaps" that simple awareness of a problem does not solve the problem. College officials and college students are certainly aware of the generation gap problem, but are they doing anything to solve it? Working together, what measures could the staff members and the students take to bridge the generation gap? What could be done to prevent the younger generation from facing the same or even a worse gap when it becomes the older generation?

12. Educator Harold Taylor stated boldly and without equivoca-

tion: "The student has become the most powerful invisible force in the reform of education—and, indirectly, in the reform of American society." Is this just extravagant praise or is there reason to believe this? What, for example, is the student doing to reform the credibility gap? What could the students or any other part of the academic community do to restore credibility in advertising? in public relations? in masscomm? in politics?

SUGGESTED READING AND LISTENING

FEIFFER, JULES, EDWARD P. MORGAN and PAUL JACOBS. "Don't Make Waves," Tape No. 193, I. Santa Barbara, Calif.: Center for the Study of Democratic Institutions, 1965.

FERRY, W. H. and HARRY S. ASHMORE. *Mass Communication.* Santa Barbara, Calif.: Center for the Study of Democratic Institutions, 1966.

GLAZER, NATHAN. "What Happened at Berkeley," *Beyond Berkeley: A Sourcebook in Student Values*, edited by C. G. Katope and P. G. Zolbrod. Cleveland: The World Publishing Co., 1966.

GOODMAN, PAUL. *Growing Up Absurd.* New York, Random House, Inc., 1960.

"Inheritor: Man of the Year: The Man and Woman Twenty-five and Under," *Time Magazine*, 89:18–23 (January 6, 1967).

LIPPMANN, WALTER. "The Tax Revolt," *Newsweek*, 70:13 (October 23, 1967).

———, ALFRED KAZIN, et al. "A Dialogue Between Generations," *Harper's Magazine*, 235:45–64 (October, 1967).

SALINGER, J. D. *The Catcher in the Rye.* Boston: Little, Brown & Co., 1951.

SAVIO, MARIO. "The Berkeley Student Rebellion of 1964," *Beyond Berkeley: A Sourcebook in Student Values*, edited by C. G. Katope and P. G. Zolbrod, Cleveland, The World Publishing Co., 1966.

SIMMONS, J. L. and B. WINOGRAD. *It's Happening*, Santa Barbara, Calif.: Marc-Laird Publications, 1966.

"Student Power on the Rise." *Newsweek*, 70:40 (October 23, 1967).

TAYLOR, HAROLD. "American Idealism, 1965," *Saturday Review*, pp. 14–16 (June 26, 1965).

"Whirl is king, having driven out Zeus."

Aristophanes

11 Ethical Issues

THE PROBLEMS WHICH THREATEN TO OVERWHELM MANKIND have been created by man. Perhaps they can be solved and perhaps not. If they can, then certainly the solutions lie within the advice given by Alexander Pope:

> "Know then thyself, presume not God to scan,
> The proper study of mankind is man."

Professor Milton Mayer suggested in his essay "To Know and To Do" that man faces not a crisis in knowledge but rather a crisis in morality, in ethics. Academic purists retreat from every social problem with the scientific dodge that more research is needed. This sounds like good counsel and would be if man had an infinity of time and if the problems would stay static until each jot and tittle of pertinent information had been gathered and analyzed. Since life is an on-going process, man has no alternative but to operate operationally. Man cannot wait until he is drowning in a sea of humanity before he takes action to stem the flood of population. He cannot continue to educate youth for the industrial revolution when it is quite apparent these youth will be living through the cybernation revolution. The largely white *haves* cannot turn back the revolution of rising expectation of the largely colored *have-nots*; as Martin Luther King warned in regard to the American Negro, the choice is rapidly becoming full integration or concentration camps. The psychologically healthy cannot deafen themselves to the cries for help coming from the alienated without, in turn, becoming alienated. If the generation and credibility gaps are not narrowed, then to some degree, each man will have to start over as Adam and, even worse, will have little faith when checking the reality of his perceptions with the other Adams who share his physical but not his psychological world.

In each social problem thus far discussed, knowledge has been needed—knowledge of the full dimensions of the problem and knowledge of possible directions to solution—yet each case demonstrated Professor Mayer's thesis: the crisis is really not in knowledge but in morality. As the biblical allegory warns, to partake of knowledge is to assume an onerous burden, for to know of good and evil requires that one act for good or for evil. It is difficult, if not impossible, to get off the hook. The biologist Thomas Henry Huxley told his students, "The great end of life is not knowledge but action." And W. H. Auden said to all who read his poetry:

> "Act from thought should quickly follow:
> What is thinking for?"

Five societal issues have been discussed in considerable detail, for each will directly touch the lives of every student and therefore each has implications for the education of every student. Five other ethical issues will be given much briefer treatment. They too will hit the generation coming to power with full force. They too require some knowledge for first awareness and deeper knowledge for possible solutions. Given this knowledge, they too become crises in ethics. They too lead to the question of who speaks with ethical authority in this society. They too raise the question of education as the source for ethical commitment.

NATIONAL SOVEREIGNTY

Professor Marshall McLuhan speaks of the world as a "global village," claiming that the cool medium of television has made New Yorkers into participants of what goes on in Israel, the Congo, or Vietnam. Since distance can better be measured in time than in miles, the supersonic stratoliners will again reduce the circumference of the earth by half, just as the jet, the propeller, and the steam engine each did in previous decades and in an earlier century. Business has become so international in scope that the French author, Jean-Jacques Servan Schreiber could in 1967 document his thesis that the *grandeur* of de Gaulle's France is largely owned by American financiers who, to add insult to injury, borrowed European capital to gain their financial control. A powerful segment of industry allies itself with the nation's military since profits are still to be had from nationalistic wars. Some cynics argue that war, being a complete waste, is the perfect means to keep production, employment, and profits high. Even if this last point were true, it would remain true only if the war gets fought in a contained way somewhere far removed from the industrial plants. Not even nuclear bomb makers are going to profit from a nuclear war.

National sovereignty has taken some strange and absurd twists in recent decades. The only countries with *de facto* sovereignty are the superpowers, namely, the United States, Soviet Russia and the People's Republic of China. The others have sovereignty within the limits allowed by the superpower under whose umbrella they stand. Ironically, the nuclear giants are somewhat at the mercy of the whims and vagaries of their satellites and of the neutrals who play off one superpower against another. North Korea can, as it did in the "Pueblo Incident" of 1968, tweak the nose of the U.S. and thereby bring China or Russia or both into a possible nuclear confrontation with the U.S. Further, there are no secrets in making A-bombs or H-bombs; any technologically advanced country willing to spend the money can make them. That means that Israel could, if it chose, compensate for the numerical superiority of the Arabs by making atomic weapons. Small countries could not win a big war, but they have it in their power to start one. The shrunken world is now so interrelated and the competition for ideological support so fierce that any minor local flare-up might quickly escalate to the point where the world is in nuclear jeopardy. The corollary to this theorem is that the superpowers fight each other by proxy, using small countries, or factions within a country, as stand-ins.

The deterrence policies of the U.S. and the U.S.S.R. predicate the maintenance of peace within the balance of terror. These policies literally puts the world's existence at the mercy of (1) the continued rationality of the two giants (inside-dopesters in the Kennedy Administration put the risk at 50:50 during the Cuban Missile Confrontation); (2) the proliferation of atomic powers (the greater the number of fingers on the button the greater the likelihood of the button getting pushed); and (3) the maintenance of the fail-safe devices (they came close to failing when accidents caused H-bombs to fall on Palomares, Spain, in 1966 and in Baffin Bay near Thule, Greenland, in 1968).

National loyalties are as strong as whip cord and are just as binding for the Afghanistani or Nepalese as for the Americans or Russians. The nation provides an in-group feeling for even the poorest and weakest. For the rich and powerful nations, citizenship brings with it all manner of material as well as spiritual benefits. Love of country has been a value cherished in every land. It has had religious overtones for many, and has been considered more sacred than one's life. It has even become justification for killing. It has been the inspiration for poets and the staple for political rhetoric. Yet, the questions grow louder and more insistent as to whether nations might not be as outmoded as tribes, whether national sovereignty might not be a dangerous illusion, and whether a world of nations locked in deadly struggle can long survive. The generation coming to power will be obliged to answer these questions.

THE WARFARE STATE

In private life, people spend money on that which they value. If the same motivation holds true for governments, then in truth the United States is a warfare state, not a welfare state. The total budget for fiscal 1968–69 called for an expenditure of 186.1 billion dollars. The military had asked for over 100 billion dollars but since this was an "austerity" budget the actual amount earmarked for current military operations (not past wars) was 76.7 billion dollars, 43 percent of the total governmental expenditure. By contrast, the Office of Economic Opportunity got 1.9 billion dollars to conduct the War on Poverty. The shooting war against communism in Vietnam was allocated a minimum of 26.3 billion dollars. The worldwide foreign aid program was limited to 3 billion dollars even though, as Fidel Castro once said, "Communism marches on empty bellies."

Former President Harry Truman said that in a nuclear age war as an instrument of national policy was suicidal. In his farewell address, Former President Dwight D. Eisenhower, warned the nation against the machinations of the military-industrial complex. News journals, not secret documents, quote figures on nuclear destructive capacity showing that the overkill ratio is sufficient to destroy not just one but several worlds. The Russian military use the justification that imperialistic capitalism must be stopped at all costs. The American military say more billions are needed to stop the communist international conspiracy. Chairman Mao Tse-tung boasts that China could sustain 300 million nuclear casualties and still have 400 million Chinese to defeat any American invasion of Mainland China.

Full comprehension of the death of even the individual is difficult. To contemplate the destruction of all life is almost beyond human imagination. Yet at an intellectual level, if not at an emotional level, it is now accepted that a major war between the nuclear powers would mean the death of all. If Russian and the United States (or China or any other new member of the "Nuclear Club") start rocketing H-bombs at each other to save the world against imperialistic capitalism or to save the world against atheistic communism, then Armageddon is at hand; to misquote T. S. Eliot, history ends with a bang, not a whimper. The option to destroy mankind is the ethical choice to end all ethical choices. And it does appear that for some time to come those living in warfare states will have to prepare themselves in knowledge, in wisdom, in forbearance, and in cool courage to circumvent this ultimate act.

FOREIGN AID

The developing countries have 80 percent of the world's population, yet 90 percent of the world's income belongs to the developed countries. This disparity is growing each year, for the population explosion in the *have-not* countries forces them to concentrate on agriculture just to feed their people. And, being beggars rather than choosers, each year they find they pay more to the *have* nations for their manufactured imports and get less revenue each year for their raw material exports.

The United Nations goal of having the rich contribute 1 percent of gross national product to the poor would bring about 8 billion dollars in aid from the U.S. alone. Instead, for fiscal 1968–69 the U.S. allocated 2.3 billion dollars. The gentlemen's agreement of 1 percent of GNP among the rich members of the U.N. was made in 1961. Since then, the total of aid from all countries has remained constant at about 6 billion dollars per year even though GNP has gone up dramatically. Even including questionable aid such as loans at 10% interest, greatly discounted military hardware, and palming off deteriorating surplus, the decline in U.S. contribution has been .87% of GNP in 1961 to .72% in 1965 to .62% in 1966 to .55% in 1967 and to approximately .27% in 1968. Donor nations, including the U.S., insist that most aid be bought in the donor country at higher than world market prices thereby making much foreign aid into a disguised subsidy to domestic exporters of manufactured or farm goods.

As far as nations are concerned, it is impossible to contradict the Marxian axiom that "the rich grow richer and the poor grow poorer." The *have-not* nations' share of world trade has dropped from one-third to one-fifth in the past decade. Food production increase in the *have-not* countries cannot keep pace with population increase so that the 16 million ton food shortage of 1967 will grow to a 42 million ton shortage by 1975 and will double again to an 88 million ton shortage by 1985. Aid in the form of loans quickly builds to the point where the debtor can hardly pay the interest. India, for example, in the next decade will need to borrow 18 billion dollars, 14 billion dollars of which will service old debts, leaving only 4 billion dollars in new aid. And the poor grow poorer, for as the technologically advanced countries create chemical substitutes (synthetic rubber is a case in point), they have less and less need for the raw materials of the underdeveloped countries.

Another ethical issue is brutalization of the well-fed as the predicted famines of the 1970's begin to dwarf even the agonies of the concentration camps of Nazi Germany. Even so, sympathy, brotherhood, compassion, and guilt appear to have worn thin and are less used as appeals by the poor nations and are less heeded by the rich nations. Instead, the militants are calling on the poor to battle the rich in a new class struggle. Neither the U.S. nor the U.S.S.R. want or could profit from chaos and anarchy in Asia, in Africa, or in South America. Yet, both the U.S. and the U.S.S.R. have been niggardly in their aid. Liberia's Minister of Commerce, A. Romeo Horton, said: "The removal of inequities between rich and poor is the key question of our times; it will decide the issue of war and peace." If he is right, the ethical issue for the affluent Russians, the affluent Europeans and the affluent Americans may be reduced to a starkly simple choice: help them or shoot them.

SCIENTIFIC PROGRESS

In the past, science and progress were considered synonymous, or at least hyphenated terms. More recently, science has come to be linked to an amoral proliferation of technology with as many evils as benefits spinning off the accelerated whirl. The serious questioning began with the philosopher-scientists, such as Albert Einstein and Robert Oppenheimer, who expressed regret for their own contribution to the ushering in of the nuclear age. The bald statement by some that scientists have no ethical responsibility for the consequences of their discoveries put a chill to previous enthusiasm. The alacrity with which the military began to first subsidize and then steer the direction of scientific investigation (17.3 billion dollars in fiscal 1968–69 for government-sponsored research and development) became a serious concern to all who distrusted the wisdom of the military. The loss of independence of research in the universities; the temptation to use whatever is discovered, be it H-bombs or heart transplants; the concentration of power in the hands of the knowledgeable elite and the loss of voice for those outside this tiny elite; the growing evidence that scientific discoveries can irreparably upset the ecological balances in nature; the minimizing of interpersonal relationships in favor of the machines—all of these elements have converted science from an unquestioned positive value into a crucial ethical issue.

Of course, scientific experimentation and discovery cannot and should not be eliminated any more than cybernation can or should be stopped. However, limits can be placed, controls can be imposed, priorities can be established, and responsibilities can be clearly defined. Some faculties and students have forced universities to turn down lucrative grants for super-secret research in exotic weaponry and in counterinsurgency techniques. Some scientists, tempered by humanism, have categorically refused to use their knowledge in research whose objectives seemed potentially harmful. Some citizens have made loud outcries against the priorities reflected in budgeting 5 billion dollars or more per year for the space research that will put a man on the moon while on earth, the air, the water, the cities, even the human psyche become polluted. Naive trust in science as an unalloyed good was lost at Hiroshima and Nagasaki. The generation coming to power faces the difficult task of establishing scientific ethics by which the powerful genii can be released for man's benefit and then rebottled to prevent man's harm.

FAITH IN THE DEMOCRATIC PROCESS

Probably the most subtle of the ethical issues, hence the one most difficult to define and illustrate, is the erosion of faith in the democratic process. This loss of faith is captured in the phrase, "You can't beat City Hall." It is reflected in the resigned shrug when the murderers of the civil rights workers Schwerner, Cheney and Goodman are only convicted of violating their victims' civil rights. It is manifested in the poor man's political advertisement: the picket line and the demonstration. It builds such a pressure of frustration that it breaks its bounds and spills out as riot and violence. It is the breath of suspicion in the U.S. and the open suspicion throughout much of the world that the assassinations of John Kennedy, Martin Luther King, Jr., and Robert Kennedy were more than just the coincidental acts of "faceless men." It is the belated protests arising from the Congress that they were manipulated by the Johnson Administration into abrogating their Constitutional power to decide for or against war. It is the general feeling of helplessness—the feeling that control over events has been taken from the individual citizen and that those in power can act with cynical disregard for the will of the majority. It is what makes some see "dropping-out" (hippies?) as the only means of salvaging one's integrity. It is what makes others (activists?) eschew dialogue and move directly to confrontation. It lies behind the increasing resort to civil disobedience, for the unresponsiveness of the power structure makes the use of due process seem like an exercise in futility.

Whether there is in fact a breakdown in the democratic

process in some ways is beside the point. As the social scientist Dr. Jon Alexander put it: ". . . this is the concept of the self-fulfilling prophecy: If men perceive events as real they will be real in their consequences." If a sizable group within the body politic perceive that the democratic process has been undermined then the citizens face an ethical crisis that can unravel the entire fabric of that society.

A NATIONAL MALAISE

At a time when the U.S. is the richest country the world has ever seen (GNP 762 billion dollars to Russia's GNP of 372 billion dollars) and militarily the most powerful (the United States has 4,500 missiles with nuclear heads to Russia's 1,000), diagnosticians of various political persuasions have kept close check on the symptoms and have reported signs of serious social illness. New York Governor Nelson Rockefeller:

> The deepest problem before America is moral and psychological. The contemporary uneasiness—especially among our young generation—reflects rebellion against the emptiness of life which knows only 'practical' problems and material goods and seems to lack a deeper purpose.

Dr. Paul Goodman:

> As people [Americans] they are decent. But they are entirely lacking in determination to prevent the causes and to solve the conditions; they do not believe that anything will be done, and they accept this state of things. As citizens they are washouts.

Walter Lippmann:

> In the more-developed countries, Communist as well as non-Communist, there are no great sustaining, unifying and inspiring beliefs, no schemes of salvation and no ardent promises of better things to come. . . . There is a growing

belief that Johnson's America is no longer the historic America, that it is a bastard empire which relies on superior force to achieve its purposes, and is no longer providing an example of the wisdom and humanity of a free society. There is, to be sure, envy, fear, rivalry in the worldwide anti-Johnsonism. But the inner core of this sentiment is a feeling of betrayal and abandonment. It is a feeling that the American promise has been betrayed and abandoned.[3]

Columnist Emmet John Hughes:

And it is a feeling—a tension in society and a stress among men—not known since the 1930's. . . . To simplify severely: The first was a crisis of need. The second is a crisis of purpose. Then, the starkest signs of trouble were economic. Now they are political. Every grave crisis in a nation springs from a particular hunger of the people. The hunger of the 1930's was for resources. But the hunger of the 1960's is for resolve.[4]

James Reston of the New York Times:

This is a divided nation today not alone over economic but over fundamental moral questions. The President is not hearing all those mutinous cries below decks because he has the ship moving, but many people think he has it moving in the wrong direction, not toward 'new and better shores' but toward the rocks.

The National Committee for an Effective Congress reported:

At all levels of American life, people share similar fears, insecurities and gnawing doubts of such an intense degree that the country may in fact be suffering from a kind of national nervous breakdown—a depression of the national spirit.

[3]Walter Lippmann, "The American Promise," *Newsweek*, 70:12 (October 9, 1967). Reprinted with permission.
[4]Emmet John Hughes, "The Smell of Crisis," *Newsweek*, 70:18 (November 30, 1967). Reprinted with permission.

Author Mary McCarthy wrote of the indifference of the majority to the moral issue of Vietnam:

> . . . the subject is treated as a minority pastime, looked on by the majority with more or less tolerance. "The country can afford it" is the attitude. Or: "It's a free country" which has come to mean "I've got mine Jack. Everybody to his taste."

Former Health, Education and Welfare Secretary John Gardner said:

> It does not seem to me that either the Congress or the public is fully aware of the alarming character of our domestic crisis. We are in deep trouble as a people and history is not going to deal kindly with a rich nation that will not tax itself to cure its miseries.

Finally, even from *Time Magazine*:

> But 1967 awakened many of its citizens to the fact that conscienceless affluence cannot only despoil the environment and drive a deprived underclass to the brink of rebellion; it can also pervade society with a sense of impotence and bring on the loss of unifying purpose."

EDUCATION AND ETHICAL COMMITMENT

This depressing catalog of ethical issues that plague the United States leads directly to the question of who speaks with ethical authority in this society? If the crisis is not in amoral knowledge but in moral wisdom, then to what institutions can the society turn to provide leadership in an ethical renaissance? In the past, religion has been looked upon as the source of moral and ethical direction and strength. No brief is made either for or against organized religion, yet the thrust of this discussion requires the comment that for many, if not most people, the role of religion is perfunctory and has little to do with the ethics of social issues.

The church as a recreational center, or the church as a place where insurance premiums against hell are paid each Sunday does not represent an ethical force within the society. Some courageous clerics risked their lives to challenge Hitler, Stalin, Mussolini, and Franco, but the verdict of history is that most were reluctant or enthusiastic collaborators. Some courageous white ministers joined their Negro colleagues in the showdown on racism in the United States, but again they were the exceptions, not the rule. Those who have lived or traveled in the South or in northern ghettos know that the most segregated time of the week is Sunday morning. Pope John XXIII and Pope Paul VI made strong statements for international peace and racial brotherhood, yet these were vitiated in the U.S. by Francis Cardinal Spellman calling for a "holy war" in Vietnam and James Cardinal McIntyre muzzling any of his priests who spoke on civil rights for Negroes. The irrelevance of religion to the ethical issues of the 1960's was underlined by the movement that had as its flip slogan "God is dead" and by the spate of articles demonstrating that "God is rich" (visible assets of the U.S. churches total 79.5 billion dollars).

The theme for this chapter, "Whirl is king, having driven out Zeus," is a line in a comic play by Aristophanes written four centuries before Christ. It attests to man's unhappy fate of having the institutions of moral authority in a state of collapse just when man needs them most. Looking at the sweep of history, Arnold Toynbee concludes that great civilizations rise and fall on the basis of commitment to an ethic usually formalized by religious dogma and structure. Of course, for many, the churches still speak with ethical authority. Perhaps for even a larger number, god-like religious personalities or commanding philosophic thinkers, independent of any formal religion, provide ethical guide posts and moral strength. Vast numbers of people would, in a vague sort of way, like their world to operate on a more ethical basis, but seeking no means to this end, they never find it.

Colleges cannot replace churches, bolster the churches, or in any significant way contribute to their resurgence as an ethical force. On the other hand, colleges cannot side step their responsibility to teach morality and ethics. It is virtually impossible to teach that which is relevant without involvement in morals and ethics. Scrupulous neutrality or even absolute avoidance do not allow escape, for "silence gives consent." Whenever evil triumphs, those custodians of the cultural heritage who failed to defend it stand accused at the bar of history. The belief that instructors are completely objective, unbiased, detached dispensers of neutral facts is an illusion of students and the public and a delusion of teachers. If such a teacher existed, he would be an ethical eunuch; no student's mind would be impregnated by his thought.

Obviously, not many students will be impressed with the message: "Be good, be moral, be ethical because we say you should be good, moral and ethical." Faculty members can, however, define and clarify the ethical issues, help the student to see what alternatives he has open to him, train him to think out what the effects of each alternative will be, and remind him that he has the freedom to make the choice, but he must accept the consequences of his decision. The authority to act as ethical advocate is not derived from any absolute source. It flows from the ancient position that there is a humanistic, a logical, and a pragmatic basis for ethical behavior. Consider three current examples: Population has to be controlled because humanity will suffer if it is not controlled. Education for meaningful leisure is required by the logic of an economy of abundance. Aiding and abetting the revolution of rising expectation is a more practical solution than a hundred-year war to suppress it.

Students know, or at least sense that ethical behavior has always had a base in humanism, in logic and in pragmatism; therefore they hold the colleges responsible for focusing upon what is relevant. In a report of a national student conference, this statement is to be found: "One criterion of a good education is relevance—relevance to the world of modern politics and social ferment, relevance to the human condition in a mass society, relevance to the doubts, fears and hopes of thoughtful youth."

For the last six chapters, there has been an insistent spelling out of one overwhelming problem after another. If the tone has been urgent, it is because it is increasingly obvious that the effects of these issues will hit the generation coming to power with full force. These problems will not be solved just by good will or common sense. It is going to require knowledge to even measure their magnitude. If they can be solved at all, which is an open question, the solutions will be found in that blend of knowledge and character that is called human wisdom. Solutions will require people with breadth of education, critical minds, and intellectual courage. They will require a generation of students who have helped design and insist upon an education relevant to the realities of the world in which they will live.

TOPICS FOR CONSIDERATION

1. Milton Mayer's thesis that man faces more of a crisis in morality than a crisis in knowledge is repeated again and again. If this is the case, why is depth knowledge of societal issues needed? Why not simply teach people moral principles and let them apply these principles as the problems arise? Does each problem have its own morality?

2. Some scorn is leveled at professors who remain noncontroversial by hiding behind a facade of scientific objectivity, indefinitely suspending judgment until all the facts are in. Does man in fact have no alternative but to operate operationally? In regard to all, or any of the problems discussed, does man have the option of waiting until all the scientific facts required for final solution have been collected, analyzed and interpreted?

3. Thomas Huxley said, "The great end of life is not knowledge

but action," and W. H. Auden echoed, "Act from thought should quickly follow./ What is thinking for?" Do these statements contradict the traditional idea that higher education should be preparation for future action? Do they support the position of the "activists" on the college campus? Is this counsel likely to lead to rashness? to going off half-cocked?

4. Assume that nationalism and the devotion to national sovereignty are as villainous in their effects as some people think them to be. Does this assumption give a college instructor the right to profess that national states should subordinate their sovereignty to the United Nations and become subdivisions within a world federation? Would most colleges tolerate such a professor? If so, what would be the reaction in the wider community? If not, does academic freedom really mean freedom to profess that which is allowable by the college and the community?

5. Warfare threatens ultimate, perhaps even imminent, destruction, yet warfare states do not appear to be going out of fashion. Does increased knowledge and increased dissemination of this knowledge appear to offer any real hope for the defusing of warfare states? What kind of knowledge would be needed? Who has ethical obligation to disseminate this knowledge?

6. Is it reasonable to think that the *have* nations will ever give substantial aid to help the *have-not* nations skip the industrial revolution and move directly into a cybernated economy? Why should any nation subsidize the development of a potential competitor for the world's markets? Is this a subject to be left to the decision of expert economists or should all citizens have a voice in the decisions? How can they qualify themselves to have such a voice?

7. Can a society allow some of its brightest young people to so concentrate their training in natural science that they never get exposed to the tempering effect of the social sciences or of the humanities? Can a society allow the great power that comes with scientific knowledge to be concentrated in the hands of a knowledgeable few? If the answer to both questions is negative, then is it justifiable for a college to require a strong bloc of general education for all students?

8. The democratic process requires those with power to respond to the will of the people. Many think there is a cynical disregard to the voice of the people by those in power; a belief that advertising and public relations will get them reelected whether they have

served the people's interest or not. Could this attitude account for the breakdown in respect for law and order? for the increased use of civil disobedience? for the defiant confrontations staged by students over the issues of the draft, political advocacy, college regulations?

9. In talking about the national malaise, what Supreme Court Justice William O. Douglas called "The Sickness of America," Mary McCarthy said the frequent response "It's a free country" really meant "I've got mine Jack. Everybody to his taste." Does this describe the student who claims his freedom is abridged when he is required to take courses that are not directly applicable to his vocational major? If a society is in fact sick, to what degree are all citizens responsible for educating themselves for its cure?

10. In answer to the question "Who speaks with ethical authority?" the position was taken that the voice of the church has been weak and largely unheeded. Is this an invalid appraisal? If so, in which of the ethical issues described has the church assumed the role of leadership? Upon what ethical basis did the church take its stand and how effective was it?

11. The thrust of the whole argument has been that the crises are in ethics, not in knowledge. If this is granted, then it seems reasonable to say that colleges should be as involved in teaching ethics as in teaching knowledge. Are knowledge and ethics separable? Can the implications of knowledge be taught without immediate involvement in ethics? Can the students' desire for relevance in education be met if the instructor restricts himself to the facts and does not venture into the implications of the facts?

12. If some students become intrigued with one or more of the ethical issues discussed in this chapter, where can they seek out depth treatment of these subjects? To what academic discipline can they turn for gaining expertise on national sovereignty? the warfare state? foreign aid? scientific progress? undermining of the democratic process?

SUGGESTED READING AND LISTENING

COUSINS, NORMAN, ROBERT MCAFEE BROWN, et al. . . . *Therefore Choose Life.* Santa Barbara, Cal.: Center for the Study of Democratic Institutions, 1965.

DE BORCHGRAVE, ARNAUD. "Scandal of the Century: Rich and Poor," *Newsweek*, 70:26–28 (October 30, 1967).

GOODMAN, PAUL, *Like a Conquered Province: The Moral Ambiguity of America.* New York: Random House, Inc., 1967.

HOROWITZ, DAVID. "World Economic Disparities." Santa Barbara, Calif.: Center for the Study of Democratic Institutions, 1962.

HUGHES, EMMET JOHN. "The Smell of Crisis," *Newsweek*, 70:18 (November 13, 1967).

LIPPMANN, WALTER. "The American Promise," *Newsweek*, 70:12 (October 9, 1967).

MARMOR, JUDD. "Psychological Aspects of Nuclear War," Tape No. 20. Santa Barbara, Calif.: Center for the Study of Democratic Institutions.

MAYER, MILTON. "To Know and To Do," *Humanistic Education and Western Civilization: Essays for Robert M. Hutchins*, edited by Arthur A. Cohen. New York: Holt, Rinehart and Winston, Inc., 1964.

MILLIS, WALTER. "War and Revolution Today," Tape No. 266. Santa Barbara, Calif.: Center for the Study of Democratic Institutions, 1965.

RAEBECK, CHARLES. "Education in a World of Revolution," *Manas*, 18: No. 12, (March 24, 1965).

SHOBEN, EDWARD J. *Students, Stress, and the College Experience*, U.S. National Student Association, Washington, D.C., 1966.

WARREN, EARL, HUBERT HUMPHREY, et al. "On World Community." Santa Barbara, Calif.: Center for the Study of Democratic Institutions, 1965.

PART 3

Practical Considerations

LABELING THIS SECTION "PRACTICAL CONSIDERATIONS" IMPLIES the other sections are not practical. That is far from the case. The Philosophic Considerations are as practical as the foundations upon which a structure is built. The Societal Considerations are the problems which will dominate the lives of the generation coming to power, therefore they should be the core of their education. Even so, there is the here and now with which students have to cope, and it is the problems here and now which become Practical Considerations.

Chapter 12 will contain some points of view and some general information pertinent to vocational choice and educational planning. This will be followed in Chapter 13 by a somewhat difficult but potentially valuable discussion of the basic principles of learning applied to the day-to-day problems in learning faced by college students. In Chapter 14, a case is made against the traditional extra-curriculum, and a strong case is made for the co-curriculum—for education beyond the classroom. Chapter 15 ends the book with a searching and sympathetic look at the mores and life styles of today's college students.

"There is nothing permanent except change."

Heraclitus

12 Vocational Choice and Educational Planning

THE MORE PLURALISTIC A SOCIETY BECOMES, THE GREATER the need for vocational guidance. In a Banana Republic, economic circumstances predetermine that most people will spend their lives working with bananas. In a caste system, those born into the fisher caste will be fishermen and those born into the cultivator caste will be farmers. However, in a complex, mobile, fluid society, such as is found in the U.S., the possibilities of occupational choice are legion: the Dictionary of Occupational Titles lists 35,550 separate jobs.

It was noted earlier that freedom is a function of knowledge. If a young person has never systematically studied his own qualities and if he has only vague familiarity with a handful of occupations, his freedom of vocational choice is indeed limited. The desire to increase this aspect of personal freedom prompted American educators and psychologists in the early part of the twentieth century to develop the process of vocational guidance. They aspired to make it into a science whereby the round peg got put in the round hole, and the square peg got put in the square hole. However, as human measurement became more sophisticated, it was discovered that those round and square pegs have infinitely more complex shapes. And neither will the holes stay put; they disappear, get plugged up, expand out of all recognition, take on the most exotic geometry and, in sum, show a complexity equal to the pegs which are supposed to fit into them. This is not to despair of the potentialities of vocational guidance. It is to disabuse those who tend to oversimplify of the notion that vocational guidance is a simple, mechanistic operation. It is to develop appreciation for vocational guidance as an ongoing process of subtlety, complexity, inexactness, and intuition, a process closer to an act of art jointly performed by counselor and counselee than to a science executed by the counselor on his client.

PREPARING FOR THE UNKNOWN

Geometric progression appears to apply to the increase of information just as it does to the upward curve of population. Knowledge breeds knowledge so rapidly in the incubators of vast college systems that the prediction of a 100 percent increase in information in the next ten years is met with nods of belief and acceptance. Considering this, not many are inclined to dispute the estimate of Labor Department analysts that 50 percent of the jobs which will occupy the labor force a decade hence are not in existence today. To be sure, the traditional professions and the age-old trades and labors will still be flourishing, but even they may be so redefined that the only thing that remains is the common name. The roentgenologist and the gynecologist are both medical doctors, and the specialist in the new math and the specialist in remedial reading are both teachers, but what an abysmal failure each doctor and each teacher would be at the other's job. The fundamental question comes to this: How does a person prepare for the unknown? How can a student train himself for a job which does not exist?

Youth, being youth, are disposed to react to this conundrum with a rather bouncy optimism. Robert A. Gross, Secretary of the U.S. Student Press Association:

> But few of us under thirty want to make a final commitment now; indeed our desire for flexibility is our dominant char-

> acteristic. We want to try out various ways of living, to test, to probe, to experiment with different values—not only while we're young but for the rest of our lives. Is it possible to continue living this way? . . . We certainly have more opportunity to do so than ever before. This country presents us a fantastic array of choices, of life styles.

Rita Dershowitz, Associated Editor of *The Yale Alumni Magazine*:

> The range of possibilities is enormous: with unprecedented economic abundance, one has the real choice of self-imposed poverty; with higher education easily available, one can choose to reject academic learning in favor of other kinds of experiences. These kinds of choices are possible because they don't depend on our parents' value systems, because they call for new judgments. The younger generation is in the process of synthesizing a new wisdom, and that is the real education.

These rather lengthy quotes from two of youth's spokesmen illustrate the confidence with which the future can be faced and provide an apt preface to what will first appear to be an antithetical attitude toward vocational choice. In truth, it is the contradictory attitude which wisely fits the contradictory problems of preparing for the unknown.

COMMITMENT AND TENTATIVENESS

In a world of rapid change, the most sound posture, the most tenable stance, the most viable *modus operandi* is that of commitment within a wider frame of tentativeness. This statement applies to vocational decision-making, to educational planning, to any kind of problem-solving which has an immediacy or urgency in the present and which has effects ramifying deep into the future.

To develop the tightness of commitment within the looseness of tentativeness seems like a contradiction in terms—and in a way they are antithetical—but the human mind is capable of tolerating seeming contradictions and pulling them together at a higher level of integration. Actually, when serious thought is given to most human problems, including those described in Part II: Societal Considerations, no real alternative for intelligent action presents itself except to develop a capacity to become committed but always within the bigger attitude of tentativeness. Perhaps definition of the key terms will give support to this last statement and will contribute toward understanding of the total concept.

Commitment is "being turned on." It is another way of saying that the person is psychologically involved. Commitment means the person values what he is doing and enjoys doing it. To be committed is to say, in effect, "That is important enough for me to make the effort." Commitment to a job, to an idea, to an activity, to a set of principles, helps to define the person. The behavior following from the commitment says to the observing world, "This is what I am," "This is what I believe," "For this I will be willing to make the struggle, pay the price." The behavior speaks not only to the outside world but also to the inside self, hence commitments become a part of the person's self-concept. They define him to himself, and they are acted out to that small audience of "crucial others" which each person carries in his mind and to whom he looks for applause or censure. That to which the person is committed becomes, therefore, the motivational base for his behavior.

To define it negatively, people who fail to arrive at strong personal commitments have the blurry quality of an underexposed film. They remain undefined to themselves and to others. They rarely feel strongly about anything, hence are without enthusiasm and are bland to the point of being insipid. In their perceptions, not much is worth the doing, not much has meaning or significance, and the unconscious question which they pose to each life circumstance is this: "If the activity, the task, has little meaning or significance, then why do it?" They cannot muster any strong belief in the value of what they are doing, hence their motivation is weak and erratic.

Tentativeness, on the other hand, means to "hang loose." It is a pervasive attitude that reflects a recognition of the flux and change in the society and the flux and change in the self. It follows from an awareness that things do not stay as they are, therefore the person should be alert for signs pointing to new directions. Some reserve of tentativeness acts as a balancing wheel keeping the person from being a "patsy" to over-enthusiasm, from being a fanatic, from being what Erich Hoffer called "the true believer." Tentativeness implies a seasoning dash of disenchantment (every life will have its evils, its nasty upsets, its loaded dice), of realism (one must learn to accept the bad with the awful) and of skepticism (if every problem of the twentieth century were solved, the twenty-first century would spawn replacements).

Applied to vocational decision, it is necessary for a student to arrive at a commitment to an occupational family, to an academic major, or at least to education in general in order to be motivated to continue. At the same time, this student must be aware that a highly specific job to which he commits himself today may become extinct, may be an occupational fossil by the time he has finished his training. The student would do well to suspect that the process of education itself may so change him that a premature and narrow commitment may simply lead him up a blind alley from which he will have to return and begin again.

How then can the college student have the motivation that goes with commitment and the maneuverability or viability that goes with tentativeness? The answer requires two insights. First, the student must increase the complexity of his perception of time so that he understands that he lives a moment at a time, in the here and now, and that the future is only problematical. At the same time, he should exercise his capacity to sense, imagine, think about the future so that the blurry but wide-angle view will act as a corrective on the myopic, tunnel vision of the present. Particular warning is made against the tendency in American society to become future-oriented, for in this delusion the present is always just a means to an ever-receding end. The student must come to see that ends simply beckon him forward, that he actually lives the means, that life is a process, that the ultimate of the ever-receding end is death.

The second insight required to reconcile the contradiction of commitment and tentativeness is that a sound general education affords the student the best opportunity to cope with whatever wicked surprises the future may bring. Introduction to the natural sciences, the behavioral and social sciences, and the humanities will help the student to see education as the process of learning to think and will reassure him that, although the content of thought will change, the method or process of thinking will be available to deal with the new content. A solid general education will provide the base upon which to build, the hub upon which to turn; it will serve as hostage to a changed fortune and will allow the student to hedge his vocational bets.

SOME DISCERNIBLE VOCATIONAL TRENDS

For use in vocational decision-making, occupational information needs to be precise, current, local, and relevant to all the factors that combine to describe the counselee. Most important, its implications must be explored in a depth interchange between counselor and student. What follows does not purport to meet these criteria. Instead, the purpose is seminal: to broadcast many seeds of thought relating to vocational trends with the hope that some will germinate in fertile minds and will be developed to meet and grow beyond the criteria noted above. Here then are some broad, sweeping vocational trends:

Cybernation has only been gathering momentum during its first decade and promises to revolutionize almost every field of work when it becomes tidal in force and magnitude.

Jobs in the public sector are increasing at a faster rate than jobs in the private sector.

Job opportunities in state and local government are expanding even more rapidly than opportunities in the Federal Civil Services.

The percentage of production-type jobs in industry is decreasing and will decrease at an accelerated rate as cybernation makes further inroads.

The percentage of farm jobs will continue to decrease in inverse proportion to the increase in automation. Agra-business occupations and services associated with farming will come to dominate the whole agricultural field.

Blue-collar jobs in all industries will be more adversely affected by cybernation than white-collar jobs, but even so, the routine desk jobs will be almost as vulnerable as the routine production line jobs.

Professional and para-professional jobs in both scientific and business computer programming will be promising for some years to come.

All types of service occupations will increase with growing affluence and with fewer workers needed in the production of goods.

There promises to be a greater number of people in existing professions, and more professions are being created as work grows more complex and requires broader and deeper education.

The increasing burden on the professionals will result in a proliferation of para-professional occupations and an increase in the number presently employed at the semi-professional level.

In the scientific and other technical fields there will be a need for approximately five technicians for every professional-level technologist.

As the population soars and as universal higher education becomes as accepted as universal elementary and secondary education, the required number of teachers at the collegiate level will double and the number of teachers at lower educational levels will also increase materially.

In an economy of abundance where leisure will be as important as work there will be increased opportunity in the performing arts, in the whole business of entertainment, and in all aspects of recreation.

Wholesale and retail trade will offer increasing job opportunities at all levels, particularly in mid-level managerial positions.

The internationalization of industry and commerce and the greater involvement of the United States in all facets of foreign affairs will require more people trained in foreign language, economics, and international relations.

The deterioration of the psychological health of the society will call for many more professionals and para-professionals in the fields of psychiatry, psychology, social welfare, counseling, and guidance.

The increased longevity and earlier retirement will create all manner of jobs associated with the health, care, and recreation of the aging.

Urban problems are becoming so pressing and are so interrelated that a coterie of urban specialists (sociologists, industrial dispersement experts, urban renewal planners, environmentalists) will be needed.

The pollution of the physical environment, the shortage of water, and all types of problems caused by or associated with the population explosion will call for many varieties of professional and para-professional expertise.

Depending upon policy decision on war and peace and on degree of involvement in space exploration, there will be expansion or contraction of occupations related to weaponry, missiles, space vehicles, and all the sophisticated electronic instrumentation associated with these fields.

Exploitation of the sea for foods, fertilizers, minerals, and desalinated water, will bring with it an expansion of existing professional and technical jobs and undoubtedly will create some new ones.

THE PROCESS OF VOCATIONAL CHOICE

Most university guidance centers offer top caliber vocational counseling but only to the small group of students who are so anguished by their indecision that they seek out this service.

Most community, or junior, colleges, on the other hand, are organized to offer, even insist upon, vocational guidance for all students. If the professional quality of the vocational counseling in many junior colleges is not the highest, as the two year Carnegie Study seemed to show, they are at least shooting toward the right target: vocational guidance should be as universal as education itself. Vocational counseling can be initial exploration for some students, narrowing of choice for a second group, decision-making for others, and confirmation or verification for the few students who have already made a definite (and correct) choice. All students, therefore, can benefit from, and should participate in, the vocational counseling process. Exploration will prod the student into doing some constructive thinking about himself and about possible jobs. Narrowing of choice may allow the student to commit himself to at least an academic major. Decision-making will clear away the obstacles and allow the student to move forward in the direction he has selected. Verification of previous decision will banish the nagging doubts and will add motivational energy to the choice which has been confirmed.

The popular notion of vocational guidance makes it akin to fortune-telling. Students often say to a counselor, "I want to take a test to see what I should be" and say it as if they had asked him to look into his crystal ball. The well-trained counselor replies to such a request with an assurance that not one but many tests may be given when they can provide needed answers and invites the student to meet with him for some freewheeling exploratory talks. These initial interviews constitute a personal assessment not so much to give the counselor all the facts as to force the student to look at himself in a very organized, systematic way and to accept the realities of what he is and what he is not.

Actually, tests are shortcuts and standard measuring sticks for what could be discerned with reasonable accuracy anyway, provided the interviews were exhaustive. So, when the student wonders about his native capacity to learn, the

Wechsler-Bellevue Intelligence Scale or some paper and pencil I.Q. test may be administered and interpreted to him. If the student's past academic grades are equivocal and seem inconsistent with the measure of global intelligence, the counselor will probably recommend that the student take one of the several reliable and valid academic aptitude tests which are available. By means of this test, the student will be able to compare himself with other college students in the basic academic tools of verbal ability and mathematic skill and reasoning. The counselor may also give him a standardized achievement battery to double-check the validity of the grades he earned in previous years and to point to academic areas of ability and of interest—and also to point away from fields where he has demonstrated weakness. In the interview sessions, the counselor and student will invariably explore vocational and academic interests, and this will lead naturally to an objective check by such instruments as the Strong Vocational Interest Test, the Kuder Preference Record and the Allport-Vernon Study of Values. Interest testing might either precede or follow measurement of vocational aptitudes secured from a battery such as the Flanigan Scales or the General Aptitude Test Battery. In junior colleges, the tests of intelligence, academic aptitudes, vocational interests, and occupational aptitudes are likely to be administered on a group basis with some group interpretation followed by more subtle interpretation by counselor to counselee. The time saved by such group work may allow the psychologically trained counselor to explore relevant personality factors through such projective techniques as the Rorschach ink blot test or the Thematic Apperceptive Test or perhaps by the paper and pencil personality scales called the Minnesota Multi-Phasic Inventory. When all this objective information is profiled and meshed with subjective data that rises to the surface during the interview sessions, both student and counselor may see, first dimly and then more clearly, the various vocational alternatives open to the student.

Concomitant with the accumulation of subjective and objective data about the student, there will occur the exploration and analysis of values. This aspect of vocational counseling is pivotal and calls for the most sensitive intuition and for depth understanding of the student, his immediate environment, and the wider society in which he lives. Technicians can give tests, report comparative scores, direct the student in his search for occupational information, and map out what courses are required for various vocational goals. It takes the basic respect, the sensitivity, the understanding, and the wisdom of the professional counselor to work successfully with the student in value analysis. The counselor does not by clever questioning expose or trap the student into revealing the values which motivate his behavior. Instead, the counselor serves as a catalyst for the student in his progressively deeper insights into the way he perceives his world and the values he attaches to each aspect of it. The counselor, having lived longer and knowing occupations better, will take an active role in defining the pattern of values required by various jobs and in comparing them with the values held by the student. If the value analysis aspect of vocational counseling is successful, the success will ramify much beyond the student's vocational decision and will affect every nook and cranny of his psyche.

Almost all students and some counselors will expect a definite, almost irrevocable, occupational decision as the end result of vocational counseling. Considering the truth that "There is nothing permanent except change," this is an impossible, and really foolish, expectancy. The whole concept of work is going to change. The nature of occupations will change even more rapidly than in the recent past. The prediction that 50 percent of all jobs a decade hence will be jobs that are not known today, will come to pass. In such a changing environment, the individual himself is going to change, to be transformed, to undergo a veritable metamorphosis. Yet, like all before him, he will have to live the days of his years; he will need to be committed for today yet remain tentative for tomorrow. Hence, vocational decision should be viewed as a process, not an event. Vocational counseling during the college years should strive for no more than a progressive narrowing of options. The student should realize, and if he does not the counselor should tell him, that he should educate himself broadly enough to keep some options open and deeply enough to qualify for an option within a job family that has most appeal and most opportunity for him in the here and in the now.

EDUCATIONAL PLANNING

There is a temptation for students moving from the narrow, prescribed high school curriculum to the broad and open offerings of college "to escape from freedom"; to turn away from the opportunity for free choice and to look to his counselor for mapping out a tight and rigid program for him. There is also a temptation for the counselor to assume this responsibility, for educational planning can be definite and precise and can make the counselor feel he is no longer grappling with a phantom. Even so, both should resist the temptation, for it is necessary for the student to be aware that he, not some functionary of the institution nor the forces of circumstance, made the grand design of his own education. To be sure, there will be required courses, prerequisites, and the usual hedges to absolute freedom, but within these limitations he should have the excitement of facing up to significant choices. And, he should be denied the easy but unhealthy escape of considering himself a victim of "the system." In the final analysis, each person has to educate himself, build his own educational edifice. Considering this, he should be the architect of the plan.

Having said this, it is also necessary to say that educational planning by the student need not be, but sometimes is, as random as a young child putting together some Tinker

Toys. There is some logic to it, some models worth studying, some ground rules, some warnings against common error, some pointers for getting started. The counselor's knowledge can be profitably exploited during the process of educational planning, and his experience should certainly be used in periodic critiques of the soundness of the educational plan. Included within the advice given by the counselor—in greater detail and made specific to the individual case—would undoubtedly be these generalizations:

The person is a human being before, during and after the time he is a worker; hence, the plan should give humanistic education some priority over vocational training.

Education should resemble a pyramid with the broad and strong base of general education serving as the footing upon which the specialization can gradually narrow to a fine peak.

Since the superstructure may become obsolete and have to be discarded, it would be wise to have the educational base broad enough to accommodate whatever new superstructure is built as a replacement.

First things must come first, and obviously the tool subjects of education take precedence over all else. The tool subjects are the media of effective communication: reading, writing, speaking, and the logical thinking involved in these, and to a somewhat lesser extent, arithmetical skill, mathematical reasoning, and graphical illustration. The student who is deficient in these tool subjects cannot progress until he has corrected this deficiency. The usual college freshman, must show continued development in the tool subjects commensurate with the increased complexity of the subject matter he is studying.

The junior college student who plans a so-called terminal program leading to the technician, mid-level management, or para-professional position should avoid classifying himself or allowing himself to be classified as either transfer or terminal. He would do well to keep all doors open, for there is a developing mobility in many of these fields that may allow him to move upward in a stairstep fashion with each step requiring a more professional level education.

Exclusive specialization will certainly create a low ceiling which will quickly block his climb.

Considering the rapid change and frequent obsolescence of tomorrow's occupations, the rule-of-thumb in educational planning should be "keep the options open." Among the best ways of doing this is to follow a core curriculum which provides the fundamental blocks of knowledge common to a whole family, if not a whole tribe, of jobs. For example, if a student in a community college takes during the first year a core program including integrated courses in physical science, technical mathematics, and graphics he will in effect have put himself on a swivel that will allow him to move into occupations anywhere along an arc describing the whole segment of physical science technologies.

Students who are not fortunate enough to have a deep commitment to education *per se* but do have a particular interest in a subject area should program themselves for one or more courses in this interest field each semester. This may buoy them up when interest lags and keep them from taking the easy exit of the dropout. They may also discover that their subject of special interest really has its roots in many other disciplines and thus find that interests expand with knowledge and knowledge expands with interests.

Whenever possible, a student should program himself for an exploratory course in a field completely foreign to him. The business administration major should take a course in music appreciation for the same reason that a person who always orders vanilla ice cream should on some occasion ask for chocolate or raspberry—to see what the other is like and possibly to expand his tastes.

The immediate protest to the above generalization will be that time limitations prohibit taking any course beyond the major and the general education requirements. That is true only if the student makes himself a prisoner of the idea that the junior college degree is a two-year program and the bachelor's degree is a four-year program. There is neither law nor even good sense that dictates this. There is no overriding reason why a student should not take three rather than two years in the junior college or five years rather than four for the baccalaureate. Actually, later entry into the labor market, a side effect of cybernation, may allow more exploration during the college years and result in a broader and more maturing education.

All of these advisory statements are generalizations that apply in the main but may not apply in the individual case. Each person's educational plan should be self-tailored. The courses should have intrinsic interest and value to the student and certainly should not be viewed by him as so many hurdles which he must jump upon command. Since each student must, in the final analysis, educate himself, each should help design the means to reach that end.

TOPICS FOR CONSIDERATION

1. Vocational decision ranks second only to marriage decision for total impact on the person's life. Yet millions of students invest years of training and thousands of dollars in preparation for an occupation about which they have not given an hour of systematic thought. Is this an accurate observation? If so, what accounts for the frequent failure of students to use the opportunities for vocational counseling? Why do people not turn to a professional counselor when they face a vocational decision in the same way they turn to a professional lawyer when they face a legal problem?
2. It was stated that the truism "freedom is a function of knowledge" applies to vocational decision just as it does to the political sphere. What does this maxim mean in the context of occupational choice? In what ways does knowledge increase a person's freedom of choice?
3. Why should money and the instructor's and other students' time be wasted by allowing some student to enter a specialty course who does not have the required ability, the special aptitudes, the interest, and the proper values to be a good risk? Would it not make sense for a college to establish verification of vocational choice as a prerequisite for entry into specialized vocational courses?
4. The estimate is quoted that 50 percent of the jobs which will occupy the labor force a decade hence are not in existence today.

Is there any logic by which to argue that this will apply to jobs which require college-level preparation? If this prediction applies primarily to semi-skilled production type jobs, then what concern should it be to those whose college education will move them beyond the semi-skilled or even skilled level?

5. If rapid change is going to make this year's commitment into next year's irrelevancy, then why become committed at all? Why not stay in a state of suspended judgment? Would it not be wiser to simply adopt a tentative attitude toward everything?

6. It was recommended that commitment within a wider frame of tentativeness be the approach in facing any and all of the problems described in Part II: Societal Considerations. How would this apply to the problem of cybernation? to the problems of national sovereignty and the warfare state? to the problem of the Negro Revolution?

7. Much was said about the necessity of having commitments and about how they become the motivational basis for behavior. But how does a person come to have these commitments? Are they more or less popular beliefs to which emotional energy can be attached? Are they philosophic conclusions which can be reached only through much knowledge and logical thought? What is the psychological process by which commitments are derived?

8. (Shakespeare's) Macbeth concluded that life "is a tale/ Told by an idiot, full of sound and fury,/ signifying nothing." If that is true, then are commitments not illusions? Are they not part of the sound and fury which signify nothing?

9. In discussing time perception, warning is made against becoming future-oriented. It is even called a delusional trap in which it is easy for Americans to fall. Since man has the capacity to fantasy the future, is it not natural for him to be future-oriented? Anticipation of pleasure is said to be more pleasurable than actual fulfillment of pleasure. Considering this, what is so dangerous or so wrong in being future-oriented?

10. Even disastrous problems create jobs for those trained to work toward their solution. Some occupational trends growing out of cybernation, alienation, and the population explosion have been suggested. What vocational opportunities will follow from the Negro Revolution? from the credibility and generation gaps? from foreign aid? from causes of the national malaise?

11. In the process of vocational counseling, value analysis was credited with being more pivotal than test administration and

test interpretation. If values are that important to vocational decision, different occupations must require different patterns of value. Does this ring true to experience? Does the typical elementary school teacher have values distinguishable from the typical retail merchant? Does the typical accountant have values distinguishable from the typical recreation director? What if the two positions are in the same job family; for example the high school teacher vs. the college professor?

12. What is the full meaning of the statement "vocational decision should be viewed as a process, not an event"? Is it possible for a person to educate himself both specifically and generally? to acquire competence in one field yet have other vocational options open to him?

SUGGESTED READING AND LISTENING

CHASE, STUART. "Are You a Specialist or a Generalist?" *Introduction to College Life*. Boston: Houghton Mifflin Company, 1966.

COLLINS, CHARLES C. *Junior College Student Personnel Programs: What They Are and What They Should Be*. Washington, D.C.: American Association of Junior Colleges, 1967.

EBEL, ROBERT L. "What a Student Should Know About Standardized Tests," *The First Years in College*. Boston: Houghton Mifflin Company, 1965.

FERRY, W. H. *The New Technology and Higher Education*, Whitewater Forum Committee, Wisconsin State University, Whitewater, Wisconsin, 1966.

GARDNER, JOHN W. "Versatility," *Introduction to College Life*. Boston: Houghton Mifflin Company, 1966.

GOODMAN, PAUL. "Jobs," *The Continuing Debate: Essays on Education for Freshmen*. New York: St. Martin's Press, Inc., 1964.

JACOB, PHILIP E. *Changing Values in College*. Evanston, Ill.: Harper & Row, Publishers, 1958.

KNOELL, DOROTHY M. *Toward Educational Opportunity for All*. New York: State University of New York, 1966.

LIPPMANN, WALTER, ALFRED KAZIN, et al. "A Dialogue Between the Generations," *Harper's Magazine*, 235:45–64 (October, 1967).

MILLS, C. WRIGHT. "The Educational Elevator," *The Continuing Debate: Essays on Education for Freshmen.* New York: St. Martin's Press, Inc., 1964.

PIEL, GERARD, ROBERT THEOBALD, and RALPH HELSTEIN. "The Bleak Outlook: Jobs and Machines," Tape No. 78. Santa Barbara, Calif.: Center for the Study of Democratic Institutions.

TIEDEMAN, DAVID and ROBERT P. O'HARA. *Career Development: Choice and Adjustment*. New York: College Entrance Examination Board, 1963.

"Whoso neglects learning in his youth loses the past and is dead for the future."

Euripides

13 Learning Principles Applied

A BASIC ASSUMPTION IN MOST PSYCHOLOGICAL SCHOOLS OF thought is that all human behavior is directed toward maintaining and enhancing the total self. It is not difficult for the layman to accept this assumption, for he dimly sees it validated in his own behavior, and he clearly sees it validated in the behavior of others. A person can maintain and enhance himself only by continuing to learn. The infant becomes the competent adult by means of learning; if he had not learned, he would have remained infantile. Therefore, the very logic of man's nature and the circumstances of life provide every man with a built-in need and desire to learn.

Babies and young children are not very discriminating in their learning and appear willing to learn anything that comes their way. As the child develops, and as more and more stimuli compete for his attention, he becomes selective and responds to that which in his evaluation will actually contribute to his maintenance and enhancement. So, progressively from grammar school to college, the student may close his ears and his eyes to education, for in his perceptions education may not seem even remotely connected to sustaining and bettering his life; learning the parts of speech may seem like learning nonsense syllables to kids who are trying to survive in the jungle of the urban slum. Put in a more positive way, students will try to learn what seems relevant. Perhaps it would be more accurate to say that the degree of effort to learn will correlate positively with the degree of relevance perceived. Of course, there are some conformists who would memorize complete gobbledygook if told to do so. And, there are those who no longer see anything as significantly contributing to their phenomenal selves and would not pay attention to directions on how to proceed immediately into a heaven on earth.

All of this is a preface to the simple truth that motivation (perceiving the relevance to maintenance and enhancement of the total self) is the key to learning. Everything else is peripheral. A student could study by a dim light coming across the wrong shoulder, in a room filled with pin-up pictures, with both radio and T.V. playing, late at night after a tiring day's work, with the crucial exam only hours away—he could commit all these sins against the injunctions in how-to-study textbooks and could still learn providing he perceived the material as being crucially relevant to his life.

Relevance, then, will be taken as the first principle of learning. What will follow will be statements of secondary, nonetheless important, principles of learning coupled with direct applications of these principles to learning at the college level. The trivial how-to advice will be largely ignored, for each student will work out details of technique compatible with his own personality once he has incorporated the basic principles of learning into his behavior.

PRINCIPLES CONCERNING MOTIVATION

Emotional as well as intellectual involvement is required for effective learning. For young children, the emotional component is largely the identification of pupil with teacher. The youngster wants the approval, even the love, of the authority figure upon whom he is dependent. This emotional relationship remains a factor even among college students; the student wants the instructor whom he respects to think well of him and may initially work hard simply to please the "significant other," only later continuing to work hard to please himself. When the intellectual content itself begins to act as an emotional excitant, then the person is hooked, the student becomes the scholar, "as if increase of appetite had grown by what it fed on." What Gordon Allport called the "functional autonomy of motives" begins to operate: The golfer who began playing just to lose weight becomes a golf addict, and the student who started his studies just to please the teacher with whom he identified becomes an avid scholar.

Intrinsic motivation is much stronger than extrinsic motivation. The student who gets active moment-to-moment pleasure from learning will eventually benefit much more than the student who jumps whatever academic hurdles are put in front of him in order to get good grades. Unless he is a thoughtless conformist, the student will eventually become as disenchanted with the extrinsic reward of good grades as the growing child becomes disenchanted with the extrinsic reward of gold or silver stars. The intrinsic reward, whether it be an interest satisfied or use put to the knowledge gained, is immediate and therefore reinforces the learned behavior pattern. Extrinsic rewards such as grades are far removed, if not disconnected, from the behavior learned and therefore do not have the immediate reinforcing effect.

Academic grinds work only for grades, and some teachers foster this confusion of the symbol with the thing. In such academic bargaining, the transaction is like a bribe by which the instructor promises and gives a symbolic reward to those who parrot back what has been "taught." In such a way intellectual creativity is smothered. Further, this kind of motivational dynamic converts learning into a competitive struggle in which some experience the satisfaction of winning, and an equal number experience the frustration of losing. To be sure, immediate intrinsic reward is not always possible, and sometimes one must resort to extrinsic motivation. The student has to learn how to spell if he wants to use written communication. Frequently, the student will find he must take Prerequisite A and Prerequisite B to be eligible for Course C. In such cases, both the instructor and the student should strive for the functional autonomy of motives, for using extrinsic reward until intrinsic reward can take over, for continuing a learning activity for the inherent value in it rather than just suffering an unpleasant means to attain a pleasant end.

Reward is a more effective agent for controlling behavior than punishment. This principle of learning is flagrantly flouted in human behavior ranging from the mother who controls the child by threats (or acts) of spanking to the superpowers controlling each other by the threats (acts would end the whole game) of nuclear holocaust. Reward acts directly to reinforce the correct response, while punishment works only indirectly at best, and does not always weaken the incorrect response. Reward carries the positive message, "Repeat that correct behavior," while punishment only carries the negative message, "Stop it," without saying what should be done. This kind of emotional suppression of behavior does not cause an unlearning of the wrong behavior. Frequently another wrong response is substituted, only this time with the further negatives of frustration and disruptive anger.

Obviously, punishment can be informative (the burned child avoids the fire), and the reward of escaping from punishment teaches a person to continue that escape behavior. Even so, the students should search for rewards in his learning and should be ingenious in creating rewards for himself throughout the learning process. The fortunate student who has had an environment fertile for the development of intellectual values and who has the mental ability to become intellectually interested will find almost any new learning rewarding—just as the baby is fascinated by any shiny or noisy object and just as most young children seem to act out the Robert Louis Stevenson jingle,

"The world is so full of a number of things,
I think we should all be as happy as kings."

As a matter of fact, anyone who gets the full impact of the message that learning is *the* means by which he will maintain and enhance his total being, will find that learning has a reward buried in it.

Emotional preoccupations and excessive anxiety can and usually do interfere with learning. To be sure, some anxiety can make the difference between being alert and being lethargic. A student preparing for a test or for giving a speech, or for any other event that puts his self-concept in some jeopardy, will naturally experience twinges of anxiety and will probably work harder and do better because of it. It is equally obvious that the shattering if vague fears of an anxiety attack will so disrupt the mental processes that the person may literally not be able to remember his own name (amnesia). Much short of this neurotic level, the student beset with emotional conflicts concerning his relationships with parents, acceptance by his peers, his draft obligations, self doubts, or personal values —the student preoccupied with any of these or similar problems, will find it difficult to focus on anything not connected to his preoccupation. And this is where the college counselor can offer substantial assistance.

Most college counselors are not clinical psychologists and certainly are not psychiatrists; therefore they are neither willing nor able to engage in psychotherapy for the neurotic. However, they are usually well-trained and widely experienced in helping normal people work through the psychological problems to which all men are subject. They are particularly adept at value analysis and can serve as the mirror by which the student can see himself and his problem in sharper focus. They can rather quickly bring the student to see the futility of constant rumination—endless beating around the psychological mulberry bush—and can be the catalyst in his exploration of alternatives leading to decision on a plan of action. If students were wise enough to use college counselors to fullest advantage, the failure rate and the dropout rate would plummet. Most students who fail or drop out from college are unnecessary casualties; they are capable of handling the work, but psychological interferences block them from doing so.

PRINCIPLES CONCERNING TECHNIQUES

In most instances, distributed learning is more rapid and is better retained than massed learning. It is this principle that prompts instructors to advise students to pace out the material to be learned throughout the semester or quarter or term. Massed learning, in this context known as "cramming," does not allow for recovery from fatigue or for consolidation of newly learned material with relevant material previously learned. It increases the interference of information most recently learned with that just previously learned (memorizing stanza two may interfere with remembering stanza one) and prevents discrimination of the important from the unimportant (minor detail must fall into the background leaving the major points as the object of focus). The qualification should be made that difficult thought problems require massed effort, although insight into the answer may come later and unexpectedly, when the inconsequential details drop from memory leaving the main points fitting neatly together in an understandable pattern. Further, massed review of previously learned material will bring *recency* and *overlearning* in as supportive allies and thereby greatly improve the student's recall (performance on a test).

Given certain reservations, learning the whole is more effective than learning the sum of the parts. This is particularly true when the whole has a unity and a meaningfulness to it and when the parts are not separable entities. Of course, if anything to be memorized or learned is very long, it must be learned by natural subdivisions and then integrated again into a whole. The more intelligent the student, the larger the entity which can be mastered as a whole. For most learning situations this related but more general principle from Gestalt Psychology is applicable:

Viewing a problem as a whole allows perceptions of the relationship of the parts and thereby facilitates solution of the problem. If a rat can see only one alley of a maze at a time, the poor animal has no alternative in learning to run the maze but that of trial and error. By reverse token, if a student can first get an overview of what is to be learned, he can quickly sort out the major from the minor and see how it all fits together to make sense. It is helpful to skim through to get the *gestalt* of a new chapter in a text; it would be even more beneficial if the student captured the organizational pattern or configuration of the whole book, and it would be immensely helpful if the instructor devoted the first day or even the first week to drawing out with broad strokes the outline, the skeletal structure, of the whole course.

Learning is fostered by knowledge of results. Since much learning, particularly problem-solving, is like a game, the participant is eager to find out how he is doing. He has more incentive to keep going if he knows he is doing well. Even when he is not doing well, if he sees his mistake before he has invested much time and effort in failure, he will be prompted to correct his error and immediately step forward in the right direction. Because knowledge of results fosters learning, students really want tests and are a little miffed if the instructor does not have the results back the next day. A student could exploit this same principle by testing himself; he could set up comprehensive questions after skimming through each chapter and answer the questions after he has thoroughly studied the chapter.

Material developed in a logical, patterned manner will be more meaningful, hence much easier to learn. It takes less effort to memorize words than nonsense syllables. It would be easier to learn nonsense syllables if they were presented in alphabetical sequence. A poem with a rhythmic beat will be mastered sooner than an equal amount of prose. A long prose passage with a compelling logic, such as the Preamble to the United States Constitution, can be remembered in essence, if not exactly, after two or three readings. This principle may be less applicable to people culturally enveloped in the mysticism of the East, but for the Westerner with the intellectual heritage of the Greco-Roman thought, that which makes up a logical, meaningful pattern can be more easily grasped, and once captured, it can be held in mind.

If there is magic to be found in any of the much-touted teaching machines, it flows primarily from the last two principles. The machine gives its user immediate results; it tells him whether he did or did not learn the material correctly. Perhaps more important, the material is programmed with a lucid logic and with a precise progression from the simple and the known to the complex and the unknown. The content is not only logically organized but also psychologically organized to force participation by the learner. It is hard for the learner not to pay attention and not to become involved. Each response gives him the results of his progress and entices him forward. This next step will be a gradual progression based on the previous logic and will probably be immediately meaningful to the student. If not, the student has the opportunity to mull it over and go back to recapture the pattern and flow of the thought. None of this is radically different from what the good teacher always did, perhaps intuitively. The programmed learning of the teaching machine simply employs the principles of learning in a more systematic way.

Since the teaching machine is already a tool in the education of the on-coming generation, two other comments, one positive and one negative, deserve to be added. The teaching machine allows the student to move at his own speed and has the healthier effect of allowing him to compete against himself rather than against the thirty or forty other students in the class. The individual differences in speed of learning are respected so the fast are not retarded by the slow and the slow are not defeated and eliminated from the game of learning by the fast.

The second, negative comment is that a vital element gets lost in the dehumanized, impersonal contact of man with machine. Some schools and colleges are so flushed with enthusiasm over programmed learning that they are trying to substitute one programming logician for x number of teachers and convert the classroom into tiny electronic learning carrels. However, most educators are listening to the criticism of students heavily exposed to this kind of learning who praise its mechanical efficiency and deplore its alienating effect. The moderates are coming to see the advanced teaching machine of the future as they now see the blackboard, charts and maps, the workbook, the phonograph, the motion picture, the tape recorder, or the closed circuit TV—as an aid to effective teaching, but not a replacement for the human relationship of teacher to student.

Although it tends to be less than expected, transfer of training can be greatly increased by consciously teaching for it. The best way to learn English is to study English directly, not through Latin. The student cannot develop his mind by exercises unrelated to the mental activity for which it will be used. Even so, if the teacher takes pains to teach the identical or even similar components—for example, the prefixes and suffixes of Latin and English—and if the teacher underscores and drives home the appropriate application of known principles to new situations, then some transfer of training does occur. Debate on this narrow issue has been largely resolved, but in a tenuous way is related to this wider and most controversial question: Should education be transmittal of knowledge for use by the student when he is an adult or should it be a rough and tumble wrestling with the implications of knowledge for "enterprises of great pith and moment"? Should only the facts of the population explosion be taught or should students and teacher go to the mat on the implications of population for the issues of birth control, abortion, foreign aid, and war and peace? Should only the statistics on cybernation be transmitted, or should the teacher also point out that an economy of abundance requires a different theoretical rationale than capitalism (or communism)? Inert facts do not lie dormant until the person is an adult and then suddenly ferment into bubbling activity. The facts do not automatically shed light on the implications of these facts. Transfer of training occurs when the instructor and the students set out to make it occur. Significant learning will occur when the instructor and the students embark on the bold and dangerous course of realistic investigation of the implications of known facts.

PRINCIPLES CONCERNING REMEMBERING AND FORGETTING

That which is perceived with clarity and understanding will be remembered. A dramatic event in a person's life will be indelibly printed, even branded, in his memory. Sensations coming through the eyes or ears which carry very little meaning will be perceived in such a blurry fashion that they will seemingly leave very little, if any, memory trace. Most of what people think they forget was never really learned. That is why it is bootless for the student to force his eyes to look at print or force his ears to listen to words which his mind is not bringing into sharp perceptual focus. Students may spend several hours in study only to fail a test on the material covered. For a person to remember a fact, or a logical pattern of thought, or implications following from facts, or even the more nebulous emotional reactions or attitudes associated with knowledge, whatever is to be remembered must emerge from the background sensations into a vivid, sharply defined figure. Remembering blurred perceptions is as impossible as taking a clear photo with the camera lens out of focus. The student must pay close attention and keep adjusting the lens of his mind to fit the subject matter crossing his consciousness. He must engage himself in a silent conversation with the author he is reading, and he must actively engage himself, sometimes in audible exchange, with the instructor to whom he is listening. If he fails to understand, to sharply delineate figure from ground, he must take the initiative to ask the questions, go back over previous material, or do whatever is necessary to adjust his mental lens so a clear image is registering. Accurate perception is an imperative, for obviously that which is not clearly learned cannot be clearly remembered.

Classical conditioning requires the reinforcement of the unconditioned stimulus; operant conditioning requires the reinforcement of some kind of reward. By conditioning, the number 81 can be associated with 9 x 9, and a complicated sequence in a chemistry experiment can be associated with the reward of an approving grade or the reward of the unknown actually being found. In such instances of learning by conditioning, the association must be repeated from time to time or the connection will become extinct, or at least very dim.

Although the various forms of conditioning are probably basic to the simple beginnings of the learning process, they do not seem very applicable to the complex learning that takes place in college. Even so, sometimes the simple carries a fundamental message. The college student should study the curve of learning and the curve of forgetting, both derived from studies on conditioning. When the vertical axis is calibrated to amount learned and the horizontal axis marks off number of attempts (learning) or time (retention), learning and retention are described by the following curves:

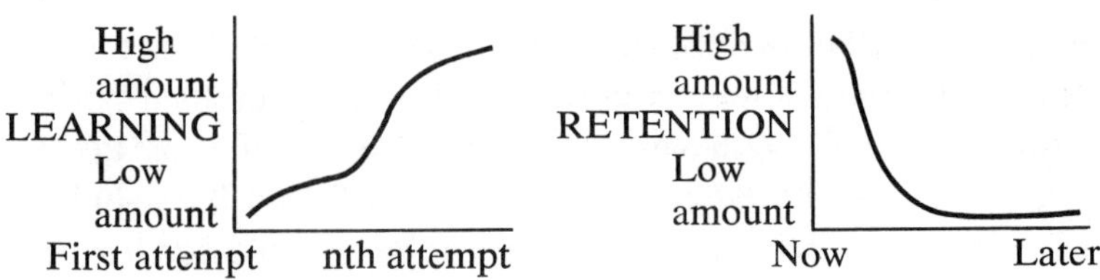

These squiggles should carry several messages to the alert student.

1. Considerable effort and repetition of attempts will be needed to make the lazy leaning S of the learning curve pop to and straighten up so the rise is rapid and dramatic.
2. The ascension cannot be a vertical line or even a straight diagonal; the student should not be discouraged by the plateaus in learning and by the eventual leveling off.
3. The drop in retention (forgetting) is discouragingly rapid. However, it is not nearly so rapid if the material is relevant to the student. The drop will be slowed or even stopped if the material is reviewed from time to time.
4. Material once learned can be relearned very rapidly so that the relearning curve would look more like a reversed retention curve than like the languid S curve of initial learning.
5. If material is overlearned, past the point of first mastery, the forgetting curve will be very slow and gradual.
6. Since the grading game has to be played, it would be good tactics to take the examination when retention is at its highest. The only way of guaranteeing retention is to first overlearn and then restore the peak of retention by reviewing the material just before the test is taken.

The various kinds of remembering—redintegration, recall, and recognition—require different levels and different approaches in learning. Redintegration means to reconstruct not only the central fact or concept but the whole context in which it was imbedded. The usual essay question calls for redintegration and therefore requires studying for understanding; rote memorization simply will not suffice. The student must first secure the big picture, the *gestalt*, then fit the major parts together in a logical pattern, and finally enrich the whole structure with illustrative detail. Redintegration requires thinking as well as dredging up the facts, for all the parts have to be related to each other making the whole greater than the sum of its parts. To study for redintegration, the student should stop at the end of each unit of learning and reconstruct the essence of what was presented.

Recall is a restatement or reproduction of a unit of memory. The question with the missing word, the filling in of the appropriate blanks, and recitation of a poem, are examples of testing using this level of remembering. Rote memorizing is a required approach to this type of learning, and repeated practice to the point of overlearning is about the only way to assure mastery. Forgetting will occur much more rapidly with learning for recall than with learning for total understanding. Relearning of that once known to the point of recall can be accomplished rather rapidly. The Boy Scout oath, memorized at age twelve and then forgotten for thirty years, can be relearned with two or three repetitions.

Recognition only requires that the person respond correctly when given the proper clue. Most true-false or even multiple-choice tests call only for recognizing that which was once learned. When people say, "I can't remember your name but your face sure is familiar," they are demonstrating the difference in level of learning between recall and recognition. Reading, underlining and possibly rereading the underlined material is usually sufficient for recognition of the right answer among the wrong.

Forgetting is reduced by active recall during learning, overlearning beyond bare mastery, and periodic review. There is not much evidence that anything thoroughly learned will ever be completely forgotten simply through disuse or passive decay. It might be blotted out by cerebral accident or by psychological repression. It may be confused by the distortion of leveling, sharpening, and assimilating of memory traces and something learned five minutes ago may be displaced by what is being learned right now (retroactive inhibition), or what is being learned right now may be interfered with by something learned five minutes ago (proactive inhibition). It is apparent—and fortunate—that we do not remember everything. It is also apparent—and unfortunate—that we forget more than we want to forget. The very best preventative against forgetting is to make the learning logical, meaningful, useful, and relevant. Then, any forgetting that might take place can be checked by active recall, overlearning and periodic review.

PRINCIPLES INVOLVING HIGHER ORDER THINKING

Learning achieved through insight can be repeated without long practice and can often be applied or transferred to novel situations. Insight experiments demonstrate that arrangement of the problem is a determinant of the ease or difficulty of the solution. It could almost be said that the answer is inherent in the questions. That is why the clever teacher can, by adroit questioning, extract such deep understanding from his students that they will even surprise themselves. That is also why the inept teacher can make such a muddle of things by his questioning that even those who previously understood become confused.

Since learning by insight inheres in the arrangement of the problem, the prudent student will take sufficient time to set up the learning situation so that insight will come quickly and will interrelate with previous knowledge so as to expand into broader and deeper understanding. In reading, the student working for insight will use some variation of the so-called P.Q.R.S.T. method. He will *preview* the chapter or section to be read. From this he will pose pertinent *questions*, the answers to be found in close *reading* of the material. Once he has finished reading, he will set the material aside and will *state*, in his head or on paper, the gist of what he has read. Finally, he will *test* himself by answering the questions he has posed and will relate the implications of what he has learned to his life situation. In lecture and discussion, the student working for insight will keep asking himself or the instructor, "Well, what is the significance of that? What relevance does that have to the subject at hand and what relevance does it have to me as an individual and to me as a part of mankind?" If, for example, in his reading or in class discussion on the organization of a beehive, the student suddenly sees that vast numbers require application of stern and rigid controls, he will not need to memorize this thought, he will just "know" it. Further, he is very likely to relate this to the human population explosion and will tie all kinds of evidence together to make the new, generalized insight that excessive population seriously threatens the continuance of democracy.

The more concrete the concept the easier it is to derive meaning from it and remember it. Abstractions are a kind of mental shorthand or symbol system. The symbols are once or twice or many times removed from the concrete thing. Unless there is constant referral back to the concrete, the thinking is likely to get as foggy as the clouds in which it is occurring. The above principle is such an abstraction. It is a shorthand way of generalizing such an idea as this: "You will better understand and remember what a chair is by seeing, feeling and sitting on it than by hearing the word *chair*." Of course, the teacher and the student must use symbols in order to communicate. It is impossible and would be a waste of time to reduce everything to the concrete. Nonetheless, the student should constantly ask the teacher to clarify abstractions: "Will you please illustrate that idea?" "Can you rephrase that in more concrete terms?" "Will you please show us how that is done?" "What is a good example of what you are saying?" In his reading, the student must ask himself the same questions and jot down concrete answers in the margin of his text, in his notebook, or at least in his head.

Reality is not independent of the language used to communicate it or to think about it. Actually, the world is conceived quite differently by those whose languages are dissimilar in meaning and structure. If Eskimos have a thousand words to describe snow and if New Yorkers have a hundred words to describe money, New Yorkers will never perceive the full reality of the Eskimo's snow just as the Eskimo will never perceive the full reality of the New Yorker's money. Language and mathematics are not just two subjects among many possible subjects which a student might take. They are the media by which thought can take place and can be communicated. Unless the student's mastery of these media is commensurate with the level of difficulty of the material to be learned, there is no possibility of his learning the material; he is defeated before he begins. Just as food and water must have priority in physical life, the symbol systems must have priority in mental life.

Most thinking occurs in the course of active or mental manipulation and exploration of the environment. That is why the much-maligned progressive educator John Dewey advised "learning by doing." In the early years of childhood, this dictum needs to be taken literally; the child learns about building by taking a hammer and nailing wood together into some form or shape. Even during the college years, the students will get a more complete appreciation of music if they play it, get more of a feel for art if they turn their hands to it, learn politics better by involving themselves in a campaign, understand why some Negroes in the ghetto riot by working awhile in the ghetto, and be disabused of the cookbook approach to laboratory science by doing some work in a laboratory where the results are crucial. Of course, all education cannot be learning by acting out. Most of the manipulations must and can go on in the mind, but it should be directed thinking, critical thinking, creative thinking, not just a free-wheeling kind of rumination and daydreaming.

TOPICS FOR CONSIDERATION

1. In this chapter the key word and overriding principle of learning was *relevance*. It was repeated again and again that if students truly saw and felt the relevance of any material to their lives they would make every effort to learn it. Is there some logical or psychological flaw in this reasoning? Do students in fact learn what they perceive to be relevant?

2. The number of college dropouts and the frequency of failure in college work appear as an indictment against the relevancy of much of what is taught. To what degree has the professional staff failed to teach that which is relevant and to what degree has the student failed to perceive relevancy even when it is really there? How can the student know what is relevant to adult life when he has not yet experienced it? Should the instructor gear the subject matter to what seems relevant to more or less inexperienced young students?

3. Assume a student in a large college knows that he still needs the motivation of pleasing the teacher with whom he identifies as a prod to make him work hard. How can he establish this identification with the teacher? How can he make him the "significant other" whose approval will prompt him toward increased effort? Would it be better for such students to enroll in very small colleges?

4. The point of view was expressed that grades are not the prime motivators that college myth would make them out to be. If the whole institution of grading were abolished, would student motivation be significantly lessened? Do knowledge and wisdom carry their own reward? Would the intrinsic rewards of learning be enough to keep students working after the extrinsic rewards had been abandoned?

5. The learning theorists and experimenters contend that punishment is not very effective in controlling and changing human behavior. Yet punishment as a deterrent is fundamental to religion, to international relations, to penology, to education—to most areas of human behavior. What would happen if hell, war, jails, and

failing grades were largely discarded as threats for controlling human behavior? Would human behavior deteriorate into an orgy of raw animal passions? Which side has the better argument, the church, the state, the police, the teacher, or the learning theorist?

6. The statement was made that most students who fail or drop out from college are unnecessary casualties who are defeated by emotional interference, not by mental deficiency. Considering this, why don't embattled students seek out their counselors as allies? Are they unaware of the help the counselor may be able to give? Do they doubt the counselors' ability to assist them? Are they ashamed to discuss personal, psychological problems?

7. In most instances distributed learning is more effective than massed learning. Does this argue against any form of "cramming" for a test? If not, under what conditions will massed learning improve performance? In what ways could a student build up power during distributed learning for making last-minute "cramming" into a booster that would rocket him to highest achievement?

8. Can the practice of grading be justified by the principle, *Learning is fostered by knowledge of results*? Do letter or number grades actually provide the student with knowledge of the results of his efforts to learn? What method other than grading could be devised to provide the knowledge of results?

9. Students should be able to expect the instructor's presentation and the textual readings or listening to be programmed in a logical, sequential pattern. Expectation and reality may be two different things. What if the presentation is not meaningful? What can the student do to extract more sense out of an instructor's discussion of a topic? What can the student do to filter the muddy waters of a turgid text?

10. The contention was made that concentration on facts without consideration of the implications of these facts is of minor value. Facts are definite and verifiable while implications are logical inferences that are not often verifiable. Should instructors risk having their bias creep into the implications? Is there any way of making education both sterile and meaningful? Can the facts be put on ice until the student is experienced enough to draw his own implications from them?

11. By what study techniques could the student straighten out and sharpen the incline of the learning curve? By what means

could the student slow down and level out the curve of forgetting?

12. Learning by insight does not require practice or repetition and one insight often transfers to many other applications so the effect is multiple. Since learning by insight seems so advantageous, how can it be fostered? How can the student set up the learning situation to maximize the chances of insight? How can he train himself to explore the transferability of any insight gained?

SUGGESTED READING AND LISTENING

BRUNER, JEROME. *The Process of Education.* Cambridge, Mass.: Harvard University Press, 1961.

DEWEY, JOHN. "My Pedagogic Creed," *The Continuing Debate: Essays on Education for Freshmen,* edited by Leslie A. Fiedler and Jacob Vinocur. New York: St. Martin's Press, Inc., 1964, pp. 169–181.

FULLER, R. BUCKMINSTER. "Education Automation," *The Continuing Debate: Essays on Education for Freshmen,* edited by Leslie A. Fiedler and Jacob Vinocur. New York: St. Martin's Press, Inc., 1964, pp. 545–562.

GILBERT, DORIS W. *Study in Depth.* New York: Prentice-Hall, Inc., 1966.

HILGARD, ERNEST R. *Introduction to Psychology.* New York: Harcourt, Brace & World, Inc., 1962.

SNYGG, DONALD and ARTHUR COMBS. *Individual Behavior.* Evanston, Ill.: Harper & Row, Publishers, 1959.

STREETER, ROBERT. "The Nature and Requirements of Learning," *Introduction to College Life,* edited by Norman T. Bell, et al. Boston: Houghton Mifflin Company, 1966, pp. 111–114.

TEAD, ORDWAY. "The Need for Significant Learning," *Introduction to College Life,* edited by Norman T. Bell, et al. Boston: Houghton Mifflin Company, 1966, pp. 133–138.

VOEKS, VIRGINIA. *On Becoming an Educated Person.* Philadelphia: W. B. Saunders Company, 1964.

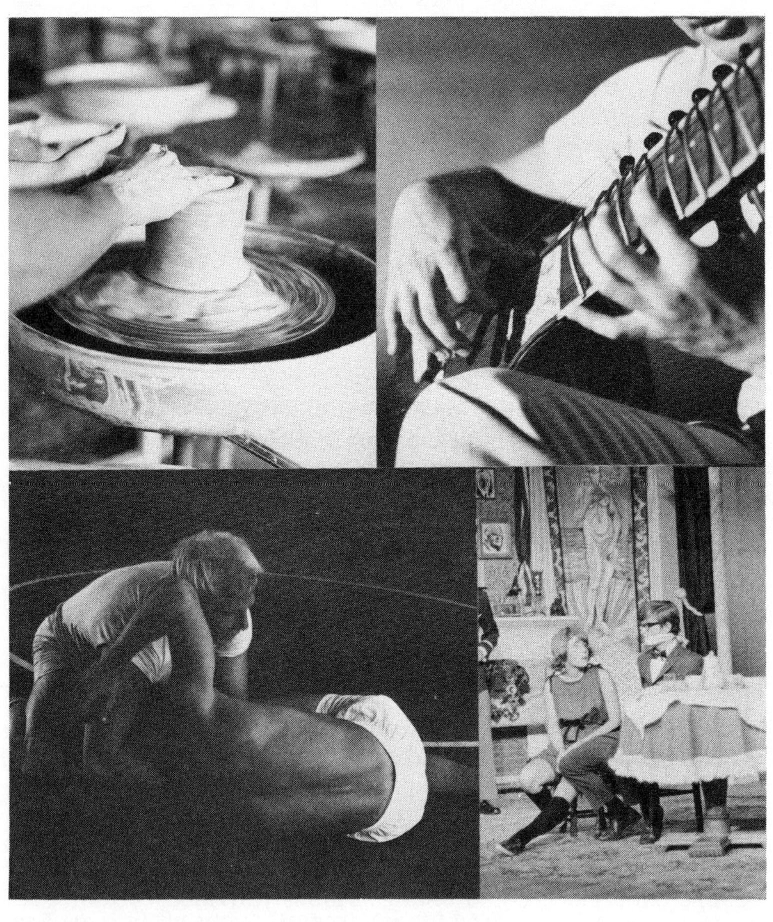

"Only so much do I know as I have lived."
Ralph Waldo Emerson

14 Education Beyond the Classroom

IN 1958, PHILIP JACOB PUBLISHED THE RESULTS OF HIS RE-search *Changing Values in College*, a book that hit the college educators who read it like a solar plexus punch. Jacob documented what the learning theorists had been saying for years; namely, it is necessary to teach for behavioral changes in values: gains in knowledge do not necessarily transfer over to change fundamental attitudes and values. Jacob found that to a discouraging degree college seniors had gone through the college experience without being changed. All too often they emerged with the same values with which they had entered. To be sure, in some instances they had put a little gloss on them, like the person who learns manners without ever learning courtesy.

Happily, the findings of Jacob's study were not universally negative. In some colleges, the students had experienced significant changes in values; hence, the conclusion that the college experience could change values provided certain conditions obtained. The *certain conditions* were, as might be surmised, the total institutional atmosphere. Street corner gang members develop street corner values because they eat, drink, and breathe them. College students develop intellectual values when they are swimming in a sea of intellectualism. Rural southern Whites absorb values regarding race as if the values soak in through their pores. Colleges that feed their students a rich cultural fare produce graduates with well-nourished cultural interests and cultural values. The indictment which Jacob really leveled at many of the colleges in his study was that they were knowledge factories in which the students checked in and out, not collegiate environments in which students were immersed. In the classroom, the students undoubtedly gained a vast store of memory traces, many of practical worth, some no doubt affecting the values of the more perceptive, and others largely worthless. Beyond the classroom, the influence of the college seemed to be nil.

It is as obvious that values can be learned as it is that the prevailing values in Harlem are different from the prevailing values on a Zuni Indian reservation. But they cannot be learned like the multiplication tables. They are learned by osmosis, by absorption, by breathing. The subject has to be totally immersed. That is why it is particularly difficult to affect the values of students in commuter colleges, in the depersonalized and diffused multiversity, and in the two-year community colleges where there is so little time to develop tradition and élan.

Valuation of the intellectual and the cultural can be taught. So can valuation of pluralism, tolerance, political activism, the different, the unique, excellence—any value that can be conceptualized and named. However, they cannot be taught by rote learning, and since they are emotional attitudes, they are not likely to transfer over from learned facts. They will be learned by constant exposure; by being confronted with them at every turn; by making them part of the expectancy, the tradition, the norm; by direct involvement, by living them: "Only so much do I know as I have lived."

THE USUAL FRONGE

Fronge is a handy word that has not yet made its way into the dictionary. It is an all-purpose word meaning the fraudulent fringe, the false frills, the fake front. It is an apt word to describe the usual extracurricular program in those colleges which have not yet come to see that what occurs beyond the classroom can be co-curricular, an educational laboratory.

The student body budget provides an open window through which one can see if the student activities program is or is not fronge. If intercollegiate athletics is the largest single item, consuming as much as 50 percent or more of the student body's money to finance a small group of athletes, then one aspect of the fronge has been exposed. It is athletic fronge run rampant if more money is allocated for athletics than for the combined activities of art, music, speech and drama. If the slice of the budget for the intermural program is dwarfed by intercollegiate competition, and if the girls only get the crumbs of that thin slice, then the fronge cannot be solely attributed to the poor judgment of youth; it takes the manipulation of coaches with the collusion of administrators. The fronge becomes royal when there is money provided for a queen and her court for nearly every dance and when dances are a synonym for college social life. It is flagrant fronge when the special interest clubs and organizations have to conduct bake sales or other childish enterprises to scrounge up their own money upon which to survive. It is discriminatory fronge when little or no money is channeled to the interests of the fee-paying adults who may constitute a fourth of all day students and three-fourths of all evening students.

The other dead giveaway of fronge is the nature of student government. More often than not, student government is without serious function or significance. It is like a kid's game on which the adults can blow the whistle at any point and change the rules when the will of the faculty, the administration, or the taxpayers is in any way challenged. Such being the case, it becomes no more than a recurring popularity contest engaged in by cliques whose members have need for institutional recognition of their popularity. Once elected, the student rubberstamps approval for a budget in permanent imbalance toward the athletic and social fronge, and spends his tenure in office complaining about that vast "out" group who are lacking in school spirit: who disdain participation in his trivial pursuits.

PLURALISM IN CAMPUS ORGANIZATIONS

Colleges, particularly open-door junior colleges, should have the same diversity and pluralistic approach to the co-curriculum as they have to their wide-ranging curriculum if they are to meet the interests and needs of their heterogeneous population. The way should be made easy for students to organize an open forum, join a religious club, affiliate with a political party, develop a cultural interest group, create an out-of-class extension of some academic area, sponsor a civil rights organization, charter a preprofessional association, activate an on-campus service club, or develop any other type of special interest group that would materially contribute to extending education beyond the classroom. The governing board and those to whom it delegates its power should be most liberal in regard to the chartering of student organizations. The major criteria for the establishment of new groups should be significance of purpose, reasonable independence from outside direction, and consistency with the basic aims of the college itself. Beyond these, the only requirements should relate to procedural matters. Such a permissive policy would reflect the pluralism of American society and yet might not give institutional sanction to such groups as the Young Communist League, The John Birch Society, The American Nazi Party, nudist colonies, advocates of use of psychedelic drugs, or other organizations which are outside the law or whose goals are inimical to the official aims and purposes of the institution. The tent would still be large enough to cover such diverse groups as the Students for Democratic Society and the right wing of the Young Republicans, the Catholic Newman Club and devotees of Zen Buddhism, the Congress of Racial Equality and the Black Muslims.

It is fruitless to say that student organizations should only concern themselves with campus matters. They should be the link that involves the student with the wider world, and obviously, the more commerce between the campus and that wider world, the better. This means that advocates of controversial and unpopular views will be invited to speak on campus. Such invitations will become the test of whether the institution is a college—a marketplace of ideas—or a training center to prepare well-indoctrinated workers. If only the safe and the innocuous can appear and speak on campus, the student organizations will be as insipid and pusillanimous as the speakers they are allowed to hear. Although it takes governing board members and administrators with tough minds to sustain it, this unequivocal policy on controversial speakers is suggested:

> On the subject of controversial issues of any nature, including those of partisan politics, the college policy recognizes the need for presentations by guest lecturers and political personalities, forums, assembly programs, etc., dealing with controversial topics of significant interest and concern so long as reasonable effort is made to make the conflicting viewpoints clear in an equitable manner.

It is ironic that such policy statements are needed at all in institutions that are supposed to carry the special blessing of academic freedom. The freedom of speech granted by the First Amendment should guarantee any kind of advocacy that does not represent "a clear and present danger." Unfortunately, the First Amendment, the traditions of academic freedom, and even policy statements like the above are frequently abridged, if not repealed, by frightened boards of trustees and administrators who do not trust the students' judgment nor respect their right to make up their own minds.

DIVERSITY IN CULTURAL FARE

Students are competent to help identify their own needs. They are also open to suggestion from mature, experienced professionals if a relationship of mutual trust and respect has been fostered. There is no great threat that, if given a chance, students will make the program extracurricular rather than co-curricular. Even though fun-loving, college students do not want to subvert the objectives of their college, particularly if they have a hand in updating and redefining these objectives. If they are truly involved in decision making, they will realize that enjoyment follows from intellectual and cultural stimulation as well as from sensual stimulation, and they will tend to strike a balance within the co-curricular offering.

A college is not a country club, a carnival, or a sports arena, and the students do not want it to be. Neither the student nor the faculty adviser has to be an educational purist to reject entertainment *per se* as one of the major aims of a college. However, the line between highbrow entertainment and education is not clear cut. Although lowbrow entertainment can at least be looked upon askance, highbrow and middlebrow entertainment and education become almost synonymous. Since the line between entertainment and education is a fuzzy one, the students must look to institutional purposes as they deliberate on how to spend student funds, or on what constitutes an appropriate co-curricular program. The choice, to use an example drawn from the field of music, will be between the Pro Arte Quartet and the Dave Brubeck Quartet: with decision going either way, would not the cultural aims of education have been well served?

Presumably, one of the desired value changes during the college experience would be the development of intellectual and cultural values. One important way of fostering these values would be to pump intellectual and cultural content into the student activity program. The content should be intellectual and cultural in the broadest definition of these terms. The scope and quality of the co-curricular program is only limited by the amount of money that can be secured to finance it. Common practice in publicly supported institutions is to share the costs among the college, the student body and the paying public. This seems defensible, for the colleges should certainly help defray the costs of that which is educationally beneficial; the students should contribute, particularly when the event is in that gray area between entertainment and education; and the public at large should be, and are, willing to pay a fair admission charge in addition to the taxes that they pay to support the total educational enterprise. With such a financing scheme, and with low-cost but high-quality events put on by the drama, speech, athletic, art, music, cinema, dance, and other departments of the college itself, a year-long series of exciting cultural events can be arranged with college funds matching the contribution made by the student body. A joint college-student body subsidization of $72,000 would easily finance the presentation of one major event plus several of lesser importance each week of the academic year. This comparatively small investment would provide such an attractive series of lectures, forums, exhibits, films, concerts, readings, dramatic performances, athletic events, recitals and festivals, that intellectual and cultural values, interests, and tastes would be part of the total environment in which the students lived. No student could escape it, and the level of excellence could be such that few would want to escape.

TWELVE FREEDOMS FOR STUDENTS

In early 1965, when much student ferment was brewing, both the American Civil Liberties Union and the American Association of University Professors gave public voice to thoughtful statements on freedoms that should be guaranteed to students. Both were official policy statements, and true to tradition, the A.C.L.U. recommendations were somewhat more liberal and less equivocal that those of the A.A.U.P. In June of 1966, the *Saturday Review* published a listing called "Twelve Freedoms for Students" in which the A.C.L.U. and the A.A.U.P. statements were not really compared but simply juxtaposed. Because of its importance, the list is reproduced here in full.

1) *Freedom of expression.* Students and student organizations: "should be free to discuss, pass resolutions, distribute leaflets, circulate petitions, and take other lawful action respecting any matter which directly or indirectly concerns or affects them." (ACLU) They "should be free to examine and to discuss all questions of interest to them, and to express opinions publicly or privately." (AAUP)

2) *Freedom of the press.* "All student publications—college newspapers, literary and humor magazines, academic periodicals and yearbooks—should enjoy full freedom of the press." Any board supervising student publications "should be composed of at least a majority of students . . . neither a faculty member nor an administrator should exercise veto power over what should be printed." (ACLU) "The student press should be free of censorship and advance approval of copy, and its editors and managers should be free to develop their own editorial policies and news coverage." (AAUP)

3) *Freedom of association.* "Students should be free to organize and join associations for educational, political, social, religious or cultural purposes . . . affiliation with any extra-mural association . . ., so long as it is an open affiliation, should not of itself bar a group from recognition." (ACLU) "Students should be free to organize and join associations to promote their common interests. . . . Affiliation with an extra-mural organization should not of itself affect recognition of a student organization." (AAUP)

4) *Freedom to choose speakers and topics.* "Students should be accorded the right to assemble, to select speakers and to discuss issues of their choice. . . . Permission should not be withheld because the speaker is a controversial figure." (ACLU) "Students should be allowed to invite and to hear

any person of their own choosing. While the orderly scheduling of facilities may require the observance of routine procedures before a guest speaker is invited to appear on campus, institutional control of campus facilities should never be used as a device of censorship." (AAUP)

5) *Freedom to protest.* "Student organizations and individual students should be allowed, and no special permission should be required, to distribute pamphlets, except in classrooms and study halls, or collect names for petitions concerning either campus or off-campus issues. Orderly demonstrations on campus should not be prohibited." (ACLU) Students should "be free to support causes by any orderly means which do not disrupt the regular and essential operation of the institution." (AAUP)

6) *Freedom from discrimination.* "Just as the college should not discriminate on grounds of race, religion, color or national origin in its admission policies, so should it not permit discrimination in any area of student life, such as housing on or off the campus, athletics, fraternities, social clubs." (ACLU) "While sectarian institutions may give admission preference to students of their own persuasion, such a preference should be clearly and publicly stated. College facilities and services should be open to all students, and institutions should use their influence to secure equal access for all students to public facilities in the local community." (AAUP)

7) *Freedom from disciplinary action without due process.* "No student should be expelled or suffer major disciplinary action for any offence, other than failure to meet the required academic standards, without having been advised explicitly of the charges against him, which at his request should be in writing. He should be free to seek the counsel . . . of his choice . . . he may ask for a hearing . . . by faculty-student (or) faculty committee . . . (he) should be allowed to call witnesses . . . and cross-examine those who appear against him . . . a final appeal to the board of trustees should be allowed." (ACLU) "In developing responsible student conduct, disciplinary proceedings play a role substantially secondary to counseling, guidance, admonition, and example. In the exceptional circumstances when these preferred means fail to resolve problems of student conduct, proper procedural

safeguards should be observed to protect the student from the unfair imposition of serious penalties," and should include, among many features, a hearing in which "the burden of proof should rest upon the officials bringing the charge." (AAUP)

8) *Freedom from arbitrary regulation of conduct.* "Regulations governing the conduct of students should be enacted by a committee composed of students, administrators, and faculty members if desired." (ACLU) "The student body should have clearly defined means to participate in the formulation and application of regulations affecting student affairs." (AAUP)

9) *Freedom to use rights as a private citizen.* "In their nonacademic life, private or public, students should be free from college control. On the other hand, the college should not be held responsible for the nonacademic activities of its individual students." (ACLU) "As citizens, students should enjoy the same freedom of speech, peaceful assembly, and right of petition that other citizens enjoy. Faculty members and administrative officials should insure that institutional powers are not employed to inhibit . . . their off-campus activities and their exercise of the rights of citizenship." (AAUP)

10) *Freedom from improper disclosure.* "When interrogated directly (or indirectly) by prospective employers of any kind . . . a teacher can safely answer questions which he finds clearly concerned with the student's competence and fitness for the job. . . . But, questions relating to the student's loyalty and patriotism, his political or religious or moral or social beliefs and attitudes, his general outlook, his private life, may if answered jeopardize the teacher-student relation." (ACLU) "Information about student views, beliefs, and political associations which professors acquire in the course of their work as instructors, advisors, counselors should be considered confidential. Protection against improper disclosure is a serious professional obligation." (AAUP)

11) *Freedom from off-campus denial of rights.* "When students run into police difficulties off the campus in connection with what they regard as their political rights—as, for example, taking part in sit-ins, picket lines, demonstra-

tions, riding on freedom buses—the college authorities should take every practical step to assure themselves that such students are protected in their full legal rights . . . (such as) fair trials in a court of law . . . speedy trials . . . that they are not abused by the police . . . that bail be sought and furnished . . . that appeals be taken when necessary." (ACLU) "Activities of students may upon occasion result in violation of law. In such cases, institutional officials should apprise students of their legal rights and may offer other assistance." (AAUP)

12) *Freedom of thought in the classroom.* "Students are responsible for learning thoroughly the content of any course of study, but they should be free to take reasoned exception to the data or views offered, and to reserve judgment about matters of opinion . . . Students are responsible for maintaining standards of academic performance established by their professors, but they should have protection through orderly procedures against prejudiced or capricious academic evaluation." (AAUP)[1]

In June, 1966, a month prior to the *Saturday Review* article, the professional journal *College Management* reported on its survey in which college presidents had been asked to react to the A.A.U.P. statements. The presidents showed up on the survey as veritable freedom fighters except on the issues of a truly free student press and on unrestricted choice of campus speakers. Many had apparently had their telephone ears bent out of shape listening to complaints about scandalous articles in the college papers and about the dangers of having communist speakers on campus. The thirty junior college presidents were the most repressive of the 200 college presidents used in the survey: "Half of the junior college presidents would not give students freedom to select campus speakers ('Our students aren't ready for it,' said one); more than one-third would curtail the college newspaper; and one out of three would disseminate records of student political activity on request."

[1]"Twelve Freedoms for Students," *Saturday Review*, 49:62-63 (June 18, 1966). Copyright Saturday Review, Inc., 1966.

STUDENT RIGHTS AND DUE PROCESS[2]

Indictment. Fundamental to the democratic idea are (a) involvement in the decision making by those who will be affected, and (b) a due process to forestall arbitrary action by the strong against the weak and to assure redress when such arbitrary action does occur. Colleges, junior and senior, almost universally flout both these democratic premises. Students rarely have a voice in making substantive decisions, and even more rarely have an established recourse to give them a fair hearing when injustices are perpetrated.

Brief. A college is, or should be, a community of scholars where basic respect is afforded to all members of that community. Respect connotes seriously listening to those who think they have something to say: this includes students.

It is within the nature and circumstances of community life for instances of disrespect to arise and to grow into violation of rights. This occurs in relations between the board of trustees and the professional staff, in relations among members of the professional staff and in relations between members of the professional staff and students. Since it is predictable that offenses will be made and conflicts of interest will arise, it is necessary that each segment of the academic community have a voice in developing policy guidelines which will minimize conflict, and that a mechanic be established to adjudicate when the inevitable conflicts do arise. The faculty senate, the whole faculty committee structure, and particularly the professional relations committee, developed in recognition of the need to give institutional sanction to the voice and the rights of faculty members.

[2]From article "Student Rights and Due Process" by Charles C. Collins, *Junior College Journal*, 37:34-36, April 1967. Copyright American Association of Junior Colleges 1967. Reprinted with permission.

The young, and not so young, adults who are students at colleges are largely voiceless in the debate over policy which directly affects them, and to make the sin against democracy more grievous, have no guarantee of a fair hearing of their complaint, or of redress. Students who feel wronged by faculty members can and do turn to administrative officers, but in truth this is turning to a partisan who is legally, professionally, and institutionally allied to the offending faculty member. For example, when a student becomes a pawn in a personality struggle between faculty members, administration is in no position to rule in favor of the student without becoming enmeshed in both legal and intrafaculty machinations.

The major lessons in ethics, justice, rule by law, and the democratic process can best be taught by doing and by example, not by precept. If students are to become involved in participatory democracy, they need to learn by participating in the debate on issues of real substance. If students are to grow into just men, they need to see justice practised. If they are to eschew rule of the weak by the strong, they must learn that when the cause is sound there is an institutionalized means by which the power of the weak and strong are equalized and within this balance, fair decision can be made.

Behavior is caused: when there is unrest among students, it is because there are real or imagined infringements of basic rights. Demonstrations are really denunciatory editorials by those who have no other media for voicing their views, for airing their grievances, and for insisting on corrective measures.

The college, the students, the aims of democratic education, the principles of justice, all would be served if structural means were developed by which (a) students had a voice in policy recommendations to the governing board, and (b) students who felt sinned against by administration or by faculty could, with impunity, present their case to an impartial panel for adjudication.

Corrective Proposals. Ultimate power and responsibility

rests with the board of trustees. This governing board is advised, however, by segments of the academic community. It has only been in the recent past that the advisory voice of faculty was added to that of administration. What is proposed here is simply that students be included in the debate on policy recommendations affecting them. Their channels to the governing board could and should be the existing channels; they should serve along with administration and faculty on the curriculum and instruction committee, the student personnel committee, and the policies and procedures committee. On matters specific to students, the student senate should speak directly to the board of trustees just as the faculty senate now speaks in matters specific to the faculty.

The companion proposal to student involvement in policy formulation is that of respecting students as full members of the academic community by assuring them the protection of due process. The proposed procedure would be as follows: a student who feels his rights as a member of the academic community have been violated or abridged may present his complaint to a screening board made up of a member of the student senate, a member of the faculty senate, and a member of administration. After preliminary hearing, this collegiate grand jury would decide whether there was enough substance to warrant full investigation. If so, an adjudication panel would be selected, composed of three faculty members (appointed by the faculty senate president), three students (appointed by the student senate president), and one administrator (appointed by the college president). The panel would conduct a quiet, thorough hearing with written or oral depositions made by all parties involved. After all pertinent data were collected and evaluated, the *ad hoc* panel would render a judgment in the form of a recommendation to the college president, to the governing board, or to both. Appeal of this recommendation by any party to the dispute could always be made to those vested with final authority, the members of the governing board.

THE CO-CURRICULUM DEFINED

The co-curriculum should complement, extend, and vitalize the curriculum. The activities should span the spectrum of student interests and growth needs, and the clubs and organizations should grow and decline on the basis of significance of purpose. The co-curricular organization should provide the mechanics by which the students become a part of the power structure of the college. The co-curriculum should aim at making the students jealous guardians of their own freedoms and rights and should give them experience by which to develop the responsibilities that go with these freedoms and rights. The co-curriculum should link the community to the campus and be the means of involving the students in the community. Diversity of experience and point of view should be fostered, and intelligent controversy should be sought, not ducked. The co-curriculum, allied with the formal curriculum, should make it difficult for a student to exit from college with the same values with which he entered. It should be education beyond the classroom.

TOPICS FOR CONSIDERATION

1. Discussion of the Jacob study carries the implicit assumption that the college experience should change the values of those who have it. Should colleges aim to change the values of those who attend? If so, what directions should the change take? What values should be taught? If not, what social institution should concern itself with the values of the maturing members of the society?

2. John Dewey's capsule advice was "Learn by doing," Emerson said, "Only so much do I know as I have lived," and Jacob found that values are changed by living in an environment where new values are pervasive. Should colleges set out to create "value situations" in which their students live and learn by doing? Should the students be made aware of what the college is doing? Should

the students have a voice in determining what kind of "value atmosphere" they will be breathing?

3. The indictment was made that a good deal that passes for co-curriculum is no more than extracurricular fronge. But who is to say what is fronge and what is not? Is it *prima facie* fronge if 60 or 70 percent of the student obody budget gets consumed in intercollegiate sports? What criteria can be established to evaluate and measure the fronge existent within the total co-curriculum?

4. Does student government often deserve being called a kid's game devoid of any significant purposes or functions? What significant purposes and functions could it have? Are these in conflict with the official power structure of the college? Are there ways of negotiating the conflicts between the student and the official power structure?

5. It is not illegal to be a member of the Communist Party, the American Nazi Party or a nudist colony. If such organizations are not illegal off the campus, why should they be illegal on the campus? How can the line be drawn to exclude the Ku Klux Klan but to admit the Black Muslims? to say yes to the Students for Democratic Society but to say no to the John Birch Society?

6. Controversial speakers seem to be booby traps which frequently explode the myth of academic freedom on college campuses. If a college is a marketplace of ideas, why should any idea be excluded? Should there not be free enterprise in the commerce of ideas as well as in the commerce of goods? Does a college have the responsibility of protecting the minds of its students from certain ideas? If so, who should say what these "certain ideas" are? Should these ideas also be censored from the books in the college library?

7. If the cultural and entertainment fare of the co-curriculum is so valuable in the total education of the students, should attendance be made compulsory? Would it be feasible to call the intellectual and cultural presentations Humanities 10 A, B, C, and D, and grant a unit of credit for each term where 50 percent or more of all such functions were attended? Should such a humanities course be made into a graduation requirement?

8. Do the students in many colleges enjoy the twelve freedoms to be found in the A.C.L.U. and A.A.U.P. recommendations? Which of these freedoms are most frequently abridged or even denied? Who is responsible for this abridgment of student freedoms, and what are their motivations? Why are junior college

students given less freedom than students in four year colleges or universities?

9. The recommendation is made to have students sit on the curriculum and instruction committee, the student personnel committee, and other policy determining committees of the college. Is this like having patients sit on medical policies boards? What would the students have to contribute? Does it take education in the profession to deal with policy questions concerning the profession?

10. What protections of due process are students ordinarily guaranteed when there is a conflict of wills or an altercation between a student and a member of the professional staff? Would the proposed due process assure more equitable treatment for students? Would it compromise the faculty member in his authority relationship with students?

11. Assume that the proposal to include students on college policy committees and the proposal to assure students an impartial hearing in conflicts with faculty were to be presented to the board of trustees or the board of regents. Who, or what groups, would champion these proposals, and who would strive to squelch them? What would be the motivation of the advocates and of the opponents ?

12. If the co-curriculum is really to be complementary to the curriculum, to be education beyond the classroom, then should it not have the same thought and planning as the development of the curriculum? Who should determine the aims that the co-curriculum is to fulfill? Who should plan its coordination with the curriculum? If it becomes so structured, then is it not just part of the curriculum? Is the fun and spontaneity taken from it?

SUGGESTED READING AND LISTENING

"Academic Freedom: The President's Dilemma," *College Management*, 1:44–45, (May, 1966).

COUSINS, NORMAN. "The Book Isn't Everything," *Introduction to College Life*, edited by Norman T. Bell, et al. Boston: Houghton Mifflin Company, 1966, pp. 141–143.

GOULD, SAMUEL B. "College Student Government," *Introduction to College Life*, edited by Norman T. Bell, et al. Boston: Houghton Mifflin Company, 1966, pp. 147–149.

HOOK, SYDNEY. "Academic Freedom and the Rights of Students," *Beyond Berkeley: A Sourcebook in Student Values*, edited by C. G. Katope and P. G. Zolbrod. Cleveland: The World Publishing Company, 1965.

NIXON, RICHARD M. and HENRY S. COMMAGER. "What Do We Mean by Academic Freedom?", *Saturday Review*, 49:12–15 (August 27, 1966).

SAVIO, MARIO. "The Berkeley Student Rebellion of 1964," *Beyond Berkeley: A Sourcebook in Student Values*, edited by C. G. Katope and P. G. Zolbrod. Cleveland: The World Publishing Company, 1965.

"Twelve Freedoms for Students," *Saturday Review*, 40: 62–63 (June 18, 1966).

". . . for the times they are a'changing."
Bob Dylan

15 College Students: the New Look and the New Morality

FRATERNITIES AND SORORITIES, BURNING LOSING COACHES IN effigy, the Big Man on Campus (BMOC), beer busts and panty raids are all from a receding past when the prevailing value structure and the whole atmosphere on campus was different. Fraternities and sororities have been kept alive since their heyday in the 1920's and 1930's by "old grads" who still thrill to "She's the Sweetheart of Sigma Chi" and by parents and even students who still think election to a Greek House is a passport to the upper class. Pro ballgames have made intercollegiate football, basketball, and baseball look too amateurish for the true sports buff. If students are going to burn anyone in effigy, it will probably be the president of the college or the President of the United States, certainly not the football coach whose ball club chanced to have a losing streak. The real BMOC is more likely to be someone like Mario Savio than the elected student body leader playing out a charade of student government. For today's students, getting "busted" has nothing to do with beer, and the punishment is certainly more than a hangover. Most college students living in what has been called *the permissive society* would look on a panty raid as a kind of infantile fetish. This is not to say that all such hallmarks of student life have been erased. Some retain a certain vitality, others hang on as anachronisms, most are considered fare for the square, and a few have become a caricature of themselves and thereby have taken on the endearing qualities of "camp."

College campuses in the 1950's were aflood with World War II and Korean War veterans. Their desire to qualify themselves quickly for jobs which buy comfort and security and the insidious fear that lingered from the McCarthy anti-communist hysteria contributed toward making them into the silent generation. The reaction against affluence, the charisma of the youthful President John F. Kennedy, and the involvement of many youth in the civil rights movement changed the picture drastically. The 1960's began with some boisterous dissent, and on campus the dissent grew louder, more insistent, and more serious as the decade progressed. The silent generation of the 1950's was replaced by the angry, frustrated activists and the disenchanted but flamboyant dropouts of the 1960's.

If the older generation wants to take a reading on the temper of the times, it should listen to the lyrics of popular music. The ethical concern which has been characteristic of college youth in this decade is reflected in—perhaps prompted by—the lyrics in the songs of Bob Dylan, Joan Baez, The Beatles, The Rolling Stones, The Doors. They sing that they are outraged with an outrageous world or that they have no truck with an absurd world. They sing the songs of social significance of the activists and the dropout songs of the hippies.

Actually, the outrage, the disgust, the nausea evoked by many aspects of the society have been the common cause spurring some students to activism and dropping others into the cult of the hippies. Although these movements seem to be the opposite of each other, they are not mutually exclusive. At least among the activists of the New Left and the hippies there is a reciprocal respect and a fraternization. The activist who has had it up to his eyeballs is likely to seek momentary refuge in hippiedom and on some issues, notably the war in Vietnam, the hippies have been known to be very disruptive in their passive resistance. Only 5 or 10 percent of college students are dedicated political activists, and since many of the hippies are college dropouts before they are society dropouts, their percentage among enrolled students would be even less. Whether the activists and the hippies are to be condemned or applauded, this much is clear: Adopting and sustaining their philosophic positions require an inordinate amount of psychological courage. Not many can venture that far from the safety of the social norm. However, if their ranks are thin, their influence has been felt way beyond their numbers. They represent the vivid extremes of a restiveness which has infected most college students and their importance flows from their impact, not from any head count.

THE ACTIVIST PATTERN

George Bernard Shaw once said that if a man were not a revolutionary at age twenty then there was no hope for him. Shaw's point was that youth inherits an outrageous world, and if he is not outraged by it during the full bloom of his vitality and idealism, think of how stupidly smug, complacent, and reactionary he will be at middle life. This is not to infer that the activism of students in the 1960's was necessarily a revolution from the left. Certainly, it was not from the doctrinaire left; those who carry the leftist label are better students of Jean Paul Sartre and Albert Camus than of Karl Marx; they are more impressed with existentialism and philosophic anarchism than with communism of the Trotskyite, Maoist, or Revisionist camp. Most emphatically, they are not in the liberal tradition. In the lexicon of the New Left, "white liberal" has come to be a dirty word for the middle-class compromiser who puts the balm of gradualism and endless debate on his conscience in order to keep his comfortable life undisturbed.

Although the student activists come in many political hues, the main thrust of student activism, the headline catcher, and the group most feared is the New Left. Telescoped and looked at from the viewpoint of the New Left, the dynamics of the movement could be described along these lines: It was triggered off by some brave Negro students who in the late 1950's defied the law and the order of the South by sitting-in at lunch counters where black Americans were refused service. This activity, along with many others, escalated into the civil rights movement in which many involved white students from the North and West felt the crunch of the white power structure. In the process, they arrived at some insights not only into evils but into the evil of countenancing evils.

The invisible poor in the land of affluence became visible to them. The Cuban missile crisis gave them a look into the grave of nuclear death. They saw that cybernation threatened not only jobs but man's power to be involved in decisions crucial to his life. They also saw that it made an economy based on scarcity seem ridiculous. The burgeoning college population made them feel as significant as a cipher and as processed as cheese. The evidence of alienation all around them made these students wonder if material affluence alone did not transform itself into dust in the hand. The generation gap visibly widened as their growing ethical concerns seemed largely ignored by parents and even teachers. To their elders, marijuana appeared to loom as a greater threat than either racism or nuclear war. To them, the credibility gap became incredible; a euphemism for flagrant lying. Due process and participatory democracy began to seem like classroom terms out of a naive past. The student leaders of the New Left found that the power brokers deal in power and without it there is no deal. And, of course, coincidental with all of these factors was the war in Vietnam, which to the New Left has been an obscenity defiling all that is good and noble in the American heritage. It has also been like an absurd version of George Orwell's *1984* where the characters declaim their lines in *newspeak*; where an American major viewing the rubble and wasteland that was once Ben Tre tells the millions viewing him on the Huntley-Brinkley News Program, "It's too bad we had to destroy the city to save it."

In a sketchy and perhaps overstated way, that is how members of the New Left, largely a loose confederation of students and other young intellectuals, would describe their increased political awareness and political involvement. The Young Republicans and other conservative groups would have a different story to tell and, although arriving at the opposite pole of the political spectrum, would share with the New Left the distinction of making the generation of the 1960's the most politically active of any in the history of American democracy. Student activism would in many ways seem like a postponed fulfillment of what Ralph Waldo Emerson wanted but found so lacking when he wrote "The American Scholar" back in 1837.

> "Action is with the scholar subordinate, but is essential. Without it he is not yet man. Without it thought can never ripen into truth. . . . Inaction is cowardice, but there can be no scholar without the heroic mind. The preamble of thought, the transition through which it passes from the unconscious to the conscious, is action."

STUDENT UNREST AND STUDENT POWER

There is a certain element of anarchy in the Student Power Movement just as there is in Black Power and just as there is in Teacher Power. Any realignment of the power structure requires some destructive forces to operate before constructive forces come into full play. That is why the more mature and less frightened observers of the current scene do not find student unrest necessarily bad. They see it as healthier and much more hopeful than student apathy, rigid conformism and slavish devotion to the status quo. These apologists make the following points.

1. Student disturbances are more cerebral than visceral: U.S. students protest against the war in Vietnam, not against the quality of food served.

2. The demonstrations put the students on the side of the angels: they can hardly be faulted for fighting for civil rights for Negroes or for defending the democratic precept of freedom of speech.
3. Disturbances often become exercises in pragmatic democracy: those who have had a bruising confrontation with the Establishment learn more about the uses and abuses of power than they ever would from a textbook in political science.

Even so, when the spokesmen for Student Power unloose some of their rhetoric, it does send a chill down the spine of the usual college administrator. *Newsweek* for October 23, 1967, carried some quotes well designed to have this effect.

> It all began, of course, with the Free Speech Movement at Berkeley three years ago. Since then student power has developed from protest against the size and impersonality of a multiversity to encompass almost every facet of student life. . . . "Student power means not simply the ability to influence decisions but the ability to make decisions," says Edward Schwartz, President, National Student Association. "Let this principle apply—he who must obey the rule should make it." Students, he adds, should help 'co-decide' curriculum, admissions and other broad policies—even investment policies. . . . Some campus leaders view student power even more directly. "We're trying to get our hands into everything that affects us," says Howard University student assembly president, Edward Brown, "be it academic, social or otherwise." "If the structure is so overbearing that it doesn't allow students to decide what issues are vital for their own interest," says Robert Narcisi, a long-haired Fordham senior who made the dean's list, "then it is time to over-throw the structure."[1]

Student activism in regard to the war in Vietnam, the draft, military and war industry recruitment on campus, and what is left of the civil rights movement—the exercise of student power on these issues captures the headlines and obscures

[1]Student Power on the Rise," *Newsweek*, 70:40 (October 23, 1967). Reprinted with permission.

what promises to be a struggle which may shatter the existing power structure in the college. When the dust has cleared, the student may be a new part of that power structure. Within academe itself, the aims of student power are to increase the relevance of that which is taught, to foster participatory democracy, to check the destructive depersonalization of education, and to assure student voice in academic as well as administrative policy decisions.

At the 1965 National Conference on Student Stress, it was concluded that "a really good education" is the prime source of student stress and that most students in most colleges felt they were not getting it. Dr. Edward J. Shoben, Jr., wrote in his report of this conference, "One criterion of a good education strongly urged by a vocal and committed group of students, is relevance—relevance to the world of modern politics and social ferment, relevance to the human condition in a mass society, relevance to the doubts, fears and hopes of thoughtful youth." The students expressed their desire to talk to professors on terms of equality and at a level of frankness where the students really knows what the instructor thinks. As one student put it, "We don't want to have our hands held or our head patted. We want a really good education." On outside issues such as whether or not to allow Dow Chemical Company recruiters on campus, faculty members have openly sympathized and even allied themselves with the opposing students.

When students' demands have brought them in conflict with the college administration, faculties have been inclined to side with the students. However, the long-term, core criticism of students is directed against faculty, not against administration. It is the faculty who determine curriculum, neglect teaching for research, protect and retain the incompetent teacher, succeed or fail in making education relevant, oppose student evaluation of teaching competency, and block student voice on the policy committees of the college. And it is the faculty who will soon find themselves pitted against the forces of student power. Paul Woodring in a *Saturday Review* article, "Who Makes University Policy?" read the handwriting on the wall:

> But when students demand changes in academic policy or control over it, when they ask for better teaching or less emphasis on research, or when they protest the dismissal or denial of promotion to a popular professor . . . they come into direct conflict with the faculty. If students are to have more influence over university (college) affairs, faculty members will have less. . . . On only a few campuses have students expressed concern for educational quality, for the competence of the faculty, or for the content of the curriculum—until recently. But now all this is changing. And because it is changing, faculties must now decide how much responsibility they should give to undergraduates. They will find the decision painful.[2]

And it should be added that the faculty may not make that unilateral decision: it may be a compromise negotiated out of the conflict of faculty power with student power.

THE HIPPIE PATTERN

The impact of the hippies can be measured by the intensity of people's reaction to them. Few are indifferent. Their wholesale challenge to the values most cherished by all the Babbitts of the middle class is so infuriating that even their characteristic beard and long hair send some opponents into a paroxysm of hate. On the other hand, for every true hippie living in the Haight Ashbury district of San Francisco or in Greenwich Village in New York or in some nameless little enclave of hippiedom, there is a clutch of young and not so young who sometimes wish they had the courage to also throw over the traces and begin to live as the inner spirit dictates.

The hippie movement will undoubtedly dissipate and pass—perhaps is already passing—but these pariahs so broke

[2]Paul Woodring, "Who Makes University Policy?" *Saturday Review*, 48:65-66 (April 7, 1965). Copyright Saturday Review, Inc., 1965.

the lockstep conformity of society, that its members, particularly the youth, will proceed at rout-step for many decades to come. The hippies stirred up a revolution in values. Value revolutions may not be as dramatic as political revolutions, but their long term effect can be considerably more potent. The very behavior of the flower children poses some disruptive questions: Who wants to be a winning rat in a ratrace? Why be what other people want you to be? Why not define yourself according to your own inner promptings? Why do those who anaesthetize their minds with alcohol condemn those who experiment with expanding their minds with psychedelic drugs? Shouldn't a person be more concerned about how he spends his time than how he spends his money or how he can make more money to spend? Why erect such big barriers over such a minor difference as skin color? Who is to say that flower power in human relationships isn't more effective than fire power? By what right should those who have made such a mess of living try to tell other people or other societies how to organize their lives? Since education helps to define a person, shouldn't he design his own education rather than be defined by some common mold?

Rita Dershowitz, a youthful participant in *Harper's* "A Dialogue Between Generations" spoke of the ramifying effect of the hippie point of view on education:

> In this instance too, the extensions of the drug culture touch more people than those who actually use drugs. The ethics of the hippie culture—indiscriminate love and openness, the dignity of the individual and the value of human relationships, the destructiveness of rigid external authority—have influenced students who are demanding flexibility and personal relevance of the college curriculum. Find your own thing, and then do it, is not just new jargon for the same wisdom. It sets up entirely new assumptions about the purposes of any educational institution.[3]

[3]Walter Lippmann, Rita Dershowitz, et al., "A Dialogue Between Generations," *Harper's Magazine*, 235:45-64 (October, 1967). Reprinted with permission.

There is no doubt at all that the hippie communities are crawling with pimps, prostitutes, pushers, panhandlers, perverts, psychotics—and that is only to list the social misfits whose names begin with the letter P. There is also little doubt that of all the utopian experiments in the history of the United States, the influence of the hippies promises to be most pervasive. Although the hippie movement is considered anathema, if not sacrilege, to many fundamentalists in religion, it is impossible to deny that the movement has a religious flavor. The hippies are in search of a new morality and a new ethic. They have the "ultimate concern" that theologian Paul Tillich said was the core definition of religion. They seek something akin to religious experience in the psychedelic drugs, the chemical expansion of consciousness. Many seek the inner peace and moral wisdom that yoga meditations promise. If they have frequently associated Christianity with the hypocrisy of the Establishment, they have been intrigued with and have often become students of the religions of the East. They have so challenged the conventional religions of the West that they have created a reaction—at least a modest resurgence of interest in Moral Rearmament and other Christian youth movements.

Such a flamboyant cult as the hippies evokes a vivid image in the mind. The usual picture is some sort of collage of beards, beads, long hair, and drugs. Beards, beads, long hair, and even the disheveled, unbathed look are, after all, rather innocent. The word *drugs* has a more ominous sound. The deleterious and addictive qualities of marijuana appear to be debatable. The rather frequent clinical reports on "bad trips" from L.S.D. and the weight of expert opinion on the barbiturates, the amphetamines and the so-called "hard drugs" leave no room for debate. To take them is to play with chemical fire. No brief is made even for experimentation with psychedelic drugs. However, the society must do more than say "No!" It is more to the point to ask "Why?" Mervin B. Freedman addresses himself to this question in *The College Experience* and concludes:

> The interest of many students in drug experience cannot be dismissed simply as a sign of delinquency, rebelliousness or psychological pathology. It represents a search for a new way of life. It indicates needs and desires that American society and education do not now meet or fill. . . . There is a quality of naivete in this quest by students. Wholeness, joy, wisdom, and love are not likely to result from a few hours spent under the influence of a chemical. The interest in drug experience informs us, however, that American society and education are doing little to contribute to the richness of life that students sense can be theirs.[4]

Most Americans over thirty, whose perceptions are rooted in the unconscious assumptions current during their own formative years, cannot understand the hippie phenomenon and do not credit it as being worth their effort to try. One American, Henry Thoreau, who died over 100 years ago, was as opposed to the Establishment and the conformism dictated by it as the most far-out hippie. He left a message of comfort to those who follow their inner prompting which may provide an insight to those who do not. "If a man does not keep pace with his companions, perhaps it is because he hears a different drummer. Let him keep pace to the music he hears, however measured or far away."

A WORD ON SEX

College students did not invent sex. They just discover it and practice some form of it. Several generations of students have lived in a society whose media has done its best to degrade women into sex objects—a commercial society that exploits sex to sell anything from cars to church bazaars. When something is so cheapened, it is usually considered trash and is given the respect which trash deserves. With such a puerile treatment of sex by the wider society, it is quite re-

[4]Mervin B. Freedmen, *The College Experience* (San Francisco, Jossey-Bass, 1967). Reprinted with permission.

markable that most college students have worked out a rather mature, if permissive, attitude and approach to sex.

The frankness and openness with which college students discuss sex does not necessarily mean an increase in promiscuity. Nevitt Sanford in his book *Where Colleges Fail* claims there is no evidence of substantial increase in the incidence of premarital intercourse among college girls. This is corroborated by the report of Mervin B. Freedman in *The College Experience*, which applauds the greater tolerance and permissiveness found among college students and even goes so far as to say,

> What is needed among youth is more eroticism rather than more obeisance to conventional repressive morality. I am not nearly so troubled by the prospect of sexual promiscuity on college campuses as I am by the prospect of a larger number of the more intelligent and sensitive college students withdrawing from participation in society.

Time Magazine's 1966 Man of the Year story "The Inheritor" substantiated some of these same ideas with less decorous but refreshingly frank and mature quotes from some co-eds.

> The (youth) do it is true, subscribe to a more tolerant morality than their elders but their mating habits have changed little. "The old submarine—the girl who's under all the time—that's wrong," says a Southern co-ed. "So is being a professional virgin." Reasons Elizabeth Crosby, a sophomore at New College in Sarasota, Florida: "Our attitudes are more an emphasis on relationship, and sex is bound up in this."

The pill and even more advanced contraceptive techniques will undoubtedly change the sexual mores of the society, just as the automobile did forty or fifty years ago. For the college authorities to simply say "Don't" is like talking into the wind. Dr. Harrison P. Eddy, speaking for his colleagues in psychiatry who wrote *Sex and the College Student* gave this advice to students and to college authorities:

> Every student has got to make his or her own choice, and there aren't any simple answers. The right answer for one student is not the right answer for another. But if one acknowledges that students are very much involved with sexual problems, it seems negligent for the colleges to turn away—to leave it up to the students to work out something so complex without help.[5]

What the students need and what they seem to want is an opportunity to explore seriously all the psychological and moral consequences which follow from increased sexual freedom. The students also deserve what the psychiatrists writing *Sex and the College Student* claim they are not now getting.

> In no institution did we find published or printed material that explicitly stated its views toward sexual conduct on the campus, yet institutions widely assume that student behavior will reflect the college rules and regulations. . . . If a college has certain expectations about sexual conduct on the campus, it has a responsibility to clarify them.[6]

THE NEW MORALITY

Those who equate morality with some narrow, puritanical, nineteenth century code centered on chastity could not give the American college student of the "Now Generation" very high marks. But when morality is viewed as those tidal forces of honesty and concern which sweep over a society washing it clean and giving it new hope, then today's youth have been their elders' mentor. It has been largely youth who have torn off the layers of masks of hypocrisy. Most of the men and

[5]Harrison P. Eddy, et al., *Sex and the College Student* (New York, Atheneum Publishers, 1965).
[6]Ibid.

women in the front lines of the battle against racism have been college students. Leaders in the National Student Association blew the whistle on the corrupting influence of the Central Intelligence Agency on student groups. Those who have acted upon the warning voiced by former President Eisenhower against the insidious power of the military-industrial complex have been youth. Far from being seduced by the glamor of war, college students have stood morally opposed to the war in Vietnam. They have acted out their rejection of the ethical drift in the United States society. The Peace Corps youngsters have polished up the tarnished image of Uncle Sam abroad just as the student volunteers in the ghettos have helped to preserve at least a remnant of respect for White Americans in the minds of Black Americans. It has been youth, particularly college youth, who have been most insistent upon, and who have led the search for, an integrating ethic that will bind the society together and will add significance to the lives of its members. *Time Magazine's* Man of the Year story on youth came to a conclusion which sums up the tough-minded morality which gives promise to the generation coming to power:

> Nonetheless, today's youth appears more deeply committed to the fundamental Western ethos—decency, tolerance, brotherhood—than almost any generation since the age of chivalry. If they have an ideology, it is idealism; if they have one ideal, it is pragmatism.

TOPICS FOR CONSIDERATION

1. It was contended that the folk-rock-jazz singers of the 1960's are spokesmen for both the political activists and the hippies. Can this contention be substantiated? How about the millions of fans who seem unaffected by any political or philosophic message? Are they just too naive to get anything more than the rhythm and the tune?

2. The statement was made that not many can venture very far from the safety of the social norm. Is it justifiable to conclude from this that it takes a gut full of psychological courage to fully adopt and sustain the role of either the political activist or the hippie? What are the negative consequences of each that would send many running back to the social norm?

3. It was estimated that less than 10 percent of the usual college population are gung-ho political activists and that even a smaller percentage would be true hippies. What influence, if any, do these two groups have in the usual public junior college? in small private liberal arts colleges? in the middle class population of large state colleges? in the prestigious, elite universities?

4. Although the right-wing camp of the Young Republicans did yeoman duty during the Barry Goldwater campaign of 1964, nonetheless the main thrust of student activism has come from the left. What accounts for this historical fact? Why do the students not follow the moderate or conservative politics of their middle-class parents?

5. Assume for the moment that Emerson was right in saying, "Action is with the scholar subordinate, but is essential. Without it he is not yet man. Without it thought can never ripen into truth . . ." Should this not apply even more to the teacher than to the students? Do college professors have an equal or better record for activism during the 1960's than their students? If not, is Emerson wrong or did most teachers fail to meet the full definition of scholar?

6. Edward Schwartz, Student Power advocate, said, "Let this principle apply—he who must obey the rule should make it." Does that sound reasonable and within the democratic philosophy? Since colleges are for students, most of the rules apply to students. Should the students, therefore, make the college rules? Should this apply to academic matters as well as student activities? Are students qualified to make the rules? Are citizens qualified to make the rules of the wider society?

7. The prediction is made that the coming power struggle will be between students and faculty. Are there fundamental issues in contention between these two groups? If so, what are they? Could these issues be negotiated now without the disruption and rancor of a full-blown battle? What are the structural means by which a negotiated settlement could be made?

8. The hippies are credited with stirring up a revolution in values which is said to be more potent than political revolution. What are the major societal values which the hippies undermined? What new values do they substitute? Could such a subculture survive in a nonaffluent society? If not, are the hippies trying to kill the goose that lays their golden egg?

9. Rita Dershowitz is quoted as saying that the hippie slogan is, "Find your own thing and then do it . . . sets up entirely new assumptions about the purposes of any educational institution." What are some of these new assumptions which would follow from taking the slogan seriously? How does the slogan affect obligations to the society? Can everyone be allowed to "find his own thing and then do it"?

10. In an article in the *Saturday Review* called "Society's Just Got to Go—We All Know That," Dr. Allen Krebs of the Free University of New York said, "The Universities of the Establishment are brothels. They're run to instill certain reactionary ideas. Hence a lot of subjects are left untaught." Among the untaught subjects presented at the Free University are "The Search for Authentic Sexual Experience," "The Literature of the Vietnam Liberation Fronts," "Hallucinogenic Drugs: Their Uses and Social Implications," "The Sexual Revolution." Is this the kind of relevancy in education for which students are looking? What untaught courses deserve to be taught?

11. Most responsible authorities say that marijuana is not addictive and leads to hard drugs only when the subject is psychologically predisposed to such a drastic form of escape. If this is true, why are the legal penalties even for possession much more severe than for the most flagrant drunkenness? Cigarettes are demonstrably poisonous. Why are they not subjected to these controls? What kinds of control should the society impose on such potential dangers as marijuana, cigarettes and alcohol? What control measures should colleges take?

12. The psychiatrists who wrote *Sex and the College Student* said, "If a college has certain expectations about sexual conduct on campus, it has a responsibility to clarify them." Why is this rarely, if ever, done? What should be the major restrictions in such a code of sexual conduct? What should the range of penalties be for violation of the regulations? What protection of due process should the accused student have?

SUGGESTED READING AND LISTENING

EDDY, HARRISON P., et al. *Sex and the College Student.* New York: Atheneum Publishers, 1965.

FREEDMAN, MERVIN B. *The College Experience.* San Francisco: Jossey-Bass, 1967.

GLAZER, NATHAN. "What Happened at Berkeley," *Beyond Berkeley: A Sourcebook in Student Values*, edited by C. G. Katope and P. G. Zolbrod. Cleveland: World Publishing Company, 1965.

KRUTCH, JOSEPH WOOD. "The New Immorality," *Introduction to College Life*, edited by Norman T. Bell, et al. Boston: Houghton Mifflin Company, 1966, pp. 69–71.

LIPPMANN, WALTER, RITA DERSHOWITZ, et al. "A Dialogue Between Generations," *Harper's Magazine*, 235:45–64 (October, 1967).

Inheritor: Man of the Year," *Time Magazine*, 89:18–23 (January 6, 1967).

SHOBEN, EDWARD JOSEPH, JR. *National Conference on Student Stress.* Washington, D.C.: U.S. National Student Association, 1966.

"Student Power on the Rise," *Newsweek*, 70:40 (October 23, 1967).

TOYNBEE, ARTHUR. "Toynbee on America," *Life Magazine*, 43:65–75, (December 25, 1967).

WAGNER, ROBERT F., JR. and ROCHELLE GATLIN. "Students Speak for Action," *Saturday Review*, 48:82–83 (October 16, 1965).

WOODRING, PAUL. "Who Makes Educational Policy?" *Introduction to College Life*, edited by Norman T. Bell, et al. Boston: Houghton Mifflin Company, 1966, pp. 175–178.